Fix Me Up

Fix Me Up

Essays on Television Dating and Makeover Shows

EDITED BY JUDITH LANCIONI

McFarland & Company, Inc., Publishers
Jefferson, North Carolina, and London

LIBRARY OF CONGRESS CATALOGUING-IN-PUBLICATION DATA

Fix me up : essays on television dating and makeover shows / edited
by Judith Lancioni.
    p.   cm.
    Includes bibliographical references and index.

    ISBN 978-0-7864-4382-6
    softcover : 50# alkaline paper ∞

    1. Reality television programs — Social aspects — United States.
2. Makeover television programs — Social aspects — United States.
3. Dating shows (Television programs) — Social aspects — United
States.   I. Lancioni, Judith, 1943–
PN1992.8.R43F59   2010
791.45'6 — dc22   2009031700

British Library cataloguing data are available

On the cover: The cast of *Queer Eye for the Straight Guy*: Ted Allen,
Jai Rodriguez, Carson Kressley, Thom Filicia and Kyan Douglas
(Photofest); background objects ©2010 Shutterstock

Manufactured in the United States of America

*McFarland & Company, Inc., Publishers
  Box 611, Jefferson, North Carolina 28640
  www.mcfarlandpub.com*

Table of Contents

Introduction

JUDITH LANCIONI

Rating is a fact of life. It is also a staple of reality television. Employers rate job seekers on the basis of business acumen — *The Apprentice* (NBC). Producers and casting directors rate would-be performers on the basis of talent — *Ted Mack's Amateur Hour* (NBC, ABC, CBS), *Fame* (NBC), and *American Idol* (Fox). We regularly rate others on the basis of appearance and personality —*Are You Hot?* (ABC). And most of us rate ourselves using similar criteria, criteria which are culturally grounded — *The Swan* (Fox) and *Extreme Makeover* (ABC).

Rating dominates dating and makeover shows, which are the subject of this book. In dating and makeover shows, rating, normally a personal or interpersonal process, becomes part of public discourse. This melding of personal and public can lead to a redefinition of both. Personal standards can lead to a re-articulation of public criteria, or vice versa, thus mandating serious scrutiny of the rating process that determines attractiveness and desirability. Does the rating process, especially as it is practiced on dating and makeover shows, support hegemonic conceptions of physical attractiveness and its importance in our lives, or does it not? The purpose of this book is to explore and evaluate the rating process as it is practiced on makeover and dating shows.

The most blatant example of the rating game and its implications was ABC's *Are You Hot? The Search for America's Sexiest People*, whose premier garnered more than ten million viewers (Bloomberg). The producers divided the country into Hot Zones, then chose 32 contestants from each zone. As the official website explained, contestants did not have to be intelligent or charming, just beautiful and sexy (*Are You Hot?* home page). Contestants were rated by a celebrity panel and by viewers, who registered their votes via the internet. At the end of the series, two contestants were crowned sexiest man and sexiest woman in America.

The television show spawned websites where anyone could post a photo and be rated by others. The show and the websites are noteworthy because of the questions they raise about standards of beauty in diverse communities and the merging of private and public standards for rating beauty. Many of the websites also blatantly link appearance and dating, not a new phenomenon, certainly, but one that makes public a rating process that was previously private. For example, Hotenough.org was established to link members with partners of comparable attractiveness. As the website advertises, "If you're finding out that you're not short of dates, but your dates are just coming up short, then you've come to the right place" ("Why"). Hotornot.com is also rating-based. This rating process has not escaped academic scrutiny. Leonard Lee and colleagues, for example, have used a similar website to study the rating of attractiveness as it impacts the selection of a partner.

Neither dating nor makeover shows are new genres. *The Dating Game* (ABC) and *Love Connection* (syndicated) are early examples of dating shows. Other examples include *Blind Date* (syndicated), *Rendez-View* (ARTV), *A Dating Story* (TLC), *Looking for Love: Bachelorettes in Alaska* (Fox), *elimiDATE* (syndicated), *The Bachelor* (ABC), *The Bachelorette* (ABC), *Average Joe* (NBC), *Mr. Personality* (Fox), *For Love or Money* (NBC), and *Meet My Folks* (NBC). Dating shows — also known as relationship shows or "reality romance" (Albertini) — are very popular. The premiere episode of ABC's *The Bachelorette* garnered 17.4 million viewers, more than the popular *The West Wing* (NBC), which it ran against. In the same week, 18.6 million viewers tuned in to Fox's *Joe Millionaire* (Levin). Over twelve million viewers tuned in to the six episodes of the first series of *Average Joe,* which ranked 25th in the Nielsen ratings. The finale of *Average Joe I* drew 17.4 million viewers, more than any other show aired that night. Over eleven million of those viewers were in the prized 18-to-24-year-old category ("*Average Joe* Earns" C4). In fact, dating games have become so prevalent and so popular that in February 2003, *The Today Show* (NBC), in recognition of the trend, conducted its own version with a bachelor whose mother, cousin, and friends were enlisted to select potential dates ("Jim Lange").

Why do so many people watch dating shows? Bill Albertini suggests that the wide appeal of dating shows stems from the passions they arouse. According to Alex Duda of *elimiDATE* (syndicated), viewers tune in because they themselves are "looking for love" and can empathize with the difficulties contestants face; they can also pick up dating tips (Pennington). Randall Rose and Stacy Wood argue that viewers enjoy comparing contestants' behavior with their own potential responses. Andrew Glassman attributes the success of *Average Joe* to the contestants' emotional appeal ("*Average Joe* Earns").

The long kisses, amorous touches, and hot tub revelations characteristic of the dating shows imply criteria by which contestants are judged by the bachelors or bachelorettes. How physically attractive are they, for example, and how open to romance? Many critics have pointed out that the group date, a staple of dating shows, feeds male fantasies. This is especially true of the hot tub dates, which feature multiple partners displaying their wares in skimpy bikinis (Albertini). On group dates, contestants only have about ten minutes each with the bachelor or bachelorette, making it very difficult to convey strong points and make a connection ("*Average Joe* Contestants"), so the impression given is that contestants are rated on looks alone.

Albertini identifies several features common to most dating shows. They equate worth with wealth and imply that romance is not possible without wealth. They portray the decision-maker in the series as royalty. This is especially true if the decision-maker is a woman, who is often treated as a fairytale princess. In the premiere episode of *Average Joe* (NBC), for example, Melana frequently remarked that she felt like a princess in a fairytale. The bachelor or bachelorette inhabits a mansion, wears expensive clothes, and travels in chauffeur-driven limousines.

The women on these shows, whether they are the decision-makers or the competitors, are conventionally attractive; their physical beauty corresponds to Western stereotypes. Often they've had surgery to correct or improve specific features, especially breasts. They are often portrayed as venal. In his real-life job as a construction worker, claimed Evan Marriott of *Joe Millionaire* (Fox), he was scorned by women (Devinney), thereby implying that women, especially attractive women, exercise both greediness and class bias. Brian Devinney, of *Reality News*, even goes so far as to provide a tongue-in-cheek ranking of female contestants on *Joe Millionaire* (Fox) based on the degree of avarice they display. For example, he christens one female contestant "the poster child of the Gold Diggers." Shows like *Cupid* (ABC) portrayed women as male bashers (Aucoin). Another stereotype reinforced by most dating shows is that women are incomplete without romance in their lives.

Men don't come off particularly well in dating shows either. The shows are constructed to display male contestants as reveling in playing the field and choosing partners on the basis of looks. As professor of psychology Laura Brown puts it, men are portrayed as "predatory, interested in the wrapping rather than the insides" (Aucoin). Unlike female contestants, males are subject to ridicule if they are too handsome or too concerned with their looks. One reviewer ridiculed a contestant on *Looking for Love: Bachelorettes in*

Alaska (Fox) because the camera caught him checking out his hair. Probably tweezes his eyebrows, too, the reviewer scoffed (Daugherty).

Contestants, in general, are portrayed as deceitful, self-serving, and sneaky. The latter impression is often the result of interview inserts in which contestants confide or complain to viewers. *elimiDATE* (syndicated), for example, used a confessional for contestants to make private comments about each other to the camera. Often such comments are scathing and put the confiding contestant in a negative light. Such confidences provide viewers with more material for rating the contestant. In fact, due to inserts, confessionals, and other editing practices, viewers would seem to be more exposed to personality traits than the bachelor or bachelorette.

Fans usually use a combination of personality and appearance to rate contestants. The results can be harsh, as in the epithets Rob Daugherty used to ridicule both female and male contestants on *Looking for Love: Bachelorettes in Alaska* (Fox). These included "Rock 'n' Roll Roadie Earrings Guy," "Void of Personality Pretty Face," "Mr. Hipness Long-Haired Guy," "Prom Queen Runner-Up," and "Grown-up Boy Snowboarder." He also remarked that one female contestant would be tolerable provided she wore little, smiled little, and shut up. Fans also regularly evaluate the bachelor or bachelorette. Melana of *Average Joe* (NBC) was ridiculed, both because of her looks (the "dumb blonde" syndrome) and because of the way her persona was constructed. Fans called her shallow. Critics derided her as "glycerin-eyed" and "smarmily sincere" (Stanley E1). "Her Royal Vapidness," as they dubbed her, was an "intellectually vacuous beauty queen" who talked in clichés (Rubinoff C4). Bachelor Rob Campos of *For Love or Money* (ABC) was described as "a lox with a bad haircut" ("Copy Cats").

DeRose, Fürsich, and Haskins demonstrate ways in which a dating show can seem to broaden our understanding of gender roles while at the same time supporting the status quo. They argue that in *Blind Date* producers use the supertext — in this case animated characters like "Blunt Guy," "Obvious Guy," and "Blind Date Producer" and wry comments enclosed in thought bubbles — to insert pejorative commentary into the reality footage and to ridicule contestants who deviate from accepted standards. That deviation is foregrounded by the selection of activities sure to show at least one of the contestants at his or her worst. The effect of that commentary is to reinforce stereotypical concepts pertaining to class, race, gender, and physical attributes (DeRose, Fürsich, and Haskins 174). Commentary on female contestants inevitably focuses on appearance, especially breasts (DeRose, Fürsich, and Haskins 178), while commentary on males concentrates on somewhat broader criteria — appearance, stature, clothing, occupation and goals (DeRose, Fürsich, and Haskins 179). Whatever the standards, they inevitably "legitimize an overall message that reinforces the perception that traits accepted by the dominant ideology are desirable, natural, and right" (DeRose, Fürsich, and Haskins 185).

Nevertheless, there are ways in which a dating show (and by extension a makeover show) might challenge the gender, class, and racial concepts of the dominant culture: by displaying contestants who don't embody hegemonic values, either in terms of appearance, attitudes, or behavior; by encouraging viewers to identify with non-mainstream contestants (DeRose, Fürsich, and Haskins 173); by employing strategies and metaphors that can be read as parody. Such strategies foreground the text as polysemous, that is a text that opens itself to a variety of interpretations. Bill Albertini believes that dating shows are polysemous, building a "complex structure of feeling that makes room for highs and lows of both indulgence and disavowal...." They are "full of holes that allow readers to find other messages within the text" based on gender, race, socioeconomic status, and so on (Albertini).

As John Fiske argues, culture and text are inextricably bound. Viewers employ their "social experience" to interpret a text and that social experience may in turn be affected by the text ("Popularity" 88). Moreover, interaction between television texts and "socially located discourses is the process by which meaning is achieved in both text and society" (89).

Like dating shows, makeovers are not a new phenomenon. The first was probably *Queen for a Day* (Mutual), which flourished on the radio from 1948 to 1957 then moved to television, enjoying a 19-year run, first on NBC from 1956–60 and then on ABC from 1960–64 before it went into syndication. Contestants would regale the audience with tales of how miserable they were and then ask for something that would change their lives, if only for one day. The studio audience would decide who deserved to get her wish and she would be crowned queen. While no plastic surgery or fashion makeover was involved, there were two similarities with current makeover shows: first the premise that changing something on the outside would affect how a person felt on the inside and second the promise that disclosing one's insecurities was the first step in getting help. The more pathetic a contestant felt, the more likely she would emerge a winner. *Extreme Makeover* (ABC) and *The Swan* (Fox) operate on the same premise and make the same promise.

Current makeover shows fall into three categories: those like *Extreme Makeover, Home Edition* (ABC), that involve renovating or redecorating a property; those like *Queer Eye for the Straight Guy* (Bravo), *What Not to Wear* (TLC), *A Personal Story* (Discovery), *A Makeover Story* (TLC), *Fashion Emergency* (E), *The Look for Less* (Style), *Glow* (Style), *Ambush Makeover* (Fox), that involve changes in lifestyle or appearance or both, and those like *Extreme Makeover* (ABC), *The Swan* (Fox), *I Want a Famous Face* (MTV), that involve cosmetic surgery and sometimes psychological counseling, fitness training, and cosmetic dentistry as well. This book focuses primarily on the last two categories. Shows in the second category have been charged with promoting consumerism and conformity. Shows in the third category have been criticized for encouraging women to rank themselves against hegemonic standards of beauty and promoting "self loathing" (Rodman).

All the makeover shows rely on a simple equation. If something is wrong with your appearance, something is wrong with your life — or vice versa. When the Fab Five of *Queer Eye for the Straight Guy* (Bravo) overhaul your hair, your toilette, your closet, and your home, you'll be a new, improved you. You'll rate yourself higher — using the standards provided by the Five. *Ambush Makeover* (Fox) shares the same spirit and some of the same tactics as *Queer Eye*. No redecorating is involved. However, a redo of hair, face, and your clothing is carried out by a team of specialists who in a three-hour period will produce a better you. The show makes a stronger link between appearance and happiness than *Queer Eye* does. Tammy, a young woman ambushed on the street, told the hairstylist who guided her makeover, "You have changed my life!" ("Shanghaied").

This is mild compared to the elation with which subjects on surgical makeover shows greet their new selves. For example, after their "reveals" (standard makeover jargon for the first view of one's new image), the reactions of the first two *Swan* (Fox) contestants suggested that they had disengaged from their "natural" selves. Rachel, a construction worker who underwent rhinoplasty, lip enhancement, chin implant, a breast and a forehead lift, and liposuction on her cheeks, chin, stomach, thighs, and back, enthused: "I feel gorgeous and beautiful. I don't look anything like that. Oh my God, this is going to take a little getting used to." Her competitor, Kelly, who opted for a forehead lift, mouth and breast enhancement, eye surgery, laser hair removal, liposuction on her cheeks, chin, back, buttocks, and legs, and collagen injections in her lips and nose, cried, " I can't believe that this is me. I feel beautiful. I don't even recognize myself. I look amazing."

Many critics have charged that the new self constructed for subjects on surgical makeover shows represents a rejection of their own identity. The best example of this is MTV's *I Want a Famous Face*, which Ellen Goodman claims turns "self-improvement into self-annihilation" (D11). *I Want a Famous Face* documents the plastic surgery chosen by people — both male and female — who want to look like their favorite celebrity. While *The Swan* (Fox) and *Extreme Makeover* (ABC) may seem conservative by comparison, those exultant words uttered at the reveals also suggest an obliteration of self.

Some have denounced the extreme makeover shows because they ignore the possible dangers of cosmetic surgery and make it "life affirming" (George). But there are additional problems. These shows, like the dating shows, have been accused of normalizing a process that supports hegemonic constructions of what it means to be beautiful and what it means to be happy, thereby encouraging viewers to rank themselves, and let others rank them, by those standards. This ranking process is not new, but its enthusiastic promotion on television is.

The personal makeover shows forge a connection between appearance and self-fulfillment. Cindy, a stay-at-home mom, had a large, unattractive nose and prominent facial hair. Change these features (and her breasts, buttocks, tummy, teeth, etc.) and she can have a new, happier life. Cindy applied to be a *Swan* contestant because she was unhappy and focused her unhappiness around two features which socially constructed notions of beauty deemed ugly. Cindy, and the producers, believed that her improved appearance would guarantee a new life. Those with features which society deems ugly have an ugly life. Those with features deemed beautiful or handsome have a lovely life.

There is nothing new about the rating system that fuels the makeover shows. The question is does television legitimize it? Do makeover shows say to contestants, "You're right. Your nose is too big and too crooked, your jowls sag and so do your buttocks. We'll fix that, and while we're at it, you need a tummy tuck, laser hair removal, braces, and teeth bleaching. Oh, and you need to lose 20 pounds."

Like all television texts, dating and makeover shows are polysemic, open structures whose potential meanings must be activated by "socially-situated viewers" (Fiske, *Television* 15–16). Viewers can infiltrate the nooks and crannies of the polysemic text and negotiate their own reading of the role of appearance, class, and gender stereotypes in the rating game, which is precisely what the authors of this book have done. They have explored "the relationship between the discursive structures in a text and those in society as they come together in the crucial moment of reading" (Fiske, "Popularity" 90).

Rating will always be with us, but the effect of dating and makeover shows is to make us more aware of the process and its relationship to social and cultural norms. This awareness is evident in the essays included in this book. Each author focuses on a somewhat different aspect of dating or makeover shows. Matthew Johnson and Narissra Maria Punyanunt-Carter deal with both genres. Some authors agree that dating and makeover shows support dominant cultural standards, while others do not. But in one way or another, each addresses the issue of rating.

The growing academic interest in audience analysis is reflected in the first five essays of this collection, which analyze the fan base for dating and makeover shows. All five employ quantitative methodologies to discern the ways in which actual — as opposed to idealized — viewers relate to these genres. For example, in "The Dating Games: Real Lessons Learned from Unreal Programs," David Gudelunas posits a strong relationship between mass media programming and its viewers. He employs focus groups to carry out his analysis of short-form dating shows to determine their relevance for their viewers. While acknowledging that these syndicated programs "sketch their contestants so thin they barely materialize," Gudelunas argues that they have a measurable effect on regular viewers between 18 and 21 years of age. Gudelunas notes that the popularity of dating programs rose even as the rate of actual dating fell. Likewise, as restrictions on sex education multiplied, mass media's portrayal of sex became more explicit. These syndicated reality dating programs, he argues, substitute for the paucity of formal sex education, but rather than teaching their viewers about dating rituals, they teach them how to negotiate sexual relations. What these shows tell us, says Gudelunas, is that dating, for this generation, is about "getting naked."

Research conducted by Elizabeth Ribarsky led to different conclusions. In "The Reality of Reality Dating: Analyzing Viewers' Perceptions," Ribarsky explores the impact of dating programs on interpersonal relationships. Based on her analysis of focus groups who viewed an episode of *Blind Date,* Ribarsky identifies five themes: voyeuristic interest in the humiliation contestants endure, awareness of the construction of hyper-reality, recognition of gender stereotypes, rejection of nonstandard sexual behavior, and the contrast between the dating behaviors displayed on the shows and their own experience. The dating shows, she determines, do not function as lessons about what to do, but rather as illustrations of what not to do. As one of her participants put it, "These people are put on there to make us laugh and to make us feel more normal." Ribarsky concludes that dating programs strengthen traditional dating behaviors; that while they enjoyed watching, viewers were not duped into accepting these shows as unscripted reality; that the genre's popularity resides primarily in voyeurism. Nevertheless, based on her conviction that television "serves as a hegemonic tool reinforcing cultural values," Ribarsky raises the possibility that viewers may eventually be desensitized to the constructed nature of the genre and begin to accept the extremes of the dating shows as the norm.

In "Women's Shared Viewing of *The Bachelor*: Generational Motives and Perceptions," Cary W. Horvath and Margaret O. Finucane seek to account for the popularity of this long-lived dating show and the sense-making process female fans engage in as they watch. Through the use of focus groups they measured the effect of viewing *The Bachelor* with friends. They also studied the possible impact of age differences on shared viewing. They found that shared viewing facilitates conversation, feelings of solidarity, and social learning. This was true across age groups. As for the show itself, focus group participants were ambiguous about its "reality," premise, and participants. Nevertheless, they watched faithfully, supporting the contestant who best matched their ideals and satisfied their desire for fantasy, "affiliation and communication." Horvath and Finucane suggest that the desire for fantasy and the need to believe that romantic love still exists enable female viewers to ignore aspects of the show they might find annoying or offensive. For these viewers, the sexism of *The Bachelor* and the issues it raises for feminists hold little interest.

In "Fans of Plastic Surgery Reality Television: Hopes and Concerns in Fan Postings," Joan L. Conners explores the degree to which the viewers of *Extreme Makeover, Plastic Surgery: Before and After* and *Dr. 90210* are inspired to undergo cosmetic procedures. Her content analysis of forty-four patient stories from three makeover shows revealed that the three makeover series diminish the potential dangers of plastic surgery while amplifying positive outcomes and their capacity to transform patients' lives. Moreover, they give short shrift to pre-operative consultations that distinguish what the patient wants and what is medically possible or advisable. Conners relates fan postings to the nature of the shows themselves. "Given the lack of attention of warnings to patients in pre-operative consultations or focus on post-operative recovery and complications in these reality programs, the lack of such discussion online is not surprising." The shows, Conners concludes, encourage the "normalization" of cosmetic procedures: "If we are not satisfied with some aspects of ourselves physically, we can fix it." Underlying Conners' comment is the nagging question of what has prompted the dissatisfaction. What aspect of our culture causes us to rank ourselves in need of cosmetic improvement?

Narissra Maria Punyanunt-Carter also focuses on audience analysis. In "Parasocial Relationships in Dating and Makeover Reality Television," Punyanunt-Carter discusses the motives which prompt viewers to form parasocial relationships with contestants on both dating and makeover shows. She discusses those cultural, ideological, and media-promulgated criteria which, according to her research, promote the formation of these relationships.

Viewers start out seeking information — about relationships in the case of dating shows and about transforming one's appearance in the case of makeover shows — and gradually develop a pseudo-personal relationship with contestants. Perhaps it is this personal connection which enhances viewers' acceptance of televisual ideology. They fantasize about the romance of the dating situations or the positive changes of the makeover in order to compensate for deficiencies in their own lives. They identify with reality show persona who either lack those deficiencies that trouble viewers or who can eliminate those deficiencies through undergoing a makeover. As Punyanunt-Carter concludes, "Parasocial relationships develop because people, in general, long to be ideal." That longing is sustained by the televisual apparatus and the ideology it embodies.

Subsequent essays in this book focus on various elements of the television texts themselves, rather than on the reactions of actual viewers. "*Average Joe* and the Not So Average Jane" incorporates elements of reader response theory into a textual analysis of *Average Joe* and *Average Joe: Hawaii*. The author poses questions about the ways in which the two shows construct the concept of average then explores the functioning of that construct within a socioculturally determined rating system. Fan commentary is used to demonstrate the ways in which the concept of "average" is influenced by interaction with the televisual texts. The functioning of these shows within the dating show genre is also explored. Finally, the possibility that *Average Joe* and *Average Joe: Hawaii* constitute a parody of the genre and a critique of the cultural norms it embodies is analyzed. The author concludes, "The selection of competitors, the exaggerated nature of the editing and the mis-en-scene suggest that the genre and the rating process it embodies are being mocked."

In "*The Swan* as Sado-Ritual Syndrome?" Christopher D. Rodkey also explores the relationship between text and society. Rodkey's goal is to detail the *Swan*'s ideological and moral implications. He denounces the unethical and patriarchal premises of the makeover genre as exhibited in this makeover show. For example, Rodkey charges that in *The Swan*, "Rhinoplasty is discussed with the ease of a cosmetologist selling eyeliner." Rodkey compares the exploitation of the "Swans" to the medical experiments conducted on prison inmates. He provides a detailed analysis of the ethical issues involved in both. Rodkey then applies these ethical principles most convincingly to *The Swan*, arguing that its contestants are "unjustly coerced by a woman-hating society to provide examples, consumer samples, to a public who are both unable to afford the medical procedures and searching for new ways to technologically reiterate its fundamental hatred of women." Thus the gynocide of *The Swan* points to a sick society that is itself in need of a makeover.

Rodkey concludes that "*The Swan*'s contestants are societal prison experiments offered by a medical establishment that wishes to convince us that we *need* our bodies to be homogenized." The reality series signifies "the deep sicknesses, the ritualized sadism, implicit in our culture."

Shana Heinricy takes a different approach to the makeover show, examining the way in which authority is constructed and then utilized to inspire trust and respect in viewers. In "The Boob Tube: Authority, Resistance, and *Dr. 90210*," Heinricy argues that the mere act of appearing on television and looking attractive confers expertise on Dr. Rey, the cosmetic surgeon who "stars" on this reality makeover show. This perceived expertise empowers Rey to make decisions about women's appearance, decisions that support dominant ideals of what constitutes ugliness and beauty. As Heinricy puts it, "Makeover television allows star experts to authorize some looks and chastise others." Heinricy discusses the case of a contestant who resisted Dr. Rey's advice. Dr. Rey reacted to this rebellion as if "his reputation, and therefore his celebrity, was materially attached to his patient's cleavage." Heinricy posits that an intersection of medicine and beauty on makeover shows strengthens the power of the expert's recommendations, which are rarely questioned by the contestant. Moreover, the ultimate goal of the cosmetic makeover is to encourage viewers to judge their bodies according to the standards established by the show and then to seek cosmetic surgery to fix aspects that do not meet the televisual norms of beauty. Heinricy concludes that television confers on makeover shows like *Dr. 90210* the power to enforce a definition of beauty whose parameters are very narrow and leave little room for personal choice; the goal is to look like "an acceptable product of society." She concludes: "Not only does televisual authority allow the beauty of participants to be judged, it also makes it acceptable for viewers to judge others by the standards expressed on the show."

Two essays in this book illustrate very different approaches to the same show, *America's Top Model*. Like Horvath and Finucane, Julie-Ann Scott is interested in the effect which a particular show has on female viewers. In "Revising Bodily Texts to the Dominant Standard: A Feminist Rhetorical Criticism of the Makeover Episode of *America's Next Top Model*," Scott argues that the makeover episode of *America's Next Top Model* "embodies the standards of the dominant beauty discourses in American culture." Contestants, she points out, are judged on their "marketability," sex appeal, attractiveness, and the degree to which they meet White, middle class standards of beauty. Contestants are made over to more completely fulfill these standards. These makeovers are tied to class issues, Scott argues. *America's Next Top Model* tantalizes its lower class and minority contestants with a combination of a fairytale existence and the fulfillment of the America dream. While Scott argues that the series promotes "the objectification and domination of women in a patriarchal society," she acknowledges that there are advantages to conforming to dominant standards for appearance and whether or not to do so is every woman's choice.

In contrast, Frank H. Wallis focuses on the impact production factors have on the show's popularity. In "Tyra Banks' Top Model: Makeover in Reality Television," Wallis presents a behind-the-scenes as well as an on-screen analysis of *America's Next Top Model*. Wallis identifies the place of the series in the history of the makeover, noting that while many of its components are different, it shares with the genre the crucial "reveal," which traditionally includes both an inner and an outer transformation. No surprise then that cycle winners regularly remarked that they felt transformed by their experience. Wallis argues that the series also borrows elements from the documentary, soap opera, game show, and talent search. Wallis' analysis makes it clear that the most important factor in *America's Next Top Model* is Tyra Banks, "the only female auteur in RTV," who created, edited, promoted, and marketed her show and acted as mentor, teacher, exemplar, and final judge. Wallis declares her a "mythic forebear for aspiring models." In concluding his analysis, Wallis argues that there is no evidence of hegemonic ideology in *America's Next Top Model* and concludes that the most relevant rating system is the Nielsens. The series is designed to sell products through advertisements and product placement and the modeling competition is designed to create the kind of drama that audiences enjoy.

Unlike many of the essays in this book, "'She Just Called You a Metro': Rating Masculinity on Reality Television" rejects the notion that dating and makeover shows promote hegemonic ideology. Matthew Johnson uses his analysis of reality television shows on MTV, TLC, and Bravo to support his thesis that there are competing constructions of masculinity on television. Makeover shows like *Queer Eye for the Straight Guy* and *What Not to Wear* promulgate a metrosexual lifestyle that stresses the importance of men's personal appearance. In doing so, they challenge traditional conceptions of masculinity, "which defines itself against femininity and homosexuality." In contrast, dating shows like *Next*, *Room Raiders*, and *Exposed* champion traditional constructions of masculinity that, by emphasizing athletic prowess, and accepting homophobia and emotional reticence, distance themselves from femininity. Johnson analyzes dating and makeover shows and their role in popular culture as indicators of "competing conversations about masculinity in the twenty-first century."

Yarma Velázquez Vargas, too, is concerned with the construction of masculinity on television, but she posits a more hegemonic text than does Johnson. In "Materialism, Disposal and Consumerism: *Queer Eye* and the Commodification of Identity," Velázquez Vargas, through close reading of key episodes, asserts that *Queer Eye for the Straight Guy* perpetuates gay stereotypes and serves the capitalist media by foregrounding consumerism, conspicuous consumption, and disposability. The program presents patterns of excessive consumption as a key to self-improvement. Velázquez Vargas notes that for the Fab Five, wastefulness is "pleasurable." Aesthetics is more important than functionality, so if a product is deemed aesthetically offensive it is discarded, whether it works or not. Consumer goods function as the means of making over a person's inner as well as his or her outer self.

Velázquez Vargas recounts one episode in which "the Five suggest that clothing, grooming, and a juicer are the essence of masculinity." Dressing, grooming, and furnishing one's home are skills that must be learned and practiced. Mastering them becomes the key to having a happy and successful life. And mastery means consuming. We are judged by what we buy. Velázquez Vargas concludes that "goods become an intrinsic part of creating an identity, creating an image and telling a personal narrative." Apparently, rating can be an expensive proposition, and transformation requires a healthy credit card balance.

In "New Blouse, New House, I Need a New Spouse: The Politics of Transformation and Identity in Television Makeover and Swap Shows," Shira Tarrant analyzes the same insidious consumerism identified by Velázquez Vargas. Buying a new wardrobe or redecorating a house will allow us to achieve self-fulfillment. Thus the makeover and swap shows encourage us to "internalize the cultural message that our old selves are not good enough." These shows, says Tarrant, "naturalize consumerism and fetishize commodities," creating "fables" that embody the dominant culture's strictures on what to wear and who to be. Tarrant's claims are supported by her critiques of *Wife Swap*, *What Not to Wear*, and *Extreme Makeover: Home Edition*. The latter two shows portray a pressure for consuming home and self-adornment products in the search to fulfill dominant standards of beauty and the promise of personal transformation. In *Wife Swap* the wives are the commodities that are traded. Tarrant also discusses the selection process by which individuals are chosen for a makeover, observing that race, class, gender, and prejudice play a covert role in this process. Moreover, the shows themselves constitute a "relentless heteronormative impulse." Tarrant concludes that makeover shows do indeed support hegemonic ideals, especially the consumerist credo that one's true self can be purchased at any mall, provided one observes the proper cultural standards.

A rhetorical approach to the study of the makeover show is exemplified by Ellen W. Gorsevski's "Revealing Western Norms of Gender Identity in *What Not to Wear*: Idealizing Femininity in Visual Culture to Win the 'War on Terror.'" Gorsevski's analysis of *What Not to Wear* explores the socio-cultural implications of the show and its relevance to the war on terror. The burqa, Gorsevski argues, stands for the West's perceived ugliness and confinement of the pre-makeover state. Through makeover shows like *What Not to Wear*, American women are encouraged to "enact their 'freedom' to reshape their bodies" either through the "least destructive" though "expensive" means or through "violent and bloody chopping, cutting, suctioning from, or, insertion of unhealthy silicone implants into their bodies." Through the makeover, the contestant is portrayed as being freed from her "psychic and physical burqa" while being made to support "Western socio-cultural norms of beauty." *What Not to Wear* enacts a "symbolic makeover" through which "a weakened national sensibility and loss of confidence is remade." Gorsevski relates this phenomenon to the important role that fashion played in maintaining morale in France and Britain during World War II and in America during the Vietnam era. She concludes that the makeover performs an ideological function and recommends future research focus on "how other social practices are represented in media in ways that serve to confirm or resist ideology." Her work illuminates John Fiske's argument that culture and text are inextricably bound.

This book would not be complete without an examination of the international impact of these genres. Makeover and dating shows are not an American phenomenon. The reality genre originated in Sweden, leading to the eventual broadcasting of the American version of *Survivor*. *Big Brother* originated in the Netherlands. In 2004, 492 new reality programs appeared in nine countries, including the United States, 111 in Britain alone, constituting 39 percent of all new programming (Caravajal). The genre constitutes 20 percent of viewership in Brazil and 24 percent in Mexico. The reality genre is growing in popularity in China and the Arab countries. These countries are not relying on the importation of American shows but instead are creating reality series of their own, some of which are dating and makeover shows. For example, *Ala al-Hawa Sawa* combined elements of *The Dating Game* and *The Bachelorette* (Lynch). Female contestants lived together while engaging in a rating of male suitors that would culminate in an arranged marriage ("Appear").

That makeover shows are an international phenomenon is attested to in "Reality Television, Body Cult and Identity Metamorphosis in Brazil and the United States." Bianca Freire-Medeiros and André Bakker compare *Extreme Makeover* and *Buying Beauty* (Beleza Comprada) in terms of the search for bodily perfection which drives both shows and permeates both American and Brazilian cultures. This similarity comes as no surprise, since both countries are world leaders in aesthetic surgery procedures, they point out. Citizens of both countries display a willingness to undergo invasive cosmetic procedures in order to redesign the body according to media-promulgated standards. This willingness to reconstruct oneself is fueled by what Freire-Medeiros and Bakker call the "look-love-life" triad. In both countries, looks are the key to social success, status, and happiness as they are represented in the media. They focus on the relationship between "the fragmentation of identity," the "desire for distinction," and the "self-constituted, reprogrammable entity" that is the body as that relationship is manifested in the media of two different cultures. They argue that in both makeover series, the body is treated as "an accumulation of components, a surface ripe for surgery" and reconstitution. It is also a surface ripe for conformity and inhospitable to individuality. Medeiros and Bakker conclude that, according to the media, beauty and the happiness it brings can only result from redesigning oneself according to experts who promulgate ideological principles that are often pan-cultural.

Together, the essays in this book illustrate the cultural complexity of dating and makeover shows and the issues these genres raise. Through the prism of rating they explore, either directly or indirectly, the interrelationship between television and society. They analyze as well the values and attitudes presented by dating and makeover programming and viewers' reactions, both theoretical and actual, to that programming. They also illustrate the variety of methodologies that can be employed in studying these genres. Finally, they contribute to the study of reality television, a species of programming that has changed the nature of television and viewers' attitudes towards it.

This collection is unique because it focuses exclusively on two genres of reality television and posits, either directly or indirectly, a cultural connection between them — ideologies and attitudes that purport to be "real" and yet are scripted, that potently impact two of the most basic factors of daily life, self-image and romantic relationships. Perhaps, as Frank H. Wallis suggests, these shows are ultimately about ratings and return on investment. Or perhaps, as Joan L. Conners, Shira Tarrant, Shana Heinricy, and Julie-Ann Scott suggest, these genres have ideological import. Perhaps, as David Gudelunas and Elizabeth Ribarsky discovered, dating and makeover shows have the potential to impact viewer behaviors. In a sense, these essays raise as many questions as they answer, but, given the growing popularity of dating and makeover shows, they are questions worth further exploration.

BIBLIOGRAPHY

Albertini, Bill. "So Wrong It's Right: The Guilty Pleasures of Reality Television." *Iris* 47 (Fall 2003): 12.

Ambush Makeover. Syndicated. Exec. prod. Chris Rantamaki. 8 Sept. 2003–9 Sept. 2005.

"Appear on Reality TV and Win an Arranged Marriage." *Guardian News & Media* 12 Dec. 2003. Buzzle.com. 11 Nov. 2008 <http://www.buzzle.com/editorials/12–12–2003–48536.asp>.

Are You Hot? ABC. Exec. prod. Michael Fleiss, Scott Enziger, Mike Nichols, Dan Goldberg, and Jennifer Bresnan. 13 Feb. 2003–2 March 2003.

Are You Hot? Home page. ABC. 23 May 2004. <http://abc.go.com/primetime/areyouhot/show.html>.

Aucoin, Don. "Those Cheatin' Gals." *Boston Globe* 21 September 2003, 3rd ed., magazine sec.: 7.

Average Joe. Co-exec. prod. Stuart Krasnow and Andrew Glassman. NBC. 3 Nov. 2003–27 July 2005 (4 series).

"Average Joe Contestants Dennis Luciani, Jay Greenberg and Craig Campbell Discuss the Show and Being Voted Off." Interview with Matt Lauer. *Today Show* 11 Nov. 2003. NBC News. Transcript.

"Average Joe Earns Above-Average Ratings." *Pittsburg Post Gazette* 11 Dec. 2003: C-4.

Blind Date. Syndicated. Exec. prod. Matthew Papish, David Garfinkle, Jay Renfroe, Thomas Klein, and Harley Tait. 20 Sept. 1999–1 Sept. 2006.

Bloomberg, David. "Are You Hot?, Episode 1: The Meat Market Begins." 15 Feb. 2003. *Reality News Online.* 23 May 2004 <http://www.realitynewsonline.com./cgi-bin/ae.pl?mode=article2757.art&page=1>.

Carvajal, Doreen. "In Europe, Reality TV Turns Grimmer." *The New York Times* 27 Dec. 2004. 30 Dec. 2004 <http://nytimes.com/2004/12/27/business/media/27reality.html>.

"Copy Cats Aren't Cool." *USA Today* 6 June 2003: E11.

Daugherty, Rob. "A Manly View of *Bachelorettes in Alaska,* Episode 4." *Reality News Online* 10 July 2002. 23 May 2004 <http://www.realitynewsonline.com/cgi-bin/ae.pl?mode=4&article2609.art&page=1>.

DeRose, Justin, Elfriede Fürsich, and Ekaterina V. Haskins. "Pop (up) Goes the *Blind Date*: Supertextual Constraints on 'Reality' Television." *Journal of Communication Inquiry* 27 (April 2003): 171–89.

Devinney, C. Brian. "*Joe Millionaire,* Episode I: Enter the Gold Diggers." *Reality News Online.* 7 Jan. 2003. 23 May 2004 <http://www.realitynewsonline.com/cgi-bin/ae.pl?mode=4&article1974.art&page=1>.

Fiske, John. "Popularity and Ideology, A Structuralist Reading of Dr. Who." *Interpreting Television: Current Research Perspectives.* Thousand Oaks, CA: Sage, 1984. 165–198. Rpt. in Leah R. Vande Berg, Lawrence A. Wenner, and Bruce E. Gronbeck. *Critical Approaches to Television.* 2nd ed. Boston: Houghton Mifflin, 2004. 86–109.

_____. *Television Culture.* London: Routledge, 2004.

George, Lianne. "Presto Chango." *Maclean's* 117 (26 April 2004): 40.

Goodman, Ellen. "Taking TV 'Makeovers' to Extremes." *Boston Globe* 11 April 2004, 3rd ed.: D11.

Hot or Not. Home page. 24 May 2004 <http://www.hotornot.com/?>.

I Want a Famous Face. MTV. Ex. prod. Lauren Lazin, Dave Sirulnick, and Brooke Gaston. 15 March 2004–17 May 2005.

I Want a Famous Face. Home page. 11 May 2004 <http://mtv.com/onair/i_want_a_famous_face/>.

"Jim Lange Hosts a Version of The Dating Game." *NBC News* 13 February 2003. Transcript.

Lee, Leonard, George Loewenstein, Dan Ariely, James Hong, and Jim Young. "If I'm Hot, Are You Hot or Not? Physical Attractiveness Evaluations and Dating Preferences as a Function of Own Attractiveness." *Social Science Research Network* 1 November 2007 <http://papers.ssrn.com/sol3/papers.cfm?>.

Levin, Gary. "Networks' Star Search Finds a Winner: Dating Shows." *USA Today* 10 Jan. 2003.

Looking for Love: Bachelorettes in Alaska. Fox. Ex. prod. Eric Schotz, Bill Paolantonio, and Scott Messick. 2 June 2002–1 July 2002.

Lynch, Marc. "Reality Is Not Enough: The Politics of Arab Reality TV."*Arab Media and Society Journal* 2 March 2009. 20 March 2009. <http://www.tbsjournal.com/LynchPF.html>.

Pennington, Gail. "Glut of TV Dating Shows Proves How Desperate We Are for Love." *St. Louis Dispatch* 7 July 2002.

Rodman, Sarah. "The Skin Game: Makeover Series Turn Self-loathing into Freak Show." *Boston Herald* 14 April 2004: O43.

Rose, Randal L., and Stacy L. Wood. "Paradox and the Consumption of Authenticity through Reality Television." *Journal of Consumer Research* 32 (September 2005): 284–296.

Rubinoff, Joel. "Let's Hear It for the *Average Joe*, A Class Act." *The Record* [Kitchener-Waterloo, Ontario] 10 Jan. 2004: C4.

"Shanghaied, Redone & Loving It! Ambush Makeover's Whatley Describes a Day in the Life of a Quick-Change Artist." *Television Week* 12 Jan. 2004.

Stanley, Alessandra. "The TV Watch. In a Made-for-Television Romance, the Most Telegenic Man Wins." *New York Times* 9 Dec. 2003, late ed.: E1.

The Swan. Fox. Ex. prod. Arthur Smith and Nely Galan. 7 April 2004–20 Dec. 2004.

"Why HotEnough?" Hotenough.org Home page. 24 May 2004 <http://www.hotenough.org.>.

The Dating Games

Real Lessons Learned from Unreal Programs

DAVID GUDELUNAS

One memorable episode of the syndicated reality program *Blind Date* ended at the conclusion of the date with a suitor not simply planting a kiss on the cheek of his date, but exposing his genitals to his date and casually asking, "Give me some opinion. What do you think? Do I get a second date? Shake it goodbye?" Welcome to the world of reality, and occasionally raunchy, dating.

Located in the fringe of both time slots and programming options, syndicated reality dating programs like *Blind Date, elimiDATE,* and *The Fifth Wheel* are notorious for low production values and arguably equally low moral values. Placed into obviously tantalizing situations involving hot tubs, massage tables, and other clichés of sexual availability, unusually attractive men and women vie not for a date, as the name of the genre suggests, but rather for sexual satisfaction (Gudelunas "Realities"). This paper focuses on short-form television dating competitions where the quest for love is contained in tidy 22-minute-or-less channel-flipping-resistant scenes. Unlike 22-episode dating programs such as *The Bachelor,* where arguably more substantive discussions may unfurl, syndicated dating reality programs sketch their contestants so thin they barely materialize.

These syndicated reality dating programs, though stretching the definition of reality, ultimately result in real lessons learned by real audiences. Drawing on a theory of formal and informal curricula about sexual education, where formal sexual education happens in classrooms and community-based sexual education programs, while informal lessons are learned primarily through informal discussions, popular culture texts, and other mediated moments, reality dating competitions will be considered a type of informal curriculum on what dating in the 21st century entails. This paper combines data about the genre itself, textual analysis of several key programs in the genre, and interviews with men and women under the age of 21 who are frequent viewers. In short, data that follow are drawn from institutional, textual, and audience realms. Ultimately, the syndicated dating reality competitions are situated as not simply a cultural outpost of exhibitionism, but rather an important source of education about lessons that typically are not learned elsewhere.

Qualitative data cited throughout this essay were gathered through in-depth interviews with fans of syndicated reality dating programs gathered through message boards and snowball sampling techniques. While not a representative sample, these audience insights allow us to move beyond simply understanding the text; instead these insights help us better understand reception of that text. All respondents were between 18 and 21-years-old and all acknowledged being frequent viewers of one or more syndicated reality dating programs. Respondents largely drove the interview process in what Kvale (5) describes as a "semi structured life world interview ... whose purpose is to obtain descriptions of the life world of the interviewee with respect to interpreting the meaning of the described phenomena." Coding was done by identifying broad themes in the initial analysis and then working to further specify these themes in subsequent analysis, using thematic analysis (Glesne). In all, 35 interviews were conducted and the interviews ended when I reached "theoretical saturation" (Glaser and Strauss).

Dating on Television: New Games on an Old Court

It is important to remember that the reality dating programs that populate fringe time slots on affiliate television stations are more evolutionary than revolutionary. Since the 1960s, variations on the format have appeared on television in various permutations. *The Dating Game* (1965–1974), *Love Connection* (1983–1995), and *Newlyweds* (1966–2000) are just some of the reality-based game hybrids that existed long before "reality" television became a prominent category of programming. If anything, the key difference between programs like *Blind Date* and *The Dating Game* is that while the latter relied on audiences imagining what a date might look like, the former actually takes the audience along on the date. Similarly, while *Love Connection* depended on contestants describing their dates for host Chuck Wollery, on *elimiDATE* we get to see the date and who ultimately ends up as the winner.

In today's world of reality dating, we no longer have to wait until the credits roll to see the guy get the girl (or vice versa); now we see the guy get the girl (again, or vice versa), and then wait until the credits roll to see if he decides to keep her. The most recent proliferation of reality television is not simply about the need of networks to fill air time with inexpensive programming, but also the increasing internationalization of genres and programming, the need to find revenue streams beyond traditional spot ad buys, the ability to integrate product placements into reality programs, and a series of other economic and technological shifts that are revolutionizing the television business (Magder; Raphael). Regardless of the exact impetus, by 1998 the dusty genre of reality dating entered a second phase with the premiere of Warner Bros.' *Blind Date*. This second wave of reality dating programs was more explicit in terms of sexual contact, more snarky in tone, and focused on a younger demographic than the previous generation of dating programs.

Hosted by Roger Lodge, *Blind Date* focused on voyeuristic surveillance of dates that placed attractive singles into a range of predictably sexy situations including outings involving body painting, drinking copious amounts of alcohol, going to the gym together, and other scenarios that allowed for maximum exposure of skin and contact. Unlike the earnest earlier matchmaking programs like *Love Connection*, *Blind Date* never took itself very seriously. From the on-screen confessions that preceded the actual date ("What makes sex good for me is when I don't have to do it with myself," revealed one dater) to a vast majority of the conversation that transpires during the course of a typical date, there is no mistaking what the focus of these reality dating programs is. The program and its host were also snide, and dates were arranged for maximum audience, if not dater, enjoyment. Some dating scenarios included pairing the Mormon with the nymphomaniac, or the porn producer with the princess. As Lodge said with great irony following one particularly painful outing, "Another perfect *Blind Date* connection." Like Lodge's comments, alternating witty and insipid on-screen graphics take the pressure off the viewer of having to critique the date. "This kid has more issues than the *New York Times*" or "Smug guy says: 'Girls are always impressed by stupidity'" are examples of on-screen pop-up graphics. DeRose, Fürsich, and Haskins argue that these graphics reinforce hegemonic norms and "the perception that traits accepted by the dominant ideology are desirable, natural, and right" (DeRose, Fürsich, and Haskins 185). This of course assumes a fairly passive audience member, something that is disputed below.

The success of *Blind Date* in the late 1990s inspired a new sub-genre of reality programs that expanded on the formula of watching telegenic 20-somethings looking for love (Mahan). Syndicated fare such as *elimiDATE*, where three men (or women) compete elimination style for the affection of the "picker," or the equally competitive *The Fifth Wheel*, where five individuals get on a bus and the entire date rolls from location to location until finally one of the five contestants is eliminated thereby leaving two winning couples, began running on network affiliate and independent television stations across the United States well outside of prime time. Alex Duda, producer and creator of *elimiDATE*, explained his take on the format this way:

> ... Attraction is key. If there's no attraction, the rest of the show is not going to work. If the picker is looking for someone tall, blond, smart and rich, then we're going to give you one of each. If there's the attraction underneath, then the game works. Unlike other shows that they set people up for conflict, we don't want conflict between the player and the picker, we want the conflict between the people who play the game ... [qtd. in McKissack D1].

Less successful reality dating programs of the period included *Shipmates* (dates played out on board a cruise ship) and *Cheaters*, which focused more on finding deceit than love, as the program's name suggests. Like the genre leader *Blind Date*, these derivative programs took advantage of generally being aired after midnight. Aisha Tyler, host of *The Fifth Wheel*, explained to *TV Guide*, "There's [sic] a lot of girls flashing their boobs at boys. It's pretty scandalous. No one's getting married off these things, so I'm just really about making it as fun and entertaining as possible" (qtd. in Cooleridge 18).

By 2005, however, the boom became a bust with just *Blind Date* still producing new episodes for syndication ("Syndie Insider" 13). While the other programs survived through reruns, in limited batches of new episodes on cable (*Shipmates* migrated to Spike TV for a brief run), and through DVD collections that showcased scenes too explicit for broadcast television, *Blind Date* was the only program still in production ("Date Reconnects"). The syndicated reality dating trend was a relatively short-lived phenomenon, but this genre of reality is interesting for reasons beyond flashing debutantes, smarmy comments, and representative shifts in the culture of television production.

Syndicated dating reality programs are interesting in part because they sit at the juncture of two significant cultural ironies in the 21st century. First, just as dating and courting as cultural practices were on the decline, the popularity of dating programs was at a zenith. Second, just as schools and other community-based sources of formal knowledge about safer sexual practices and healthy relationship building were being restricted by conservative cultural impulses, mass media were becoming ever more explicit when it came to discussing relationships. Both of these ironies are discussed in more detail below. Ultimately, the real importance of these syndicated reality dating programs is that in the absence of other formal education or instruction about courtship, the made-for-television antics of these sexually charged studs and vixens is an important primer in what is expected to successfully navigate the singles scene. The "date" in these reality programs becomes synonymous with foreplay as men and women try on different partners hoping to locate sexual if not emotional compatibility, suggesting to audiences that getting naked is oftentimes the first successful step in getting a date.

The Media–Dating Connection: I Just Play a Dater on Television

Despite seeming like a timeless tradition, dating as rite of passage for American youth is actually a cultural ritual that has existed for a relatively short time period. Dating as a youth ritual was not popular until early in the 20th century when labor laws, mandatory schooling, economic conditions, and broader cultural shifts provided the space and impetus for newly minted teenagers to meet and mingle outside of parental supervision (Schofield Clark 698). Of course, courting in various guises has always existed, but dating as a youth ritual is something that did not happen until teenagers had the time and resources to "try out" potential partners.'

Mass media has always been intrinsically connected to dating rituals in America. From the movie palaces that provided a dark and unsupervised place for necking to the movies and television texts themselves that explained and glamorized what it meant to "go on a date" at the start of the 20th century, the ritual of dating has always been connected to our media habits. Today's syndicated reality dating programs are no exception, but the exact relationship between media and dating practices has changed.

Dating today is a ritual past its prime. Dating has recently come to define a category more so than an act. That is, individuals may consider themselves "dating" (as a sort of category that proceeds more definitive commitments like engagement or marriage), but the practice of actually going on a "date" is something that Generation-Y largely sees as anachronistic. As one 18-year-old female explained:

> I have never gone on a date. I have a boyfriend, and have had boyfriends before this one, but I have never actually been on a date. We met in school and that was it. We go out, but we go out with friends. He doesn't ring my doorbell, meet my dad and then take me to the drive-in or anything like that. That's what my parents did, not me.

Another respondent, a 19-year-old male, said:

> Since I was in high school I've had a consistent girlfriend. I mean I guess we
> went out on some dances or stuff, but mostly we go to parties, chill with
> friends, you know just hang out. On [my college] campus a lot of the guys
> have girlfriends but I think unless you're having sex you're not alone too much
> with them. I don't have money to be going to a dinner every Saturday or noth-
> ing.

Ironically this same demographic that does not actually go on dates
comprised one of the largest audience segments for syndicated reality
dating programs. Aired after even the late night talk shows wrapped, programs like *Blind Date* and *elimiDATE* became must-watch programming
in dormitories after studying (and partying) ended. As one female college
sophomore put it, "Every girl on my floor dropped everything at midnight
to watch *Blind Date*. The guys would watch too. There's not much on at 1
A.M."

At 1 A.M., these college students made mandatory viewing of syndicated
reality dating programs that took the quaint notion of dating and made it
into a postmodern spectacle. These mediated texts, however, were not providing scripts that instructed audience members how to date; rather these
scripts become instructive in how to negotiate sexual relations. Moreover, if
the audience didn't actually go out on dates, they enjoyed watching others
experience this cultural ritual. Just as the producers understand that these
neatly packaged 22-minute dates are not a place to find true love, audience
members are more likely to root for humiliation and sensational moments
of spectacle than romance. Unlike the first generation of reality dating competitions, this second wave never made any pretense that the competition
was about finding love. Frequent viewers had no trouble articulating what
kept them returning night after night to their favorite programs:

> Some of the girls are hot. And when they fight over a guy, especially if they
> are in a bikini, well, I mean, who doesn't love that? [20-year-old male dis-
> cussing *elimiDATE*].

> The dates are hilarious. It is these guys who are total creeps trying to get with
> these chicks who are complete sluts. Basically it's a contest to see who can out
> skank who [19-year-old female discussing *The Fifth Wheel*].

> We joke that the contestants on *Blind Date* were just released from jail. They
> meet their date and it's like you can see the hormones revving up. They are
> complete horndogs and have no shame whatsoever. They basically are like
> "Will you sleep with me?" [21-year-old male discussing *Blind Date*].

> The dates aren't as much dates as they are make-out parties. These people have
> no shame, they say hello and then, like, they have a tongue down someone's
> throat. It's kinda hot [20-year-old female discussing *Blind Date*].

These programs, in other words, were seen by audiences not as a place where contestants went to find love or a relationship that extended beyond the physical; rather these programs were precisely about the physical. Sex was the prize. As one 19-year-old female explained: "The competition is brilliant. What better prize can there be than sex, right? I'm not sure what anyone wins, and ... who would want to win some of those losers? But the competitive part makes it fun. We root for people to basically get laid."

Competition and the challenge of sexual satisfaction are key. Though *Blind Date* follows a more traditional date in documentary style, *elimiDATE* and *The Fifth Wheel* are explicitly competitions where there are winners and losers. Even *Blind Date*, however, which features only the two daters, was considered a contest by audience members, who would choose a side in the date and hope that someone "won." Many audience members, in fact, noted the competition was a reason they watched so regularly. While competition is nothing new in reality dating programs, the level of competition has certainly escalated because bachelors clamored to come up with the best answer to "What's your ideal Saturday night date?" Instead, on *elimiDATE*, contestants introduce themselves to the audience in interstitials that make it clear they are there to do battle.

One episode of *elimiDATE*, as an example, began with women speaking to the camera explaining, "I'm Jennifer and I can be really mean," and "I'm Alba and I live life without any restrictions," or perhaps more explicitly, "I'm Rena and I am open to anything" and "I'm Eva and I have a big booty and I'm not afraid to use it." The lines drawn, the women then go to meet their date and battle it out first in a lackluster game of wiffleball and then over drinks in round two at a Manhattan nightclub. In each round of the date, one woman is eliminated until two remain in the third and final round. Inevitably the date turns into a screaming match between the women, who spend a majority of the episode denigrating one another with swipes at everything from weight to hair highlights. Not coincidentally, the male "picker" is removed from all criticism. One audience member explains, "It is not unlike an episode of *Jerry Springer*, but these people aren't missing so many teeth."

The real competition on a typical episode of *elimiDATE* comes when during the final round the date moves to a more intimate setting (think hot tub or private room at a nightclub). It is not uncommon for the final contestants to have extended make-out sessions with the "picker." Consequently, it is also not uncommon for the results of the contest to be based on one's ability to make out. People are regularly eliminated from competition on *elimiDATE*, or kicked off the bus on *The Fifth Wheel* when, in fact, they refuse to participate in the sexually charged antics that these programs require. A recent entry into the *Blind Date* "Hall of Shame," as an example, was a dater who refused to take off his swim trunks during a hot-tub-based game of truth or dare after his date did.

Unreal Texts, Real Lessons

Flipping the traditional dating program model on its head, competition in the second generation of reality dating programs is not about winning a date and possible physical contact; rather here physical contact is the first step in getting a date. More than an update on the traditional show model, this new generation of program literally inverted it. For audience members (most of whom were familiar only by name with previous dating reality programs), this idea of exchanging saliva before actually winning the date was actually par for the course. Asked if it was odd that someone would be expected to perform physically to win a dating competition, audience members had a variety of responses that clustered around the central notion that physical compatibility precedes any sort of emotional or other relational compatibility:

> I have never had a girlfriend I started dating before I at the very, very least made out with [20-year-old male].
>
> How would you know if you should bother going out on a date with a guy if it isn't going to, you know, click in the, well, sexuality department? [19-year-old female].
>
> I don't think I ever met a guy who I ended up dating that I didn't first at least get a little physical with at a party or something like that [20-year-old female].
>
> I don't think these programs are representative of what goes on in my life, or like in lives of the kids at [college]. It's exaggerated and edited for maximum funny effect. On the other hand the fact is these shows have it right ... you make out with someone at a party ... you know when you're drunk or just ... and then if it's all good maybe the next weekend you'll go to a movie or something [21-year-old male].

Of course it is unlikely that any of these respondents learned these lessons from watching syndicated reality programs, yet we should not ignore what lessons reality dating programs do teach us. As Justin Lewis notes, "Television is not a social abstraction — we cannot systematically pluck those hours of the day we spend watching it and disregard them as nothing more than a vicarious, second hand class of experience" (292). While each of the respondents cited above were at least 18-years-old and living away from home at college, many more audience members are much younger. This highlights the second great irony of reality dating programs. At a time in American culture where high schools are reluctant to devote even a semester to talk about sex, and community sexual education advocates are locked in fierce battle with proponents of abstinence-only sexual education, syndicated reality dating programs are discussing relationships almost entirely in the context of sexuality.

As Janice Irvine notes, sexual morality in the United States is most frequently controlled by policing talk about sex. She says sexual education "breaks a silence. It introduces talk about sex into the regulated space of the public school" (Irvine 4). Talk about sex within this regulated space happens infrequently. The George W. Bush administration increasingly tied federal funding for education initiatives to abstinence-only sexual education in public schools. While exactly what goes in the classrooms across America is murky at best, all 50 states have some form of abstinence-only sexual education on the books (Rosenberg 67). While comprehensive sex education advocates battle with folks who favor abstinence-until-marriage education in the classroom and other community-based educational settings, it is clear that outside of the classroom this battle is largely irrelevant. In 2001, the year when the syndicated reality dating programs were experiencing some of their best ratings, 61 percent of high school seniors reported that they had sexual intercourse, four million teens were diagnosed with sexually transmitted diseases, and teen pregnancies hovered around nine hundred thousand yearly (Henry J. Kaiser Foundation).

In the formal curriculum, such as the nation's classrooms and other community-based forums, there is no discussion of sexuality. Meanwhile, in the informal curriculum, such as conversations around the water cooler, in the cafeteria, and even on the playground, as well as through the mass media, talk about sex has been increasingly graphic (Gudelunas, "Confidential" 11). In short, Americans are not just having sex, they are talking about it. While the frequency and level of detail in which Americans talk about sex in the informal curricula stands in stark contrast to the restricted discussions about sex in the formal curricula, we should not assume that interpersonal conversations or mediated texts can be as informative and instructive as more formal sexual education (Gudelunas, "Confidential" 18).

French philosopher Michel Foucault's now well-cited linkages between sexuality, knowledge, and power in the modern age help to explain this disconnect between the formal and informal curricula. Foucault argues that although discourse concerning sex has proliferated since the eighteenth century, sex itself has been codified into an object of knowledge. Specifically, sex has become a site of scientific inquiry as well as a fodder for confession.

Moreover, Foucault posits that sexuality is not repressed by power but rather sexuality is power. That is, sexuality serves society by distributing certain kinds of power. The various discourses that have multiplied around sex and sexuality (e.g., educational, psychological) are important because although they increase the amount of talk regarding sex, they also serve as a means of social control. Interestingly, Foucault discusses how to maintain our own sense of "healthy" sexuality; we are eager to police the behavior of others (Gudelunas, "Confidential" 19).

For many audience members who identified as heavy viewers of reality dating programs, Foucault helps us understand how the informal curriculum of the mass media is actually quite instructive.

> I don't think I learn anything by watching *elimiDATE*, no ... these programs are not educational by any stretch of my wildest imagination. But you know, I guess it makes me feel not so horrible about the fact that maybe like I made out with someone Thursday night and forgot his name Friday night. These girls are letting some skeezy dude put his hand up their shirts before they are on the second martini [20-year-old female discussing *elimiDATE*].

> Those girls have it right. They cut right to the chase, they're not sitting there talking about their cat or sister or whatever ... they are like "Lets go twist tongues" [21-year old male discussing *The Fifth Wheel*].

> I think *Blind Date* lowers expectations. I haven't been on a date in a while, but wow, I hope whoever it is that I do go on a date with doesn't think these dates are acceptable. I'm not getting in a hot tub topless on the first date. Who does besides the girls who want to be on TV? [20-year-old female discussing *Blind Date*].

Conclusions

While respondents did not specifically indicate they learned any lessons from dating reality programs, these programs not only served as a sort of cultural barometer where audience members could compare and contrast their own behaviors, but also these dates and contests gave respondents a chance to critique the behavior of others. Rating contestants, in other words, allowed audience members to rate themselves. As one 20-year-old female explained, "When we watch, and I don't think I ever watched with fewer than two roommates, we definitely spend a lot of time asking 'would I do that' or 'what about [roommate's name]' when it comes to some of the more scandalous stuff." Syndicated dating reality programs of the late 1990s and early 2000s marked a remote, but not insignificant, outpost of the television landscape. Dating programs such as *Blind Date*, *elimiDATE*, and *The Fifth Wheel* appealed to audience members who, having abandoned dating as a cultural practice themselves, still enjoyed watching others look for romance. Audience members devoted considerable time critiquing the dating habits of others, and this helps explain part of the appeal of these programs with young audience members. The ability to rate the behavior and morals of others (as well as themselves) was a major draw for the younger audience demographic.

This second generation of reality dating programs, unlike earlier versions such as *The Dating Game* or *Love Connection*, took viewers along for the date and changed the rules of the game so a date was won only after contestants proved their sexual prowess. In this new breed of reality dating competitions, dating is more akin to foreplay than anything else. These dates, as it turns out, were little more than contests to prove who could be the most promiscuous.

There is nothing wrong, of course, with sexually liberated young adults, and audience members understood these programs to be humorous takes on reality as much as documentary views into the mating habits of 20-somethings. However, at a time when our culture is severely divided on when, where, and to what extent to talk about sexuality in an educational setting, informal discussions about dating, relationships, and sexual norms like those found on reality dating competitions are well worth paying attention to. After all, the lesson learned from reality dating programs is often simply that to get a date, you first have to get naked.

BIBLIOGRAPHY

Blind Date. Syndicated. 2002.

Cooleridge, Daniel. "Talk Soup's Hot Dish." *TV Guide.* 1 April 2002: 18.

"Date Reconnects with NBC Uni." *The Hollywood Reporter.* 7 June 2005: 18.

DeRose, Justin, Elfriede Fürsich and Ekaterina V. Haskins. "Pop (up) Goes the *Blind Date*: Supertextual Constraints on 'Reality' Television." *Journal of Communication Inquiry* 27 (April 2003): 171–89.

elimiDATE. Syndicated. 2002.

The Fifth Wheel. Syndicated. 2002.

Foucault, Michel. *The History of Sexuality: Volume 1: An Introduction.* New York: Pantheon, 1978.

Glaser, Barney, and Anselm Strauss. *The Discovery of Grounded Theory.* Chicago: Aldine, 1967.

Glesne, Corrine. *Becoming Qualitative Researchers: An Introduction.* Boston: Pearson, 2006.

Gudelunas, David. *Confidential to America: Newspaper Advice Columns and Sexual Education.* New Brunswick, NJ: Transaction, 2008.

_____. "Realities of Reality Dating." *American Sexuality Magazine.* 27 July 06. 10 Oct. 07. < http://nsrc.sfsu.edu/MagArticle.cfm?Article=621&PageID=0>.

Henry J. Kaiser Foundation. "Teen Sexual Activity." Menlo Park, CA: Kaiser Foundation, 2003.

Irvine, Janice. *Talk Abut Sex: The Battles Over Sex Education in the United States.* Berkeley: University of California Press, 2002.

Kvale, Steinar. *Interviews.* Thousand Oaks, CA; Sage, 1996.

Lewis, Justin. "The Meaning of Real Life." *Reality TV: Remaking Television Culture.* Ed. Susan Murray and Laurie Ouellette. New York University Press, 2004. 288–302.

Magder, Ted. "The End of TV 101: Reality Programs, Formats, and the New Business of Television." *Reality TV: Remaking Television Culture.* Ed. Susan Murray and Laurie Ouellette. New York University Press, 2004. 137–156.

Mahan, Colin. "NBC U Goes Out on Another *Blind Date.*" TV.com. 7 June 2005. 12 December 2007. <http://www.television.com/blinddate/show/7595/story/308.html?>.

McKissack, Fred. "*elimiDATE* Sets Its Sights on Mad Town." *Wisconsin State Journal* 6 August 2003: D1.

Raphael, Chad. "The Political Economic Origins of Reali-TV." *Reality TV: Remaking Television Culture.* Ed. Susan Murray and Laurie Ouellette. New York Universtiy Press, 2004. 119–136.

Rosenberg, David. "The Battle of Abstinence." *Newsweek* 9 December 2002: 67.

Schofield Clark, Lynn. "Dating on the Net: Teens and the Rise of "Pure" Relationships." *Gender, Race and Class in Media.* Ed. Gail Dines and Jean M. Humez. Thousand Oaks, CA: Sage, 1995. 696–707.

"Syndie Insider." *Broadcasting and Cable* 21 June 2004: 13.

The Reality of Reality Dating
Analyzing Viewers' Perceptions

ELIZABETH RIBARSKY

The media, in particular television, play a significant role in influencing individuals' perceptions (Cohen; Gerbner, Gross, Morgan, and Signorielli). As the television has become one of the most widely accessible mediums (Bagley), television programming serves as a hegemonic tool reinforcing cultural values. This issue is complicated by the onslaught of reality television, "one of the most significant developments in recent U.S. media" (Glynn 2). Popular reality television programming, such as *Survivor*, *Big Brother*, and *Blind Date*, places ordinary individuals in extraordinary circumstances (Syvertsen), creating a hyperreality in which the real and the fictional become indistinguishable (Glynn). This ambiguity becomes precarious, as individuals attempt to understand cultural values of real individuals in constructed realities.

Although reality television depicts people in numerous constructed realities, Americans are obsessed with dating (Hestroni). Reality-dating programs have become one of the most popular and growing reality television segments (Poniewozik). Although these programs vary in the level of absurdity and sexual promiscuity, many of the dating shows are filled with atypical sexual advancements. Through media reinforcement (Jagger), emphasis has been placed upon finding a mate for physical fulfillment (D'Emilio and Freedman) rather than long-term relationships. Unfortunately, viewers may perceive the television programming as an accurate reflection of expected or mainstream behavior (Morgan), creating greater sexual expectations for men and women (Aubrey, Harrison, Kramer, and Yellin; Ward). Thus, it is imperative to explore how viewers perceive and interpret reality daters' behaviors.

Television — Shaping Culture

Television plays a significant role in shaping individuals' perceptions and in developing a shared culture. Television has become the "dominant medium of social discourse and representation in our society" (Hall 75). Cultivation theorists argue that as they are exposed to repeated messages, such as those portrayed on television, individuals will begin to adopt the messages they see and hear into their interpersonal lives (Gerbner et al.; Jupiter). Despite the fictional nature of many television programs, the repetition of messages influences what individuals believe to be true, regardless of the veracity of the statements (Schwartz). Therefore, as individuals view repeated episodes involving the same/similar situations, they may begin to believe the television content is real. Thus, the program's content and characters may shift viewers' cultural concepts of what is acceptable (Abt and Seesholtz). This adoption is alarming considering the anarchic, corrupting (Davies and Machin) and sexually laden television programming (Greenberg, Sherry, Busselle, Hnilo, and Smith). For example, students who were exposed to sexually-oriented television adopted notions of earlier and more varied sexual activities (Aubrey, Harrison, Kramer, and Yellin) and endorsed the presented sexual stereotypes (Ward). These often fictional accounts on television are shaping cultural values. However, this issue becomes more complex with the introduction of reality television.

Reality Dating Television

With rising production costs and threats of writers' strikes in the early 1990s, producers began focusing on "reality-based" programming (Glynn). This change in television production quickly became wildly popular, as it gave individuals a sense of participating with "real" individuals (Glynn; Syvertsen). In particular, reality-dating shows sprung up in great numbers from *Blind Date* and *elimiDATE* to *The Bachelor* and *Change of Heart* (Austin). These shows gained rapid popularity, as they appealed to human instinct and a desire to view individuals at their most vulnerable and private moments. There are two significant issues that have been instrumental to the popularity of reality-dating shows: naturalizing surveillance and the appeal of humiliation.

NATURALIZING SURVEILLANCE

It is human instinct to desire to invade individuals' privacy (Tunstall and Dunford). Although this invasion is usually seen as negative, reality television viewers are drawn to the ability to safely participate in voyeuristic activities (Andrejevic). Individuals are able to invade private moments of reality participants' lives, creating a sense of participation without violating established moral codes regarding privacy. Viewers even can delve into participants' romantic rendezvous, interactions in which most people would desire some form of seclusion and privacy. Reality dating programs have created a legalized form of "peeping Toms." The prevalence of reality television normalizes the use of surveillance, eliminating many morality issues surrounding voyeurism. "Currently, we are living in a society that is becoming increasingly tolerant of, used to, and even positive about the widespread presence of video surveillance" (Dority 13). Although this naturalizing of surveillance has significant cultural implications, it also remains a popular form of television, allowing the audience to feel like part of the scene (Glynn). This sense of participation may influence viewers' perceptions of reality daters' behaviors.

THE APPEAL OF HUMILIATION

One key aspect of voyeurism is viewing individuals at their most vulnerable moments, including escalating a romantic relationship. Frequently, participants in reality dating shows are subjected to extremely humiliating situations (Poniewozik; Syvertsen), leaving many individuals wondering why anyone would subject themselves to that type of invasion and embarrassment. Individuals are placed in socially and sexually awkward situations, such as being asked to feel women's breasts for implants or being paired with someone with a clashing personality. Although the participants may partake in the reality show for prizes or fame (Syvertsen), viewers thrive on engaging in others' embarrassing moments. Embarrassment becomes a popular pleasure as it allows individuals to see mainstream people falter (Fiske). Rosenzweig said, "This may be the most serious consequence of these kinds of television shows — that they reduce the comedies and tragedies of life to nothing more demanding than a consumer product choice. And because we are fascinated, we will watch and allow that to happen" (48). Seeing reality show participants make fools of themselves, including on dates, makes the participants seem increasingly accessible and entertaining to the viewers.

Perceptions of Reality Dating Shows

Because reality television blurs the real and the fictional, viewers' perceptions of reality, including dater behaviors, may be skewed. The traditional dating script focuses on stereotypical dating behaviors typical of the 1950s (Rose and Frieze). These traditional dating behaviors are often simple and innocent, such as dinner and a small activity. And, sexual activity is appropriate after a couple is married.

Reality-dating shows rarely follow the traditional dating script. Some dating shows depict atypical sexual advances, such as engaging in sexual contact within 30 minutes of meeting one another. And, it is not uncommon for reality daters to engage in extravagant dates that extend beyond the norms of the traditional dating script, such as wine tasting across the French countryside or sailing on a luxurious yacht. Producers have made atypical dating situations look normal on the reality show. If dating shows portray what dating and/or love "should" look like, many viewers may not be able to live up to the expectations put forth by the programs (Glynn). And, if viewers do adopt these "reality" dating behaviors, it may have significant social implications. Thus, one must question if viewers perceive these shows to be an accurate reflection of reality. Therefore, the researcher posed the following research question:

> RQ1: How do viewers perceive and interpret the extreme behaviors depicted on reality-dating television?

Methodology

PARTICIPANTS AND PROCEDURES

For the purposes of this qualitative investigation, the researcher conducted hour-long, tape-recorded focus group interviews with 29 students (males = 13; females = 16) from a large midwestern university. The participants varied in age from 19 to 23 (M = 20.13), including 24 European Americans, 4 Asian Americans, and 1 African American. Focus groups included between four and six individuals. In these focus groups, the participants first were shown a 22-minute video clip of *Blind Date*, a popular reality show that depicts atypical dating behaviors. Although *Blind Date* epitomizes reality dating that violate the traditional dating script, the show includes one unique feature. *Blind Date* utilizes a supertext that chastises atypical behavior (DeRose, Fürsich, and Haskins). The supertext often appears as a cartoon-like thought bubble coming from the daters or observers. In these supertexts, pop-up commentary sarcastically jabs at an individual acting bizarre, such as noting how a male dater has not looked anywhere but at his partner's chest. Thus, the supertext highlights the daters' nontraditional dating behaviors.

The particular episode of *Blind Date* used for this study included two dates. The first date consisted of two white daters in their early 30s. The woman was very clean cut and attractive while the man had greasy long hair and wore a biker jacket. The daters attended a cooking class where the man continually offended the women by making rude comments, including sexual innuendos and an account of how he likes to beat up homeless individuals. The date ended at a restaurant where the conversation became increasingly awkward, as the man continued his abrasive comments and displayed his disgusting eating habits. The second date included two white divorcees in their early 30s. Through the pop-up supertext, the man was ridiculed for being overly positive while the woman was noted to be cynical with a "nice rack." The daters engaged in several activities including side-by-side massages, the woman modeling lingerie for the man, and dinner. After the focus groups viewed these dates, the researcher facilitated an in-depth group discussion regarding feelings and reactions to the show and dating behaviors depicted. After each focus group, the interviews were transcribed.

GENERATING THEMES

Thematic analysis of these transcripts was conducted using Polkinghorne's four-step method of thematic generation. First, the researcher conducted an initial reading of the transcript to familiarize herself with the content and nature of the interviews. The second step involved an additional reading in which the researcher started examining recurring themes among the focus group interviews. In the third step, the researcher conducted additional readings to finalize themes by reducing redundancies and extracting further evidence from the interviews. Finally, the researcher utilized these themes to draw conclusions regarding the current investigation. Through this gradual process, the researcher allowed themes to emerge rather than forcing transcripts into set categories.

Results

A thematic analysis of the focus-group interviews revealed five key themes:

1. Sexually-extreme reality dating shows provide an outlet for natural voyeuristic curiosity of others' humiliation.
2. Viewers watch reality dating shows with an accepted sense of a scripted reality.

3. The audience easily discerns the prevalence of gender stereotypes.
4. Viewers resist the behaviors portrayed on sexually extreme dating shows.
5. The absurdity of the reality dating shows normalizes viewers' lives and behaviors.

THE NATURAL APPEAL OF VOYEURISM AND HUMILIATION

As it is human instinct to desire to invade individuals' privacy (Tunstall and Dunford), reality dating shows provide a perfect outlet for individuals to safely invade other individuals' lives. One woman exemplified this feeling by stating, "I like getting an inside look." Another woman noted, "I like watching people and how they interact ... just watching their behaviors."

In particular, individuals crave seeing people in awkward situations. One man noted, "I like watching people in predicaments that I wouldn't normally be in." In addition, the participants recognized that the producers purposely select predicaments that are apt to create some awkwardness. Several participants noted that these behaviors were unrealistic, especially for a first date. One man said, "I could never imagine calling a girl up and saying, 'Hey, how'd you like to model some lingerie for me on Saturday?'" Another man said, "I know that they make these situations purposefully sexual. The producers are trying to make things awkward, especially for the couples that don't get along."

In particular, the producers spur individuals into awkward situations through the use of alcohol. One woman stated:

> ... I think that the producers encourage them to drink. Ya know, they probably send alcohol right to the table and when you need another one, they're probably right there. I think that they want people to loosen up more. I think typically people on a date don't get drunk and that they want to remember what's going on....

Another woman noted a similar observation of the role of alcohol. She said:

> ... When they go to dinner, they'll have a drink. Then, they'll go to a bar and have a drink. Alcohol is always involved. They usually get drunk. I've seen episodes in the past were people get drunk and just everything happens....

The unusual behavior spurred by the alcohol serves as a catalyst for humiliating behavior. The participants noted that these humiliating scenes were particularly enjoyable. One man said, "Ya know, the drunk guy is the entertaining one." Another man noted that humiliation on television was entertaining because there is a sense of safety involved:

> I think that we kind of like watching stuff fail sometimes. It's kind of a twisted mentality, but like, why does *America's Funniest Home Videos* last for like 35 years? You see some guy fall off a ladder or get kicked in the balls. You know they're okay, so it's okay to laugh.

Reality dating shows remain widely popular as they enable the viewers to engage in a safe form of voyeurism. The viewers are able to enjoy the participants' humiliation, as they are provided a sense of security knowing that something humiliating or dangerous can only be humorous if a network deems it safe for viewer consumption. Essentially, the viewers are given an unwritten guarantee that if something is shown on television, the participants will be safe in the end.

ACCEPTANCE OF A SCRIPTED REALITY

As the participants noted the producers' use of alcohol to spur entertaining television, many of the participants explained that they accept that reality television is not really real. A man stated, "No reality show is really reality. It's larger than life." In fact, many of the participants explained an acceptance of the scripted nature of reality television. Participants noted that the shows are skewed on three levels: participants, setting and editing.

First, the shows are scripted due to the producers' selection of certain individuals to appear on the show. A woman noted, "They choose certain people, like the bitch, like, ya know, the nice one, so that there are so many dramatic people." One man stated, "They're not just going to have some average Joe on there. They're going to have someone who's a total loser or has something crazy about him." This particular drama-driven selection creates a falseness surrounding the shows' daters.

Further, the scripted nature of the show is demonstrated through the scene selection. Many *Blind Date* episodes take the daters through an intricately planned day-long date filled with multiple restaurants and activities. A man stated, "It's just too well planned out," while another said, "There's no way any regular person could afford to date like this. It's completely fake." One woman explained, "They put them in places to get their reaction. Who would go to a lingerie shop on their first date?"

Finally, the editing plays an important role of creating a sense of a scripted reality. One woman noted, "They pick and choose what they put on the air. They actually portray people to be something that maybe they only are a fourth of the time, but on the show, they're that way all the time." A man questioned, "I always wonder how much extra footage they cut out." This editing process challenges viewers to decipher what is real and what is created. This sense of a scripted reality epitomizes the notion of a hyperreality, in which the viewer can no longer distinguish between the real and the fiction (Glynn). Although the viewers accept the scripted nature, it is difficult to draw the line between the script and reality.

Prevalence of Stereotypes

Though the interviews did not focus on stereotypes, several of the participants were quick to discern their presence. One woman noted, "Some of the things they say are really demeaning." Gender stereotypes in the video clip used for this study were present in two forms: the woman as the sexual object and the man as the sexual aggressor. However, both men and women framed the stereotypes as explicitly harmful to the men while negating their effect on women. One man said, "The first pop up you see says like, 'Nice rack!' They stereotype the men in a bad way." A woman noted, "They showed his eyes staring at particular areas. They're just trying to get you to form an opinion of him." While there is stereotyping of both the men and the women throughout the show, the participants seemed to be more offended by the depicting of the male sexual aggressor.

Resisting Daters' Behaviors

By viewing the strange dating behaviors, the participants explained that the show essentially serves as lessons of what not to do on a date. One woman noted, "It's showing you what you don't want to happen." A man said, "I think they're intentionally editing it to see people do stupid things, teaching people not to do stupid things through humor." The participants took these shows as dating lessons that they were able to apply to their own lives. A man said after viewing a woman on a bad date eating very quickly, "I'll definitely watch how fast my date eats from now on. If she's eating really fast, I'm screwed." Another man explained, "They're pretty much just showing you how to act or not to act." Therefore, as participants view the daters' behaviors as atypical, the viewers actually conform to traditional dating behaviors.

Normalizing of Viewers' Lives

Despite the absurdity of many of these dating shows, viewers still find them relatable. One woman said, "We've all had bad dates. We can compare ourselves to that." But, as Glynn noted, reality television and talk shows focus on the bizarre. This focus tends to normalize viewers' behaviors, as the viewers engage in social comparison with the reality television characters. Some of the behaviors depicted in these shows are so extreme that even a viewer's bad dating experience, suddenly may seem normal. One man said, "These people are put on there to make us laugh and to make us feel more normal." A woman said, "They probably make you feel better about yourself too, that you're not crazy like that." Through the focus on seemingly crazy individuals or instances that viewers can relate to, the viewers felt that their own lives were remarkably normal.

Discussion

The results not only support previous findings regarding reality television but also provide significant insight into the understudied realm of reality-dating television. From these results, four significant conclusions can be drawn regarding viewers' perception of reality-dating television.

THE REINFORCEMENT OF TRADITIONAL DATING NORMS THROUGH RESISTING REALITY DATING

When the participants in this investigation viewed a reality dating show in which the daters engaged in atypical dating behaviors, such as getting massages and engaging in a mini lingerie show on a first date, the participants were quick to develop resistance messages. Many of the viewers discussed feelings regarding "what not to do on a date." Because the resistance messages oppose atypical dating behaviors, individuals are actually conforming to traditional dating norms. With the strong sexual content on *Blind Date* and similar reality dating shows, one must question if viewers also resist reality-dating shows with more conservative themes, such as *The Bachelor*. Where is the point at which viewers relate to and adopt characters' behaviors or reject the actions of reality television characters? Further, if viewers continue to be exposed to these bizarre dating behaviors, will they be desensitized to the extreme content? Will these extreme dates begin to appear more acceptable, and in turn, possibly change the traditional dating script?

GENDER STEREOTYPES

Although stereotypes are plentiful in television (Glynn), gender stereotypes play an interesting role in reality dating shows. Both men and women are negatively stereotyped with women being sexual objects and the men being sexual aggressors. However, the viewers admittedly were more offended by the male stereotypes. Though both the male and female stereotypes were equally demeaning, the participants only reacted negatively to the stereo-typing of the man. One must question why both male and female viewers more readily discerned the male stereotypes.

Women have long been portrayed as sexual objects, and therefore, it is not surprising that few participants even noted the demeaning portrayal of women. Television series, music videos and reality television have become increasingly sexually laden (Glynn). Thus, viewers may have been inoculated to the presence of women sex objects. As the participants viewed the man in a role that may not be as readily accepted, the participants may have been more apt to note this unfamiliar portrayal. Additionally, if viewers believe these portrayals of men are an accurate view of reality, there could be significant social implications if men attempt to act out these crude and sometimes dangerous sexual behaviors.

ACCEPTANCE OF A HYPERREALITY

The accepted role of the producer becomes an increasingly pertinent factor in the viewing of reality television. Participants are quick to note that the producers "can edit what they want" and "choose interesting characters" to create a show which will keep the audience interested. This editing process creates a hyperreality in which the real and the fictional are no longer distinguishable (Glynn). Though the producers cannot control what the participants say or do, they can control what the audience views. Through careful editing, the producers can create a scene that may have never even occurred by using splices of other recorded situations. For example, an individual who may be sad only five percent of the time while on a show could be portrayed as someone who is clinically depressed by splicing together clips of the few moments of sadness an individual experienced. Though the participants recognized this process, it did not detract from their viewing enjoyment. However, as individuals view and interpret these shows, scholars must examine how viewers determine where the fiction stops and the real begins.

NORMALIZING SURVEILLANCE

This study supports Andrejevic's previous findings that reality television maintains its appeal by creating a safe and distanced form of voyeurism. The prevalence of reality television increasingly has normalized surveillance of everyday activities. Reality shows, such as *Big Brother,* blatantly address the normalizing of the surveillance of everyday individuals. The continual viewing of these reality shows may reinforce to the audience the right of others to engage in surveillance of people's private lives. Thus, as reality television continues to grow in popularity and surveillance becomes more readily accepted, producers may continue to push the envelope, delving into exposing even more personal activities. Further, if surveillance through reality television becomes increasingly acceptable, one must question if viewers may become more tolerant of surveillance, even by governing bodies. This normalizing of surveillance may have significant ideological consequences.

Conclusion

Reality dating television may have significant social implications, influencing what people view and accept as societal norms, including dating behaviors. This intersection between the media and interpersonal relationships is a pertinent issue that demands further exploration. Reality dating shows have become a cultural phenomenon, challenging the way in which we view television and our relationships.

BIBLIOGRAPHY

Abt, V., and M. Seesholtz. "The Shameless World of Phil, Sally and Oprah: Television Talk Shows and the Deconstructing of Society." *Journal of Popular Culture* 28 (1994): 171–191.

Andrejevic, M. "The Kinder, Gentler Gaze of Big Brother: Reality TV in the Era of Digital Capitalism." *New Media and Society* 4 (2002): 251–270.

Aubrey, J. S., K. Harrison, L. Kramer, and J. Yellin. "Variety Versus Timing: Gender Differences in College Students' Sexual Expectations as Predicted by Exposure to Sexually Oriented Television." *Communication Research* 30 (2003): 432–460.

Austin, E. "In Contempt of Courtship." *Washington Monthly* June 2003: 40–43.

Bagley, G. "The Television Text: Spectatorship, Ideology, and the Organization of Consent." *Critical Studies in Media Communication* 18 (2001): 436–451.

Cohen, J. "Parasocial Relations and Romantic Attraction: Gender and Dating Status Differences." *Journal of Broadcasting & Electronic Media* 41 (1997): 516–529.

Davies, M. M., and D. Machin. "It Helps People Make Their Decisions: Dating Games, Public Service Broadcasting and the Negotiation of Identity in Middle-Childhood." *Childhood* 7 (2000): 173–191.

D'Emilio, J., and E. B. Freedman. *Intimate Matters: A History of Sexuality in America,* 2nd ed. Chicago: The University of Chicago Press, 1988.

DeRose, J., E. Fürsich, and E.V. Haskins. "Pop (Up) Goes the Blind Date: Supertextual Constraints on 'Reality' Television." *Journal of Communication Inquiry* 27 (2003): 171–189.

Dority, B. "A Brave New World or a Technological Nightmare? Big Brother Is Watching!" *Humanist* 61 (2001): 9–13.

Fiske, J. *Understanding Popular Culture.* London: Routledge, 1989.

Gerbner, G., L. Gross, M. Morgan, and N. Signorielli. "Growing Up with Television:

The Cultivation Perspective." *Media Effects.* Ed. J. Bryant and D. Zillmann Hillsdale. Mahwah, NJ: Earlbaum, 1994. 17–42.

Glynn, K. *Tabloid Culture: Trash Taste, Popular Power, and the Transformation of American Television.* Durham, NC: Duke University Press, 2000.

Greenberg, B. S., J.L. Sherry, R. W. Busselle, L. Hnilo, and S.W. Smith. "Daytime Television Talk Shows: Guests, Content and Interactions." *Journal of Broadcasting & Electronic Media* 41 (1997): 412–426.

Hall, S. "The Rediscovery of 'Ideology': Return of the Repressed in Media Studies." *Culture, Society and the Media.* Ed. M. Gurevitch, T. Bennett, J. Curran, and J. Woollacott. London: Routledge, 1982. 56–90.

Hetsroni, A. "Choosing a Mate in Television Dating Games: The Influence of Setting, Culture, and Gender." *Sex Roles* 42 (2000): 83–106.

Jagger, E. "Marketing Molly and Melville: Dating in a Postmodern, Consumer Society." *Sociology* 35 (2001): 39–57.

Jupiter, B. C. "Ideology of the Witch: Cultivating the Witch through Repeated Representation in Television and Film." Selected paper from the annual meeting of the National Communication Association, Nov. 2004, Chicago.

Morgan, M. "Television, Sex-Role Attitudes, and Sex-Role Behavior." *Journal of Early Adolescence* 7 (1987): 268–282.

Polkinghorne, D. *Methodology for the Human Sciences.* Albany: State University of New York Press, 1983.

Poniewozik, J. "Hot Tubs and Cold Shoulders." *Time* 12 Aug. 2002: 56–58.

Rose, S., and I. H. Frieze. "Young Singles' Contemporary Dating Scripts." *Sex Roles: A Journal of Research* 28 (1993): 499–509.

Rosenzweig, J. "Consuming Passions." *American Prospect* 6 Dec. 1999: 46–48.

Schwartz, M. "Repetition and the Rated Truth Value of Statements." *American Journal of Psychology* 92 (1982): 399–407.

Syvertsen, T. "Ordinary People in Extraordinary Circumstances: A Study of Participants in Television Dating Games." *Media, Culture & Society* 23 (2001): 319–337.

Tunstall, J., and M. Dunford. "Light Entertainment." *Television Producers.* Ed. J. Tunstall. London: Routledge, 1993. 138–53.

Ward, L. M. "Does Television Exposure Affect Emerging Adults' Attitudes and Assumptions about Sexual Relationships? Correlational and Experimental Confirmation." *Journal of Youth & Adolescence* 31 (2002): 1–15.

Women's Shared Viewing
of *The Bachelor*

Generational Motives and Perceptions

CARY W. HORVATH AND
MARGARET O. FINUCANE

ABC's *The Bachelor* portrays one bachelor's gradual elimination of potential mates from an original pool of 25 women. Each season debuts a new bachelor, portrayed as a prize catch by traditional standards: rich, handsome, athletic, or otherwise successful. Previous bachelors have included a prominent football player, a physician, an heir to the Firestone family fortune, and a real-life prince. Throughout the season, the bachelor gets to know each young woman through a series of meetings and dates, episodically eliminating some of the women. Notably, at the end of each show, he dramatically selects favorites with a ceremonious bestowing of roses, and some bachelorettes are not selected. The season finale anticipates a marriage proposal to his true love — the last woman standing.

According to Yep and Camacho, *The Bachelor* reinforces patriarchal, heterogendered stereotypes. Problematic is the consistent portrayal of the all-powerful male, stereotypical standards of male and female beauty and attractiveness, women as objects for male gaze, female rivalry, women as subservient caretakers, and fairytale language and imagery (339). Streitmatter, too, contends such shows glorify casual sex and infidelity, and turn bodies into sexual objects (225). Not surprisingly, feminists swiftly criticized the show as old-fashioned and demeaning to women, but female audience members tuned in — in droves. In the first five weeks of the show's 2003 season, 64 percent of the viewers were adult women (Pendelton 25). The show is "a powerhouse in attracting women. Each installment consistently scored as a top 10 performer among females age 18 to 49" (Pendelton 25). Recent ratings indicate the show's continued popularity; the May 2007 finale resulted in *The Bachelor* again winning its time period in total viewers and adults 18 to 49 (Rocchio and Rogers). The November 2007 finale in which the bachelor chose "none of the above" enraged fans — and provided the show its highest rating of the season. The following "After the Rose" retrospective won its 10 P.M. time slot and was the highest rated "After the Rose" ever (Hibberd, "'Bachelor' Finale," "'Bachelor': After").

Thirty-nine-year-old Mike Fleiss dreamed up the show with women in mind, believing "the show's appeal lies in its elaborate romantic fantasy dates, tempered by the common emotion of heartache. I wanted it to have a bigger, larger-than-life, dream date sort of quality" (Pendelton 25). Women's enthusiastic viewing of this show is curious, as the program presents such a seemingly sexist portrayal of relationships. Therefore, this research seeks to answer two logical questions:

RQ1: Why do women watch *The Bachelor*?
RQ2: How do women make sense of *The Bachelor*?

Initial anecdotal information indicated that women commonly watched the show with other women, discussing the show during and after the viewing. Watching the show as a shared event seemed to complement and add enjoyment to the experience. Previous research has found that shared television viewing benefits personal relationships in a variety of ways. Couples often perceive television as a positive element in their love relationships (Finucane and Horvath 314; Gantz, "Exploring" 75; Gantz, "Conflicts" 314). For example, couples report that viewing television together provides a shared activity, an opportunity for conversation, and a chance to relax together. Gantz found that couples reporting higher marital satisfaction perceived television as a shared activity (76).

Kubey (317) found shared viewing was perceived as a more social, cheerful, and challenging experience than solo viewing. Family members reported a greater desire to watch television with someone else, rather than alone. Lemish found that college students' coviewing of soap operas was more of a social activity than students' interest in the program content (289).

Finucane and Horvath (318) found couples' positive perceptions of television could be explained in part using Lull's (201) typology of social uses. The relational purposes include viewing to facilitate communication (e.g., conversational entrance, agenda for talk), viewing for affiliation or avoidance (e.g., family solidarity, conflict reduction, relationship maintenance), viewing for social learning (e.g., behavior modeling, information dissemination), and viewing for competence/dominance (e.g., role reinforcement, intellectual validation, argument facilitation). In this study, we found women view *The Bachelor* for similar purposes and outcomes.

Method

Women who shared viewing of *The Bachelor* participated in focus groups. The research was approved by the institutional research boards affiliated with both authors. All women were informed of their rights and signed consent forms prior to their participation. Identified through purposeful sampling, the groups consisted of two groups of traditional college students ($N = 11$, ages 20–23) and two groups of older women ($N = 9$, ages 37–41). All women were identified as Caucasian and all resided in Northeast Ohio. All groups had watched together several seasons and planned to continue. Participants responded freely to a host of questions about motives for shared viewing, as well as perceptions about the show itself.

Results

Generally, women expressed belief that shared viewing has a positive effect on their friendship. Shared viewing commonly had a party atmosphere, including food and drinks. Strikingly, very few differences emerged between any of the groups. Older women engage in more shared viewing via telephone and tended to talk more about relationships and behavior, whereas younger women talked together more about contestants' physical appearance. Otherwise, answers were nearly identical. Across groups, women share the same annoyances about the show's repetitive formula (e.g., "This is the final rose," "Never pick my girl!"). The women also commonly share and discuss other programming (e.g., movies or other television such as *Dawson's Creek*, *90210*, *General Hospital*, *American Idol*, *Extreme Makeover*, and *the Newlyweds*), but they reported that none of these compared to the intensity of sharing *The Bachelor*. Analysis of the data resulted in three themes common to all women who watched *The Bachelor*: communication facilitation, affiliation, and social learning.

COMMUNICATION FACILITATION

Lull (202) suggested that television facilitates communication, providing conversational entrance and an agenda for talk. *The Bachelor* serves as a reason and a catalyst for talk among women; talking together is an important outcome of the experience:

> "Instead of talking on the phone it's better to watch together ... it's more fun to be together so you could say something every couple seconds rather than every 15 minutes."
>
> "I hate watching by myself ... it wouldn't be as fun ... you couldn't talk about people ... I would be talking to myself. I'd be like, 'You're stupid!'"
>
> "Those 15 minutes between commercial breaks are hard for me, not to call somebody when something happens right away, but the general rule is that we don't talk during commercials. I could be saying something the entire time, no doubt about it. I really could be talking about it for the whole hour."
>
> "I can't stand not relating to someone while I'm watchin' it ... sometimes we watch whole TV shows on the phone."
>
> "We don't shut up the whole show. We even miss things they say sometimes because one of us are saying something the whole time."

Participants also frequently talked to women by phone during the show (often one another or sisters or mothers):

> "We're calling each other ten times."
>
> "Everyone, other people call."
>
> "We call each other after watching our shows and we talk all about the show."
>
> "If no one's here, then every phone is ringing and I'm getting beeps ... if I'm home watching with my husband, he hates me, cause I'm on the phone the whole time."

They also reported talking to each other about the show during commercials, and at other times during the week, and to anyone else who watched the show:

> (during commercials) "We usually are still talking about the show."
>
> "Whenever it comes up."
>
> "We always talk about it."
>
> "They all sit around at lunchtime and talk about it; we talked until the water cooler guy came in."
>
> "I do hair and so if clients watch it I talk about it with them too."

AFFILIATION

Another common reason for shared viewing is affiliation, including increased feelings of solidarity, conflict reduction, and relationship maintenance (Lull 203). Comments generally indicated the desire for affiliation and relationship maintenance:

"It was an excuse to get together and hang out."

"I've never watched it alone."

"I don't watch TV alone."

"It's made our friendship better than it would have been had we not had this show in common ... right. Then you find other things in common."

"We're always together! We were both really excited about it.... I think the whole thing about watching together is you have to watch with someone who's just as interested in it as you."

Most important to the shared viewing experience was a need for opinion solidarity among the women. Although all of the women claimed to have differences of opinion about the show, solidarity reigned. They were nearly unanimous in their opinions, speaking often in unison, and frequently using the word "we" when expressing beliefs or attitudes:

"We don't always agree but there are some elements of it that are in common."

"You could just tell from our conversation that we were as addicted as one another."

"We're gonna find something wrong with every single bachelorette that there is [laughter] especially if we're jealous of them, then we're like, 'We hate you ... we don't like her.'"

They also wanted to know that their opinions were shared by others watching the show:

"We get outside information from everybody, outside opinions."

"You can express your opinions ... see how your opinions measure up."

"One time my neighbor Tonya called also during commercial, said, 'I want to stab, I want to gouge her eyes out with an ice pick' [laughter]. I was like, 'I concur'" [laughter].

"If we think someone's stupid, we need someone else to agree ... we're all, like, 'Yes!'"

"There are a lot of people that we like too, you know, 'We love her,' that kind of thing."

"Kinda get their opinion to see if they think the same thing we did."

"You know what is funny, if you listened to us talk back and forth about it, you probably wouldn't be able to understand one word we're saying but we'd both end up at the same conclusion.... Yeah, a lot of times we'll be talking at the same time about completely different things and we can understand each other and still continue on with our point."

"It is a scream to watch those stupid girls; we scream at it like that last time Bob picked one of the girls we were yelling at the TV we were so mad. We swore we were never going to watch it again and then we did."

"Our favorite character never gets it. It doesn't happen like we want it to."

Many of the shared opinions revolved around criticism of the other women:

> "It's a bunch of women that we can make fun of."
>
> "How fake the girls can be ... yes. I like to see how many psychos there are. I notice that right off the bat."
>
> "Women like seeing pretty women — like, 'Oh, I like her hair.'"
>
> "And how the other girls act with guys."

Furthermore, the women hinted that opinion deviants were punished:

> "Me and my one girlfriend always end up arguing because she always likes the opposite person I do. Of course, every time we think someone is stupid my other girlfriend likes her, so then I yell at her [laughter]. 'Stupid, I can't believe you like her!'"

SOCIAL LEARNING

People also share viewing for the purpose of social learning (Lull 204). Together, they make sense of characters and portrayals for the purposes of behavior modeling and sharing information. With regard to reality television, Hall found that in addition to viewing for interaction with friends, people also watch for the enjoyment of unpredictable, comedic and bad behavior, and vicarious enjoyment of happy endings (206). We see some of that here, where women struggled together to explain their attraction to the show's content and their conflicted views about its validity. For example, they acknowledged their love of "girly" fantasy and romance in the shows:

> "Sucking face all the time, you know, that's kind of strange."
>
> "It's a situation that we probably all have thought at one point ... boy, that would be really fun, but no way could I ever do it."
>
> "I think we're all living vicariously through these women that are there having a good time, living in this house, meeting new friends, going out with a hot guy, being on television, all that stuff that we would be so chicken to do."
>
> "It gives us something exciting to look forward to, you know, after you put the kids to bed, and you know, you live your normal mom life."
>
> "There's always, like, the fairytale one in there where one of the girls has a Cinderella dress on and he's in tuxedo and they're in a mansion, like that kind of thing goin' on. You always know there's going to be the big outdoorsy one where they're parasailing or mountain climbing, or you know, that kind of stuff is pretty general now, you know, but I love it."
>
> "We don't care; we watch it anyways [sic]."
>
> "They make the main person out to be like a fairytale person that everyone would want to be with."
>
> "Good point" [laughter].

"A happy ending."

"I don't think men are very interesting in dating shows in general, or romantic movies, or girly stuff."

"It's just a girly thing."

"I think all women like to see dating, in general."

"Yeah, I mean, in all honesty, as far back as I can remember, I have been all about obsessing with relationships, you know, whether it be my friends or my family or what's on television or whatever, so this is right up my alley."

"The same reason women like to watch romantic movies or read romantic books or watch soap operas — because you like to see how it's supposed to turn out."

"Men don't do that as much. I don't think they're that much into it."

Nabi et al. found that voyeurism was a significant predictor of enjoyment of *The Bachelor/Bachelorette*; however, it did not predict enjoyment of other reality television genre. The findings suggested reality genres are distinctly different from one another in the way they're used and enjoyed (441).

Kilborn noted much of the success of reality television can be attributed to pre-launch publicity, press releases, interviews with leading characters, websites, chat rooms, and other interactive technologies (85). Although the shows claim "real life" interaction, the desire to produce heightened drama leads reality television producers to fabricate the truth, blurring boundaries between factual and fictional genres. At the same time, "audiences are becoming increasingly knowledgeable (and probably cynical) about the strategies employed in the construction and delivery of various forms of factual entertainment" (16). Not surprisingly, women simultaneously expressed conflicting opinions about the show's "reality":

"They're real people. It's not like they're actors on TV, you know, it's not real when you're watching those other shows. You know, these are real people with real feelings."

"So this is like, this is for real, so maybe that's why we get so crazy about it."

"I know in the back of my head that it's not really real, but I still pretend that I think it is, you know?"

"It's bad to think that someone — that you could, like, end up with for the rest of your life — was picked at random."

[about husbands] "They just don't even believe in it. They don't believe for a minute that these people are really there trying to find true love. They have not fallen for the whole thing like I have."

"He's been proven right cause everybody's broken up except for one person."

"Well, nothing's worked out yet for all of them."

"Except for Trista."

"Yeah. Trista and Ryan, but they'll probably divorce."

"You gotta wonder if it's really real."

"Yeah, cause they're editing everything."

"It was scripted."

Ambivalence about the show's reality is understandable given that media send conflicting messages about whether true feelings are represented in the program. Magazine and Internet readers are encouraged to believe that true romances result and continue after programming ends. One couple, Trista and Ryan, actually married and now have two children. Papacharissi and Mendelson studied reality television without regard to specific genre and found that "affinity for the reality genre cannot develop unless the audience, to a certain extent, accepts the reality of what is being presented" (368). Viewers commonly "acknowledge that producers stage events, but suggest that the behavior of the cast members within the context of those events is real" (Hall 201).

So, what "real" behaviors are being presented and endorsed? Ferris et al. conducted a content analysis of reality dating shows, including *The Bachelor*, which revealed three central attitudes toward dating that occurred 14 to 15 times per hour: men are sex-driven, dating is a game, and women are sex objects. Furthermore, all three sentiments are more often rewarded than punished on the shows. Viewers who commonly watched reality dating shows and saw them as realistic, especially men, tended to endorse the three sentiments. The authors also found a positive relationship between viewing and endorsing some of the dating behaviors depicted on the show, such as drinking and hot tub use (504). Together, the findings suggest it's possible that reality dating shows cultivate perceptions about dating and even motivate social learning about useful and proper dating behaviors.

When asked about gender portrayals and the show's overall premise, the women expressed ambivalence, apathy, and even disdain for the female participants:

"If you think about it, it's like cattle marching in."

"They just want their 15 minutes of fame."

"They are like so fake and so dramatic and it's just ... I think they play to win and not to get the guy."

"It shows that the woman needs a man to be complete ... he's the knight in shining armor on the white horse and she's not complete with out the man."

"It still comes down to the girl getting proposed to."

"They knew what they were doing when they got into it. It wasn't like they were going against their will; they knew exactly what they were doing."

"I'm not sitting there, like, thinking about how these women are getting treated. You know what I'm saying? It's just pretty much casual ... just for fun."

"I could probably come up with reasons why it doesn't make women look good or, you know, the whole situation. But I don't think about that kind of stuff. I really don't want to."

"The only thing I think is it's not something that I would ever do. I can't imagine myself fighting with 25 other people for a guy. That, to me, is just desperate."

"I actually don't think it's something I'd want to be involved in."

"Sometimes it's embarrassing to women in general how they act; some of them are very pathetic."

A final question asked whether the women thought *The Bachelor* showed positive or negative portrayals of women:

"NEGATIVE" [all chorused, long pause].

"I think to some extent it is true [laughter]. It's just what it is all about."

"Yeah; all girls get catty [laugher]."

Discussion

Reality television offers a powerful means to study all four functions of the media: surveillance, correlation, transmission of culture, and entertainment (Lasswell 203). Women's viewing of ABC's *The Bachelor* provides a compelling example of this point. In watching the experiences of other people, women learn how to navigate their own relationships, how to interpret the environment, and what their culture values. Profound life lessons are communicated through a veil of innocuous entertainment.

Consistent with the results, Papacharissi and Mendelson found that greater liking for reality television resulted from more frequent watching for entertainment, habit, relaxation, companionship, and social interaction (367). The authors suspected, however, that different demographic groups watch reality television differently, concluding "qualitative interviewing or ethnographic study of smaller communities of reality viewers could help us understand more complex behavioral tendencies" (268). This study attempted to do just that.

The focus groups with older and younger women helped to answer why women watch *The Bachelor* and how they understand it. One of the most striking findings of the study was the identical nature of the answers regardless of the age of the participants. Three of Lull's (202) social uses of media were clear sources of motivation for shared viewing: communication facili-

tation, affiliation (especially opinion solidarity and relationship maintenance), and social learning. Watching together is an end in itself, a reason
to "hang out," talk and laugh; however, it is also a means to discovering
deeper truths. Together, they make sense of themselves through the experiences of other women. They search for validation of their perceptions related
to attractive and ethical behavior, common fantasy, and perceptions about
what's real. This study did not find support for Lull's (205) competence/dom-
inance function of coviewing; women do not watch together to compete or
show superiority among one another. However, it can be argued the coviewing experience enabled them, as a group, to feel superior to women on the
show (e.g., "If someone has a messed up life, TV makes you feel better about
your own life," "Everyone on those shows looks stupid — I mean, that's why
you watch it").

Lancioni lamented the failure to empathize with reality television characters. Instead, we use them to fill boring evenings, mock their stupidity,
and laugh at their dysfunction. In this, we devalue ourselves as well as them
and become desensitized to others' pain or embarrassment. The passive audience is a false paradigm — when we condone, even cheer for, unethical behavior in our favorite characters, we condone it in real life. Active viewing is
ethical. As we watch, "we need to constantly remind ourselves that although
the situations are contrived, the people are real" (155) and that "the people
we see on the screen have been constructed from thousands of feet of raw
footage, most of which we never see" (Lancioni 156).

Unfortunately, contradictions among the women's opinions indicated
their ambivalence, even apathy, about what's real and about feminist issues.
The women in this study were conflicted about the show's reality; they want
to believe that happy endings and true love are actual outcomes of the show,
but realize production techniques falsify its content. They watched for the
love of fairytale and romance, but had negative opinions of the show's overall premise and characters. The key strategy used to reduce their dissonance
was to eliminate the importance of the issue (e.g., "I don't think about that
kind of stuff," "It's just for fun").

Douglas contended that women view *The Bachelor* for much more than
mere amusement. Women viewers root for the woman who best validates their
own sense of womanhood. If the bachelor chooses her, he validates her own
identity. His choice perpetuates patriarchy because it indicates what type of
woman can survive in a world run by men. All the women are slim, pretty,
and most are blonde. "Women who railed against the sexism of the Miss America pageant, TV detective shows and Mr. Clean commercials on the early '70s
must not believe what they are seeing" (Douglas 61). Yet the show has been

a smash among young women. Douglas asks, "What the hell has happened to this generation of young women?" (62). Based on the above findings, one might add, "What happened to their mothers?"

Douglas argues for women, the show is not about the bachelor; it's about the women. "Female viewers see an array of personas, identifying with some and rejecting others, as they calibrate what kind of woman succeeds in a world where appearance and personality still powerfully determine a woman's fate" (62). They place themselves on a "post-feminist scale of femininity" and tune in to see if the show validates their suspicion that men choose women based on superficial standards, or that patriarchy has become more "enlightened" and sensitive (63).

A look at similar programming can help shed light on our findings. Maher discussed women's addiction and obsession with TLC's programming, especially with *A Baby Story* and *A Wedding Story.* The shows reinforce traditional gender roles and "nothing-without-a-man ethos" (199). They reflect and create typical childhood fantasy stories, full of references to romantic love and fairytales (e.g., "prince" and "princess"). Every bride and groom in *A Wedding Story* is announced as "Mr. and Mrs. Insert Male First Name and Last Name Here" (202). Most online fan-site participants are married women. One fan of *A Wedding Story* said that her husband can't understand why she continues to watch the show. "A plethora of recently married women soon respond, and there is a general agreement that once again, husbands just don't understand" (210). Online postings about TLC's programming reveal "the complicated nature of female longing for love, dissatisfaction with that love, and a need to be reassured that love is still possible" (212). Women's reactions to *The Bachelor* echo these values.

Women's attraction to *The Bachelor* can be explained apart from notions of feminism. The mere thrill of exciting competition is one factor. Mittell labels *The Bachelor* a "reality drama" genre of reality television with others such as *Real World* and *American High.* This genre relies "on shorthand techniques of montage sequences, musical cues, and strategic casting of character types to maximize dramatic pleasures for audiences who are used to the pacing and style of fictional storytelling" (197). These pleasures are heightened when "conflicts and goals are extreme" (198). Pleasures of viewing are also wish fulfillment and identification with characters, as in "horror and gangster films," but it doesn't mean that viewers necessarily want to be on the show themselves.

Similarly, the appeal to fantasy is another attraction. Reiss and Wiltz argue reality television is attractive to viewers because it enables "fantasy about gaining status through automatic fame" (27). It's easy to imagine that you, too, could be a celebrity on television — to experience the secret thrill that an ordinary person could become important to millions. Boorstin posited that Americans crave illusion, the contradictory and impossible. Society has shifted attention from real events and facts to pseudo-events, blending and confusing the real and unreal. Pseudo-events are carefully orchestrated with intent for reproduction and mass interest. Their appeal is in "whether it really happened" (11).

Shifting cultural use of media can also explain why women use the show to fulfill needs for affiliation and communication. Andrejevic contended reality television is symptomatic of a post modern society characterized by heightened surveillance and need for mutual monitoring (cell phones and the Internet are characteristic of this, also) to replace the loss of daily mutual monitoring in traditional communities long gone (26).

All this, together, can explain why women are drawn to *The Bachelor,* one of the most blatantly sexist programs on television. Affiliation, solidarity, social learning, excitement, validation, and fantasy combine together to compel women's attention. Add a dash of apathy toward notions of feminism, and you have the makings of a huge hit.

BIBLIOGRAPHY

Andrejevic, Mark. *Reality TV: The Work of Being Watched.* New York: Rowman & Littlefield, 2004.

The Bachelor. ABC. Exec. prod. Mike Fleiss. 25 March 2002–.

Boorstin, Daniel. *The Image: A Guide to Pseudo-Events in America.* New York: Harper Colophon, 1971.

Douglas, Susan. "Young Women Learn Harmful Gender Stereotypes from Reality TV." *Reality TV.* Ed. Karen F. Balkin. Farmington Hills: Greenhaven, 2004. 61–63.

Ferris, Amber, et al. "The Content of Reality Dating Shows and Viewer Perceptions of Dating." *Journal of Communication* 57 (2007): 490–510.

Finucane, Margaret, and Cary Horvath. "Lazy Leisure: A Qualitative Investigation of the Relational Uses of Television in Marriage." *Communication Quarterly* 48:3 (2000): 311–321.

Gantz, Walter. "Conflicts and Resolution Strategies Associated with Television in Marital Life." *Television and the American Family.* Ed. Jennings Bryant and J. Alison Bryant. Mahwah, NJ: Erlbaum, 2001. 289–316.

_____. "Exploring the Role of Television in Married Life." *Journal of Broadcasting & Electronic Media* 29 (1985): 65–78.

Hall, Alice. "Viewers' Perceptions of Reality Programs." *Communication Quarterly* 54 (2006): 191–211.

Hibberd, James. "'Bachelor: After the Rose' Wins Hour." *TV Week* 21 Nov. 2007. 30 Nov. 2007 <http://www.tvweek.com/blogs/james hibberd/2007/11/bachelor_after_the_rose_ wins_h.php>.

_____. "'Bachelor' Finale Hits Ratings High." *TV Week* 20 Nov. 2007. 30 Nov. 2007 http://www.tvweek.com/blogs/jameshibberd/2007/11/bachelor_finale_hits_ratings_h.php>.

Kilborn, Richard. *Staging the Real: Factual TV Programming in the Age of "Big Brother."* New York: Manchester University Press, 2003.

Kubey, Robert. "Television and the Quality of Family Life." *Communication Quarterly* 38 (1990): 312–324.

Lancioni, Judith. "'Survivor' in the Vast Wasteland: The Ethical Implications of Reality Television." *Desperately Seeking Ethics.* Ed. Howard Good. Lanham, MD: Scarecrow Press, 2003. 145–160.

Laswell, Harold. *The Structure and Function of Communication and Society: The Communication of Ideas.* New York: Institute for Religious and Social Studies, 1948.

Lemish, Dafna. "Soap Opera Viewing in College: A Naturalistic Inquiry." *Journal of Broadcasting and Electronic Media* 29 (1985): 275–293.

Lull, James. "The Social Uses of Television." *Human Communication Research* 6 (1980): 197–209.

Maher, Jennifer. "What Do Women Watch? Tuning in to the Compulsory Heterosexuality Channel." *Reality TV: Remaking Television Culture.* Ed. Susan Murray and Laurie Ouellette. New York: New York University Press, 2004. 197–213.

Mittell, Jason. *Genre and Television.* New York: Routledge, 2004.

Nabi, Robin, et al. "Emotional and Cognitive Predictors of Reality-Based and Fictional Television Programming: An Elaboration of the Uses and Gratifications Perspective." *Media Psychology* 8 (2006): 421–447.

Papacharissi, Zizi, and Andrew Mendelson. "An Exploratory Study of Reality Appeal: Uses and Gratifications of Reality TV Shows." *Journal of Broadcasting & Electronic Media* 51 (2007): 355–370.

Pendleton, Jennifer. "Trafficking Among Dream Bachelors." *Television Week* 10 Nov. 2003: 25.

Reiss, Steven, and James Wiltz. "Fascination with Fame Attracts Reality TV Viewers." *Reality TV.* Ed. Karen F. Balkin. Farmington Hills: Greenhaven, 2004. 25–27.

Rocchio, Christopher, and Steve Rogers. "'The Bachelor: Officer and a Gentleman' Ends with a Ratings Bang." *Reality TV World.* 31 May 2007. 20 Nov. 2007 <http://www.realitytvworld.com/news/the-bachelor-officer-and-gentleman-ends-with-ratings-bang-5263.php> .

Streitmatter, Rodger. *Sex Sells! The Media's Journey from Repression to Obsession.* Boulder: Westview Press, 2004.

Yep, Gust, and Ariana Ochoa Camacho. "The Normalization of Heterogendered Relations in *The Bachelor.*" *Feminist Media Studies* 4. 3: 338–341.

4

Fans of Plastic Surgery
Reality Television
Hopes and Concerns in Fan Postings

JOAN L. CONNERS

According to statistics from the American Society of Plastic Surgeons (ASPS), nearly 12 million cosmetic surgery procedures were performed in 2007, a 59 percent increase in procedures since 2000 ("Plastic Surgery Procedures Maintain Steady Growth in 2007"). The ASPS press release reporting such statistics included the following quote from Richard A. D'Amico, ASPS President: "The report tells me Americans are devoted to looking and feeling their best." This quote reflects the perception of cosmetic surgery in America in the 21st century, that if we are not satisfied with some aspects of ourselves physically, we can fix it. A primary source that reinforces these messages is the portrayals of plastic surgery in television entertainment, including reality programs such as *The Swan* (Fox) or *Extreme Makeover* (ABC), or fiction such as *Nip/Tuck* (FX).

The top five cosmetic surgical procedures conducted in 2007 according to the ASPS are ones frequently seen on plastic surgery reality programs: breast augmentation, liposuction, nose reshaping, eyelid surgery and a tummy tuck ("Plastic Surgery Procedures Maintain Steady Growth in 2007"). One analysis of *The Swan* in 2004 is consistent with these statistics, as 11 of 17 contestants underwent breast augmentation, 16 had liposuction, and 13 had work done on their noses (Kuczynski 1).

To what extent do plastic surgery reality programs result in increased interest in undergoing cosmetic surgery? In "Makeover Madness" Granatstein states, "Rising consumer interest in nose jobs and brow lifts has translated into hit reality shows like Fox's *The Swan* and ABC's *Extreme Makeover*" (26). Although interest in cosmetic surgery may have resulted in the creation of such TV programs, the cause-effect may take place in the opposite direction: Do plastic surgery reality programs increase public interest in cosmetic surgery, and willingness to undergo procedures? Reality TV may not be the only source of such motivations for viewers, as Blum suggests that "given so many fictional episodes of beauty risen from the ashes of homeliness, we might start thinking that it's our duty to our own identity to confirm it through some bold ritual, say cosmetic surgery" (193). It is likely a cycle of both, that the popularity of plastic surgery resulted in the popularity of plastic surgery reality television, which may be motivating more viewers to consider cosmetic surgery procedures.

The plastic surgery narrative offered in television programs such as *Extreme Makeover* and *The Swan* suggests we as viewers have flaws that can be fixed, that the ideal body image can be fulfilled in reality courtesy of cosmetic surgery procedures. We see patients, regular people, who express dissatisfaction with their physical appearance to the extent that it may have hindered their self confidence or their relationships. We then see their spirits lifted when they are able to pursue a physical transformation; courtesy of "television time," procedures and recovery appear rather efficient and painless. The narrative of such programs concludes with the dramatic reveal to one's friends and families their new selves, their new bodies, their new outlooks. There are never regrets, second guesses, or complications.

A critique of the plastic surgery industry reflects a similar concern with the message the public is receiving about cosmetic procedures. According to Jordan:

> Over the course of the last century, plastic surgery advocates have engaged in a concerted, commercial effort to redefine the human body as a plastic, malleable substance which surgeons can alter and people should want to alter in order to realize their body image ideals. These messages convey to the public the apparent ease and wonder of plastic surgery and associate body augmentation with individual empowerment, making surgery a desirable solution for individuals with body image issues [328].

Some plastic surgeons themselves have been concerned with the message plastic surgery reality television conveys to the public, in particular to teenage females. In the height of popularity of many such programs in 2004, ASPS president Dr. Rod Rohrich stated, "The new wave of plastic surgery reality television is a serious cause for concern. Some patients on these shows have unrealistic and, frankly, unhealthy expectations about what plastic surgery can do for them" ("New Reality TV Programs Create Unhealthy, Unrealistic Expectations of Plastic Surgery").

Concerns regarding viewers of plastic surgery reality television, expectations from plastic surgery and patients' poor body images may be justified,

as recent research suggests. While Kubic and Chory acknowledge a number
of factors contribute to eating disorders, their analysis found that exposure
to TV makeover shows correlated with self perceptions common to those
with eating disorders, such as lower self esteem and high body dissatisfaction (288). An experiment that exposed college students to either an episode
of *The Swan* or a non-makeover reality program found that those who
watched the plastic surgery reality program had lower self-esteem after viewing, especially those who had internalized a thin-ideal perception (Mazzeo,
Trace, Mitchell, and Gow 396). Both studies suggest viewers of plastic surgery reality television may already have poor body image or low self-esteem
prior to viewing such programs, or may decline as a result of viewing such
programs. Plastic surgery alternatives in their own lives, as presented in the
reality program narratives, may therefore become a more desirable "correction" they consider taking. However, the risks and consequences of undergoing such surgical procedures, which are typically neglected in the narratives
in such reality programs, are also likely ignored by most viewers who become
potential patients.

Content Analysis of Plastic Surgery Reality TV

To explore the messages of risk present in reality programs on plastic
surgery, I conducted a content analysis of episodes of plastic surgery reality
programs *Extreme Makeover*, *Dr. 90210*, and *Plastic Surgery: Before and After*
that aired in 2006 (Conners 73). A total of 12 patient stories were analyzed
from *Extreme Makeover*, 14 patient stories from *Dr. 90210*, and 18 patient
stories from *Plastic Surgery: Before and After*. Online fan discussions of these
programs will be the focus for the present study, but it is relevant to compare the content of these programs to understand what differences and issues
may emerge in fans' comments.

Extreme Makeover has aired on the ABC network since 2002 and then
the Style Network on cable since 2006. Two patients are featured in each
episode, each providing explanations for their desire for plastic surgery. Once
the patient is surprised with the announcement that they will be on the program, the audience then sees them meeting with doctors and stylists as the
beginning of their transformation that may take as long as six or eight weeks
before they return home to their families. The climax of *Extreme Makeover*
episodes is the dramatic reveal to one's family and friends back home after
recovery. *Dr. 90210* airs on the Style Network, and features the patients and
doctors of a Beverly Hills plastic surgery office. Two patient stories are fea-

tured in each episode, but considerable program attention is focused on the personal and professional lives of the plastic surgeons. *Plastic Surgery: Before and After* airs on the Discovery Health channel and features four patients' stories in each hour-long episode. Unlike the other two programs described, this reality show does not feature patients' dramatic reveals to family and friends, and no additional attention is paid to the doctors conducting the procedures. The program utilizes computer graphics to profile what procedures are being performed on each patient, and features a full body comparison of before and after pictures at the conclusion of each patient's story.

While these three reality programs attend to different issues of plastic surgery, two patterns are consistent across these programs: the degree to which they downplay the potential consequences of undergoing cosmetic surgery, and the extent to which they glamorize surgical procedures and focus primarily on the patients' desire for transformation, and the outcome of their procedures. In this assessment of three plastic surgery reality TV programs of 2006, this was a general conclusion reached about the different portrayals of patients:

> *Extreme Makeover* focuses attention on the patients' dramatic emotions as they anticipate and undergo their transformation. *Dr. 90210* devotes much program time to the doctors' private lives but also features patients discussing procedures with doctors and then undergoing surgery. *Plastic Surgery: Before and After* attends very little to patients' emotional experiences or their doctors' lives; instead, this program profiles more patients and procedures in each episode [Conners 81].

Plastic surgery reality TV programs rarely focus on preoperative consultations beyond a patient expressing desire for what they want changed; "the focus of such segments is not the surgical risk the patient faces but his or her anticipated cosmetic transformation" (Conners 82). Recovery segments in such programs were very brief and often featured the patient being wheeled out of surgery groggy with a doctor explaining the surgery was successful. *Extreme Makeover* shows patients recovering in an upscale hotel, with doctors visiting them a day or two after their procedure, but otherwise recovery is all but ignored in such programs. *Extreme Makeover* usually includes a follow-up to remove bandages and check a patient's progress, but the program focuses much more attention on the dramatic reveal to a patient's family and friends. *Plastic Surgery: Before and After* offers a full physical comparison of a patient prior to and following surgery, and *Dr. 90210* often features patients returning to the doctor's office months after surgery to express their satisfaction with the process, and their gratitude toward their doctors.

It is apparent from this content analysis that while these three programs are all considered plastic surgery reality television shows, they differ considerably from each other in theme, the focus of attention on patient and doctor, and messages they convey about plastic surgery procedures. Although they each celebrate the transformation plastic surgery patients undergo, they vary from each other in the additional messages regarding patients' decisions, risks of plastic surgery, and the recovery process.

Analysis of Comments by Plastic Surgery TV Fans

Do fans of plastic surgery reality television discuss the types of issues raised above with each other, and do they do so in an online communication environment? Before getting further into the analysis of fans' comments, it is important first to consider issues of fandom, and online discussions by fans.

Considering the nature of television fans, Jenkins states:

> If the term "fan" was originally evoked in a somewhat playful fashion and was often used sympathetically by sports writers, it never fully escaped its earlier connotations of religious and political zealotry, false beliefs, orgiastic excess, possession, and madness, connections that seem to be at the heart of many of the representations of fans in contemporary discourse [12].

We know of faithful fans of television programs and rabid sports fans, and the growing popularity of fan fiction is a particular activity for involved television fans. Online discussions among fans are also a growing source of communication and fandom.

While reality television garners substantial viewing audiences, the vast majority of viewers do not discuss their impressions of the programs or questions about the content in online venues, such as fan boards (sponsored by the network or station producing the program, or by other groups not affiliated with the program). Bielby, Harrington, and Bielby studied different sites of soap opera fan activities, include fan clubs, daytime magazines, and electronic bulletin boards in the late 1990s (36). They found through these resources fans take ownership of the program narratives by commenting on storylines and accuracy in programs. The potential immediacy of reaction through online bulletin boards increases the potential for such discussion and debate, as compared to letters being published in a fan magazine. Similarly, an analysis of X-Files fans, and particularly the online discussion of the possibility for a romance between lead characters Fox Mulder and Dana Scully, was examined in 1998 through online discussions in a Usenet newsgroup and an AOL *X-Files* Forum (Scodari and Felder 239).

Online bulletin boards continue to be a primary source for electronic fan discussions, although fan blogs and social networking groups in MySpace and Facebook have also developed since some of this "early" fan discussion research. More contemporary examples include research on fan activism, such as that conducted on a ten-year campaign to keep the soap opera *Another World* on the air. Scardaville found that online fans not only connected more easily with one another than in other venues offline, but were able to increase the size of their movement rapidly, and therefore their potential influence through online activism to save their beloved program (885).

The current analysis takes the next step following the content analysis of plastic surgery television described above. Beyond how the programs represent plastic surgery and its risks realistically and accurately, what concerns do fans of plastic surgery reality TV raise in their online postings? To assess this question, the viewer postings regarding *Dr. 90210* from the website Fans of Reality Television were collected, as well as viewer postings on *Plastic Surgery: Before and After* from the Discovery Channel website.* The purpose of this analysis is to understand what issues are salient for viewers of plastic surgery reality programs, and whether or not viewers have simply accepted the programs' framing of plastic surgery as a risk-free option for improving oneself.

A total of 461 posting were gathered about the program *Dr. 90210* between July 2, 2004, and November 26, 2007, and 731 postings were collected about the program *Plastic Surgery: Before and After* from June 8, 2004, through November 13, 2007. For this analysis, fan comments regarding concerns over plastic surgery procedures, in terms of risks, recovery, follow-up, or additional surgeries were identified for further analysis, to track the patterns of comments with the findings of the previously reported content analysis. General themes of other postings were noted, but not quantitatively or qualitatively analyzed further in this study.

Of the more than 400 comments posted about the program *Dr. 90210*, 8.5 percent of comments addressed some issue or question about risk of plastic surgery, pain in recovery, or other issues relevant to considering undergoing such cosmetic procedures. Postings either raising questions or addressing them included issues on getting a qualified plastic surgeon to per-

---

Online discussions of Extreme Makeover *were not found in any similar proportions to those of the other programs, and therefore were not collected for this analysis. The program has concluded airing on ABC and shifted to the Style Network, but it was not apparent if new episodes were being produced.*

form one's procedures, as well as the need to find a board certified plastic surgeon. This was a relevant discussion, as Dr. Robert Rey, the primary plastic surgeon featured on *Dr. 90210*, is not board certified, which was posted to the discussion. One former patient, "ScarlettM," responded, "I had a quite a lot of surgery done by Dr. Rey and he really is devoted to his patients.... His devotion paid off—I got perfect results!!" (July 23, 2004). As additional questions were raised about what it meant to be board certified, "ScarlettM" responded again, "Well ... I went to Dr. Rey and he is Board Eligible. He just has to take the final exam. If you look at his training and qualifications, he's better trained and educated than most other plastic surgeons" (August 1, 2004).

Other issues raised in these discussions involved the use and risk of anesthesia, the need to get multiple opinions before selecting a plastic surgeon, pain from injections, scar tissue, and risks to patients with low potassium levels, to name a few primary areas of discussion of concerns. The following questions by "Bearcata" on post-operative care after breast augmentation is representative of many of these postings of concern: "Isn't there a lot of pain involved in breast surgery? Isn't there a lot of post operative care that the patient has to do? I got the impression that you have to massage your breasts to get them to be soft and natural looking? Doesn't it take 3–6 months for all the swelling to come down so they look more natural?" (August 2, 2004) Similar questions expressed apprehension of aspects of cosmetic surgery procedures by potential patients.

As a response to such postings of anxiety, some comments shared favorable experiences, particularly with the doctors on *Dr. 90210*. Besides the comments from one of Dr. Rey's patients mentioned above, another posting by "artfullady" shared her daughter's favorable experience with another plastic surgeon in the same practice, Dr. Linda Li. The posting states, "My daughter had a breast augmentation from Dr. Li last year and she is very happy with her work. Dr. Li was very caring, careful and artistic! My daughter felt confident with her from the consultation on through the post-op check-up" (March 11, 2005).

In the medically related questions and comments in these postings, a variety of medical issues were raised; there were neither many "horror stories" of problem surgeries shared, nor was a pro-surgery bias conveyed consistently. Early feedback online by viewers of the program *Dr. 90210* was quite favorable for its portrayal of plastic surgery. For example, one posting by "gaby" stated, "The thing that sticks out to me with this show is they are not going for the gore. Nor are they selling as if all your problems are going to be cured with a body over haul [sic]" (July 21, 2004). Similarly, one viewer was reluctant about the program but became a fan; "Bearcata" posted, "Originally I wasn't going to watch this show because some of these makeover shows depend so much on plastic surgery that they act as if it is a cure all for all your problems. Regardless, I liked how they put the show together" (July 21, 2004). The overall conclusion of the theme from these postings was one of caution, with relevant questions being raised and answered by other viewers with both positive and negative experiences to share.

The vast majority of *Dr. 90210* postings were not on the surgical procedures themselves, the risks of them, or a patient's satisfaction with their cosmetic surgery. Rather, the majority of *Dr. 90210* postings were about the doctors themselves, and their families. This is consistent with findings from the content analysis, in that this program compared to others focuses considerable attention on the plastic surgeons and their lives outside of their medical practice. The show attends in many scenes to Dr. Rey's life and family, in particular his wife Haley, their children, their dogs, and their home. The personal lives of other plastic surgeons are also featured, such as the wedding plans of Dr. Jason Diamond or Dr. Li's pregnancy with her first child, but such storylines were quite infrequent compared to the attention devoted to Dr. Rey. Many comments focus on how he treats his patients (favorably and unfavorably) or concerns for his underweight and unhappy wife Haley. It is no surprise then that the majority of postings were the about the doctors and their families on the program *Dr. 90210*, rather than on plastic surgery itself.

From the more than 700 postings analyzed on online bulletin boards about the program *Plastic Surgery: Before and After*, 15 percent addressed issues when considering plastic surgery or concerns with procedures. This is nearly double the proportion of such postings regarding *Dr. 90210*. However, the format of the two programs explains the difference; while *Dr. 90210* attends to the plastic surgeons lives and families for much of the program, the primary focus in the stories aired on *Plastic Surgery: Before and After* is on the patients. The doctors are introduced, and scenes of them meeting with patients are included in each episode, but that is the entirety of what a viewer learns about any individual doctor. Additionally, patients are profiled from across the country, so no single plastic surgery practice is featured as the office on *Dr. 90210* is.

Postings about the plastic surgery reality program *Plastic Surgery: Before and After* were submitted under one of three categories: "Personal Experiences with Plastic Surgery," "If You Could...," and "Talk About the Show." A few comments specifically criticized plastic surgery reality programs in general for not being more attentive to discussing such issues as risks of procedures and recovery times. For example, "dd0416ak" commented, "I'd just like to say that I think there should be more warnings about the risks of this procedure.... If you're considering the surgery please consider the risks. I wish more of these plastic surgery shows would talk more about the risks, the things that your dr [sic] doesn't tell you. Life might be different for me now had I been more properly informed" (Feb. 25, 2006). While such comments were extremely rare, they do suggest some viewers' desire for more realistic portrayals of plastic surgery procedures on such reality television programs. Similarly, "pbawkin" describes her experience with a tummy tuck procedure, and argues that neither plastic surgery reality television nor her own doctor informed her properly:

> I love all the excess skin that's gone after my weight loss, but really — couldn't they have told me about the swelling beforehand. They sure don't mention it on the show and all the doctors I saw before deciding on one never mentioned it either. They could be a bit more honest about how long the whole process takes.... My hope would be that Discovery Health and any other shows, as well as plastic surgeons, would be honest with their patients as to how long recovery takes [Dec. 25, 2006].

In the more than 1,100 viewer comments gathered and read for this analysis, only these two specifically commented on the accuracy of plastic surgery reality television, and what viewers should be told and shown versus what they do see on such programs.

The above comments may reflect a particular type of online respondent to such discussions, the disgruntled or dissatisfied patient. Such plastic surgery "nightmare" stories were more common in the collection of responses regarding *Plastic Surgery: Before and After* than those posted about *Dr. 90210*. Such postings commonly shared experiences of poor results with breast augmentation, infections, the need for additional surgery to correct problems, risks of silicone from breast implants, as well as other complications. However, many postings also attempted to alleviate others' fears by sharing their experiences of short recovery times, little pain, a high degree of satisfaction with one's procedures, and improvements in one's life following plastic surgery. The majority of postings that addressed risks and concerns were questions from potential or future patients, in terms of how long will recovery from surgery take, how much pain will a patient experience with particular procedures, and a few questions about anesthesia and risks related to it. The following posting from "aahawks" is typical of such concerns:

> I just returned from a consult for lipo[suction]. The doctor says that he uses general anesthesia for his surgeries. I am a little worried about this kind of anthesia [sic] because I have never used it before. Have any of you had gen-

eral anesthesia for liposuction. I am having lipo under the chin and chest. Are their [sic] any thoughts on the best anesthesia to use, local or general [May 3, 2005].

The majority of postings did not address particular concerns with procedures, but they often addressed one of a few primary topics. One common theme was the cost of procedures and if insurance covered any expenses. A second frequent category of posting was the "pick me for the show" stories, where potential patients would describe in some detail their desire or need for plastic surgery, their wish to be selected to be on *Plastic Surgery: Before and After*, although no one affiliated with the television program ever responded in these online discussions.

A third popular topic beyond the risks and concerns of plastic surgery was "medical tourism"; that is, travelling primarily to Latin or South American countries to undergo cosmetic surgery procedures for considerably less cost than would be charged in the United States. For example, "freddias" frequently posted messages similar to the following: "Please, go and check in www.mednetbrazil.com. You can join the forum there and change some ideas with post op that came to Brazil. The owner of the website is a post op as well and you can talk to her. Good luck!" (Feb. 20, 2005). Few questions about problems, risks, or the qualification of doctors were raised in response. In some cases, the response was "Who wants to go?" It was clear that participants were regularly posting promotions of such travel plastic surgery, especially in response to postings about concerns with the cost of procedures.

Implications

This study finds that concerns and questions of risk of plastic surgery are relatively uncommon in two online discussions of particular plastic surgery reality programs, *Dr. 90210* and *Plastic Surgery: Before and After*. Only 8.5 percent of postings for *Dr. 90210* and 15 percent for *Plastic Surgery: Before and After* express concern or apprehension about plastic surgery, its risks and recovery from procedures. Given the lack of attention of warnings to patients in pre-operative consultations or focus on post-operative recovery and complications in these reality programs, the lack of such discussion online is not surprising. These programs' narratives do not commonly suggest such issues, but rather they focus on the transformation to one's body, body image, and life that can occur following cosmetic surgery.

While popularity of plastic surgery reality television has grown, as has interest in plastic surgery, online discussions do not demonstrate any corresponding increase in the number of questions viewers raise. Perhaps prospective patients are asking more questions in doctors' offices, as they witness procedures and the outcome of them in these patient stories on television. But the concern persists that plastic surgery reality television contributes to the "normalization" of plastic surgery in society, that is commonplace to do, if not desirable, and that viewers evolve into likely patients.

One limitation to acknowledge in this study involves the nature of online fan discussions. Viewers of programs such as *Dr. 90210*, *Extreme Makeover*, *The Swan*, and other plastic surgery programs who are willing to pursue the activity of online discussions are fans; they enjoy the programs, the dramatic transformations they present, and the "characters" on them (patients as well as doctors). They are likely to be regular viewers of the programs they discuss online, so they may not be as skeptical about the representations they see as non-viewers. While there are also anti-fan online discussions, the internet postings studied here originate from typically dedicated viewers of plastic surgery reality programs. They enjoy what they see being portrayed and may not have serious questions about the stories. Rather they participate in online discussions as an extension of their viewing, as an opportunity for social interaction about the programs with other plastic surgery reality television fans.

BIBLIOGRAPHY

Bielby, Denise D., Lee Harrington, and William T. Bielby. "Whose Stories Are They? Fan Engagement with Soap Opera Narratives in Three Sites of Fan Activity." *Journal of Broadcasting and Electronic Media* 43 (1999): 35–51.

Blum, Virginia. *Flesh Wounds: The Culture of Cosmetic Surgery.* Berkeley: University of California Press, 2003.

Conners, Joan L. "Pain or Perfection? Themes in Plastic-Surgery Reality Television." *Women, Wellness and the Media.* Ed. Margaret Wiley. Newcastle: Cambridge Scholars Press, 2008. 73–88.

Dr. 90210. E! Exec. prod. Donald Bull. 11 July 2004–.

Extreme Makeover. ABC. Exec. prod. Howard Schultz, Kimber Rickbaugh, Paul Miller. 2002–2008.

Granatstein, Lisa. "Makeover Madness." *MediaWeek 6* 28 June 2004: 26.

Jenkins, Henry. *Textual Poachers: Television Fans and Participatory Culture.* New York: Routledge, 1992.

Jordan, John W. "The Rhetorical Limits of the 'Plastic Body.'" *Quarterly Journal of Speech* 90 (2004): 327–358.

Kubic, Kelly N., and Rebecca M. Chory. "Exposure to Television Makeover Programs and Perceptions of Self." *Communication Research Reports* 24 (2007): 283–291.

Kuczynski, Alex. "A Lovelier You, with Off-the-Shelf Parts." *New York Times* 2 May 2004, sec. 4: 1.

Mazzeo, Suzanne E., Sara E. Trace, Karen S. Mitchell, and Rachel Walker Gow. "Effects of a Reality TV Cosmetic Surgery Makeover Program on Eating Disordered Attitudes and Behaviors." *Eating Behaviors* 8 (2007): 390–397.

"New Reality TV Programs Create Unhealthy, Unrealistic Expectations of Plastic Surgery." *American Society of Plastic Surgeons.* 30 March 2004. 18 Jan. 2007. <http://www.plasticsurgery.org/media/press_releases/New-Reality-TV-Programs-Create-Unhealthy-Unrealistic-Expectations.cfm>.

Plastic Surgery: Before and After. Discovery. Exec. prod. Janice Engel and Thom Beers. 2002–2008.

"Plastic Surgery Procedures Maintain Steady Growth in 2007." *American Society of Plastic Surgeons.* 25 March 2008. 14 April 2008. <http://www.plasticsurgery.org/media/press_releases/Plastic-Surgery-Growth-in-2007.cfm>.

Scardaville, Melissa C. "Accidental Activists: Fan Activism in the Soap Opera Community." *The American Behavioral Scientist* 48 (2005): 881–901

Scodari, Christine, and Jenna L. Felder. "Creating A Pocket Universe: 'Shippers', Fan Fiction, And *The X-Files* Online." *Communication Studies* 51 (Fall 2000): 238–257.

The Swan. Fox. Exec. prod. Arthur Smith and Nely Galan. 7 April 2004–20 Dec. 2004.

Parasocial Relationships in Dating and Makeover Reality Television

Narissra Maria Punyanunt-Carter

Reality television has become increasingly popular. Some of the most popular reality programs are ones that deal with dating, such as *The Bachelor, Next, Dismissed, Meet My Folks, Cupid,* and *The Bachelorette;* and makeovers, such as *The Biggest Loser, Extreme Makeover, The Swan, Queer Eye for the Straight Guy, What Not to Wear,* and *A Makeover Story.* Viewers watch the programs because they feel a connection with the personas presented therein. Viewers develop parasocial relationships with these personas. Investigation of reality dating and makeover television shows will provide several explanations for why parasocial relationships transpire. These programs promote several cultural ideals, such as the notion that you cannot be happy unless you are beautiful — according to cultural standards (hence the makeover). Only the beautiful find romance and only the most beautiful man or woman wins (hence, dating shows are so popular because they are usually filled with extraordinary-looking people).

Another cultural principle that such programs promote is the idea that if you're not a winner, you're a loser. Thus, losers end up alone and this is considered taboo, especially for women. The programs perpetuate viewers' ideas that they should follow similar ways of thinking and doing as suggested in the programs. Ultimately, cultural, ideological, and media-promulgated criteria used to develop parasocial interactions will also be proposed.

Parasocial Relationships

Horton and Wohl describe parasocial interaction as the illusionary "face-to-face" relationship that develops between a television persona and a television viewer (215). According to Horton and Wohl, parasocial relationships are created and managed by the television persona and develop in the audience over time. Viewers acquire a bond with television personalities that are similar to their own social networks.

Pekka Isotalus explained that parasocial relationships are not contingent on the program, persona, or type of medium. Isotalus posited that personas "try to establish parasocial relationships with their viewers, because it will increase the viewers' willingness to watch the performers' program" (61). Isotalus also noted that performers' attempts at establishing parasocial relationship with viewers influences the viewers' intent to watch and affects the viewers' perceptions of amiability toward the performer. Both dating shows and makeover shows have personas that viewers can identify with and that affect how they perceive the reality program. For instance, the shows usually have characters with whom the audience can identify because the producers choose people who are similar to the viewers of the program. Involvement in parasocial relationships may include seeking advice from a media person, developing a friendship with the person, or trying to feel included in the program (Norlund).

Viewers of dating shows and makeover programs may watch to learn more about relationships and transformations. Eileen Zurbriggen and Elizabeth Morgan discovered that male college students watched dating reality programs to learn about dating more often than female college students did. This suggests that reality programs can provide information on an area that may be unclear for viewers. In turn, viewers develop a bond with the character to understand what stages of development will occur in romantic relationships.

Often, viewers talk to characters on the screen or to each other about the content (Rubin and Perse). Sometimes, when viewers watch dating or makeover programs, they feel so connected to the characters' transformation from the beginning of a relationship to the end that they feel they should share their opinions openly. Some makeover programs and dating shows provide clips where certain personas give the viewer a more detailed account of what is going on in their minds. These revelations provide viewers with more insight about the personas and encourage more loyal viewing of the program.

Parasocial activity is the result of perceptual actions and reactions within viewers who grasp and then create meaning out of watching television (Caughley). Some members of the television audience actively select and use the content of the program to satisfy their information curiosity (Caughley). For example, Zurbriggen and Morgan noted that most viewers of reality dating programs are less sexually experienced. Hence, dating programs might provide them with more information on love, sex, and romance. Turner showed that parasocial relationships are likely to develop among viewers who have the same attitudes. Makeover programs usually show individuals who are unhappy with themselves in some way and, like the contestants, want a transformation. Viewers may look to makeover programs hoping to get information on how they can make similar transformations.

All in all, people watch television for different reasons (Rubin 37). These reasons include: escapism, voyeurism, to pass-time, to get information, and even for companionship (Rubin). There are several genres in which parasocial activities have been studied. These genres include, but are not limited to, reality television genre such as dating shows and makeover shows.

Dating Shows

Some scholars have suggested that romantic expectations may be influenced by mass media representations (Bachen and Illouz; Punyanunt-Carter; Segrin and Nabi). Chris Segrin and Robin Nabi noted that reality television shows tend to idealize romantic relationships. They discovered that exposure to romantic television programs had a significant impact on viewers' expectations about romance. Moreover, Reiza Rehkoff found that there were significant connections among romantic expectations, parasocial relationship strength, and relationship satisfaction. Individuals who watched more romantic television programs were also more likely to fantasize about romantic relationships. Results also indicated that individuals who had parasocial relationships also had more romantic beliefs, but were experiencing low levels of relationship satisfaction. This suggests that romantic television programs help fulfill emotional needs while raising romantic expectations.

Perhaps the reason why so many viewers watch reality dating shows is because it fulfills the need for romance in their own lives, romance that may be less satisfying and/or nonexistent. Many singles may be longing for a relationship like the ones portrayed on television. Thus, they watch the programs hoping to gratify a need for a romantic relationship. Several dating shows also attract couples who are married. Married couples could be reflecting on how their dating experiences were similar or different from the characters portrayed on dating reality programs. It is also possible that couples want to live vicariously through the actions of these reality characters.

Tim Cole and Laura Leets discovered a significant relationship between individuals who have a desire for passionate romantic relationships and the formation of parasocial relationships. Parasocial relationships are similar to social relationships, but may lack salience and some behavioral components (Cohen 516). Therefore, for some viewers, dating reality programs fulfill a need for a romantic relationship. If they are not able to have a relationship, they can still sympathize with the characters on dating shows. On dating shows, such as *The Bachelor* and *The Bachelorette,* there are several eligible men and women with the same goal: to find their ideal mate. Dating reality programs tend to glamorize each of the dates. On the *The Bachelor,* the producers have created exotic destinations and unique situations for the dates. For instance, one season of the show was taped in Italy. Each week, the bachelor took the ladies to different locations around Europe and let them dress up in expensive evening wear. In another situation, the bachelor gave his date jewelry worth a million dollars to wear on their date. The producers of the show created once-in-a-lifetime moments where the bachelor and his date would have a private concert and see a personal show of fireworks. Viewers who watch the program become infatuated with the idea of experiencing similar romantic moments.

Identification with program characters is commonly linked to the development of parasocial relationships (Rubin and McHugh 279). People tend to form relationships with others that they feel they have something in common with (Cathcart 207). Situations on the reality dating shows may be similar to issues and experiences of the audience. Each of the dating reality shows displays the normal stages of relationship development from the first impression to the first kiss. The programs also show how relationships may terminate because two people may not be compatible in some fashion. Viewers can identify with the feelings of either bonding with someone and/or ending a relationship. On websites such as buddytv.com and fanforum.com, many fans of dating shows have voiced their perspectives and opinions about the show. For instance, when discussing the bachelor Brad Womack, one viewer called janetlovesherdoggy, wrote:

> As much as I do not believe that this show is a good forum for finding "love," and as much as I hated to see the final two get so hurt, I don't think that anyone, including Brad, is bad, or "sucks." I don't think Brad is full of B/S either. Weren't you listening to Brad? He said it as clear as day. He believes, and has believed, apparently, all of his life, in the hopeless romantic, knock you off of your feet type of love, and, since he was not able to feel this way w/either woman, he decided to hold out for that. At the same time though, I think he is realizing, and more so through this experience, that maybe his idea of what love is, and how it develops may need some further exploration, thus, him admitting that he may also need to work on himself. Aside from that, I believe that Brad was "trying" and guess what? He said that. He was trying, because

he really wanted to find love, he was trying, because the show puts pressure on you, and he had no choice but to take the show to it's [sic] very end. I think that he had the right intentions all along, but in the final moment, he just couldn't do it, pure and simple. Do I think he needs to grow a lot? Sure. But he's no bad guy, like some are making him out to be.

In this example, the viewer is clearly trying to empathize with the character on the show. She is trying to also understand his behavior. Individuals in parasocial relationships will tend to assume certain distinctions about the characters on the show. They also have certain ideas about how the show should end. In the recent season of the *The Bachelor,* a fan called Ms. NoraStrom writes,

> This guy has some serious issues, he obviously didn't get it..he IS SUPPOSE [sic], to choose one girl, that's the concept of the show ... why not just choose and date the girl for a few weeks and then break it off IN PRIVATE. It IS the honorable thing to do. Then tell the girl in private, not in front of millions of people. His dilution of honesty is warped THIS IS MY LEAST FAVORITE BACHELOR, because of the way he handled it. It's a total waste of time and furthermore, makes him look like a total fool!.... WHAT A FOOL!...

Another example of a fan expecting a certain outcome is from metoo45, who stated:

> Blah Bah Blah...true to his heart?..First off if Brad felt love Means "thunderbolts and Lightening..He needs a Serious Reality Chek ..He played with these Girls emotions and to have the Audacity to say to Deanna at the end of the re-cap show..after Dumping her...."ill miss you more than you will know?.What a insensitive thing to say..I guess GUILT makes one say Stupid things..Brad Knows he's got Emotional Issues..he admitted it..FIX your Issues dude, before you mess around with women you know yu cant COMMITT to. [sic]

It is apparent that the actions of the characters on this show have an effect on viewers' perceptions about how characters should have acted or how they should behave on television.

Perse and Rubin (368) found that people pay attention to messages that have personal relevance. As a result, a viewer who personally identifies with one of a program's characters may eventually form a relationship with the character (Perse and Rubin 367). Once this connection is formed, the viewer may feel sympathy, empathy, or sorrow for any event that may occur within that character's life the same way as they would care for someone they know on an interpersonal level (Perse and Rubin). For instance, on the final episode of *The Bachelor,* the bachelor decides on his final bachelorette. He must decide between two women. The woman who is not chosen is usually hurt and disappointed. Thus, the viewers feel sympathetic towards her, because she was not the final bachelorette.

Perhaps this is the reason why so many viewers watch the *The Bachelor*. Over time, viewers have gotten to see the bachelor's traits and his eligible prospects. Viewers are allowed to hear the opinions, beliefs, values, and viewpoints of the bachelor and his potential mates. In addition, viewers are given an opportunity to see how the relationship develops in such a short amount of time from the initial meeting, group dates, a single date, a date in an exotic location, a date to meet the family and/or friends of the bachelorette, a date to meet the family and/or friends of the bachelor, to the final proposal for marriage/serious commitment or termination of the relationship. It is exciting for viewers to try to guess whom the bachelor may choose and how the bachelorettes will vie for his affection/attention. Viewers enjoy the anguish of how difficult it may be to end a romantic relationship with one of the bachelorettes. Viewers also find it exciting to see how the bachelor responds to each of the bachelorettes, his dates, and their feelings. Some bachelorettes reveal very personal things to him and some reveal very personal emotions.

In one episode of this show, a woman wrote a love poem for him on their very first date. This was quite unexpected and he did not know how to react. In the end, she did not get a rose and did not get to stay on the program. The bachelor felt that she was opening up her feelings to him rather quickly without really getting to know him.

Makeover Shows

A new line of parasocial research has emerged related to the use and effectiveness of forming parasocial relationships with makeover shows (Schiappa, Gregg, and Hewes 92). Makeover shows typically show a person's transformation from point A to point B. The makeovers usually deal with physical appearance and sometimes mental well-being and self-esteem. The makeovers are fun for viewers to watch because, similar to dating shows, they bond with the characters on the show. They can identify with feelings of insecurity, uncertainty, and/or desire to change/improve in some way. Viewers can develop attachments and relationships with certain characters on the makeover programs because they might have similar personal backgrounds.

From a few of the message board, fans have stated:

> I would love to be on a program like this. These people are so much like myself. I would do anything to be on that show. Every person on that show knows what it is like not to feel right. I want to be accepted.

Makeover programs highlight how people may feel inadequate about themselves. Viewers may watch the programs hoping to use the character as an ideal of what they should strive to become.

The Swan, was a makeover program where the producers selected women who had poor body image and low self-esteem and who had been teased for looking a certain way. The women on the show would be altered both in body and mind. Then, the women would compete in a beauty pageant. Many viewers were amazed with the transformations. Viewers would have parasocial relationships with these characters because in the end, they would choose their favorite to win the beauty pageant. Some viewers even desired desperately to be on the show. For instance, a viewer on a message board wrote:

> my name is wendy. i am just wondering how much low self-esteem, and ugliness one person has to have to be a swan or a second chance. i have had low self-esteem since elementary school. being picked on in elementary school because i had bad teeth, braces in high school, 3 kids, got pregnant my junior year of high school, stretchmarks, adoption with my second child, divorce at 18, married in to the military, a great man in my life, but i can't seem to get over my body to get past alot of our fighting in the bedroom, being away from my family, my husband and 5 year old iis in alaska, and my 8 year old is in georgia, i am in florida, i can't go to the beach because i won't wear a bathingsuit. if you could please comment back, help me and tell me what to do next. thanks mrs. warren [sic]

Another viewer writes:

> I'm 29 yrs old I'm puertorican woman with 3 wonderful kids, unfortunately I have ugly stretch marks, acne and more so then ever now crooked teeth. I don't hate myself at all I just wished that I could afford to fix life's flaws I know who I am, it's just sometimes it gets to me my personal appearance I don't to be perfect I just wanna look and feel good and show like swan and extreme makeover really makes a difference in somebody's life you know if I was quick enough then maybe I could've go on either shows but that's just my luck well I hope your company can come back maybe I'll get a chance again. Thanks [sic]

Makeover programs provide women with hope and they long to be like the contestants they see on the program.

Perse found a direct correlation between parasocial activity and information-seeking. She found that parasocial interactions may be associated with entertainment, informational viewing motives, perceived realism, and exposure. This could also be another reason why viewers pay attention to makeover shows. Viewers may want to get more information about how to transform their bodies and minds. Not only are makeover programs entertaining and informational, they also give viewers hope that they will be able to accomplish similar transformations. People who watch makeover programs tend to believe makeovers are life-changing.

The amount of exposure to makeover programs may also influence viewers' perceptions. Dittmar found that viewers who were identified as having clinical depression watched twenty more hours of television in one week than did the control group. Dittmar also noted that serious television viewers tend to feel less satisfied about their own lives and are inclined to have lower self-concepts than those who are not heavy viewers. Thus, heavy viewers of makeover programs may have lower self-esteem as well. Dittmar also explained that heavy viewers have reduced social skills and often view characters on television as friends. Dittmar believed this exposure may be an important precursor to the formation of parasocial relationships, and the reason many heavy viewers associate with contestants on makeover shows.

Makeover shows typically portray how lives are flawed, imperfect, and/or inadequate in some way. Makeover shows constantly give viewers impressions about how their lives are lacking or deficient because of either lifestyle and/or appearance. The shows fulfill a need for viewers who already feel flawed, and offer information on improving quality of life through makeovers. Makeover shows can have a very powerful effect on the formation of parasocial relationships.

Conclusion

Parasocial relationships occur among viewers who watch dating and makeover reality programs. There are several cultural, ideological, and media-promulgated criteria used to create parasocial interactions. As the literature shows, many people consider parasocial interactions to be of the same relevance and quality as interpersonal interactions. Most everyone is looking for companionship. Most people seek contact with people that they can touch; however, some people seek relations from people they can only see or hear via mediated ways. For the latter group, parasocial activity is just as fulfilling and worthwhile as all other relationships.

We live in a society where mass media images tell us that we constantly need improvement. Media tells us that we need to look a certain way (e.g., have shiny hair, whiter teeth, a flatter stomach, sexy legs, clear skin). The makeover shows usually highlight individuals who feel uncomfortable or inferior about themselves in some way and want to improve. Makeover shows stress that society will respond differently to a person who is prettier, younger, and more attractive. Viewers tend to perceive that what is beautiful must also be good. Therefore, they long to be more attractive and search for ways to accomplish those goals through a harsh physical fitness regime, plastic surgery, minor revisions, and/or altering their entire wardrobe.

Our society is influenced by fairy tales, where young girls think that they have to be pretty to get Prince Charming and live happily ever after. Media tell us that the perfect bachelor will find true love and his soul mate over the course of a few weeks. Media also imply that we need to be involved in a romantic relationship. Dating shows perpetuate the idea that individuals should not be alone, but rather searching for their soul mate, like the bachelor or bachelorette. Most programs highlight romantic couples and do not showcase people who are lonely and unattached. McClanahan notes that our society is influenced by a thought that women who are not with someone are not living a fulfilled life. At the same time, men who are single are just not with someone and it is acceptable. Men who are not involved in a relationship are seen as career driven and women who are not in a relationship are seen as peculiar. Hence, culture, ideology, and media all promote the impression that we are not complete until we have found our soul mate. This impression is what fuels the popularity of the dating shows. Dating shows idealize the possibility that beautiful people can find romance and avoid the cultural stigma of being alone.

Glebatis argues that dating shows also promote the idea that one can fall in love at first sight. The audience wants to believe that love can happen instantly. Thus, viewers watch to see if love at first sight can actually happen. Finally, audience members use dating shows to fantasize about their own romantic relationship.

Reality is very different from reality television. People do not always have the time and/or in some cases the money or resources to have a complete makeover or go on a dream date to Paris. Moreover, many of the characters on reality television fail to maintain these changes after the show has aired. There have been numerous bachelors that failed to continue their relationships with the bachelorette that they selected at the end of the show. There also have been many individuals from makeover programs that went back to their previous lifestyles. For instance, some of the contestants from *The Biggest Loser* who lost a lot of body weight on the show slowly gained it back after the show aired. Thus, reality television programs provide some sort of fantasy for viewers. In turn, viewers develop a relationship with contestants, hoping in some way to emulate or live vicariously through the contestants' actions. The experiences of the contestants are what make the attachment strong enough that viewers watch and reflect on them. Media producers are clever in choosing contestants for the programs that people can in some way identify with. The programs have something viewers long for, whether it be an ideal mate or an ideal change. Parasocial relationships develop because people, in general, long to be ideal.

BIBLIOGRAPHY

Bachen, Christine, and Eva Illouz. "Imagining Romance: Young People's Cultural Models of Romance and Love." *Critical Studies in Mass Communication* 13 (1996): 279–308.

Cathcart, Robert. "Our Soap Opera Friends." *Inter/media, 3rd ed.* Ed. Gary Gumpert and Robert S. Cathcart. New York: Oxford University Press, 1986. 207–218.

Caughey, John L. "Social Relations with Media Figures." *Inter/media, 3rd ed.* Ed. Gary Gumpert and Robert S. Cathcart. New York: Oxford University Press, 1986. 219–252.

Cohen, Jonathan. "Parasocial Breakups: Measuring Individual Differences in Responses to the Dissolution of Parasocial Relationships." *Mass Communication and Society* 6 (2003): 1–12.

_____. "Parasocial Relationships and Romantic Attraction: Gender and Dating Differences." *Journal of Broadcasting and Electronic Media* 41 (1997): 516–529.

Cole, Tim, and Laura Leets. "Attachment Styles and Intimate Television Viewing: Insecurely Forming Relationships in a Parasocial Way." *Journal of Social and Personal Relationships* 16.4 (1999): 495–511.

Dittmar, Mary Lynne. "Relations Among Depression, Gender, and Television Viewing of College Students." *Journal of Social Behavior and Personality* 9 (1994): 317–328.

Glebatis, Lisa M. "'Real' Love Myths and Magnified Media Effects of *The Bachelorette.*" *Critical Thinking about Sex, Love, and Romance in the Mass Media: Media Literacy Applications.* Ed. Mary-Lou Galician and Debra L. Merskin. Mahwah, NJ: Erlbaum, 2007. 319–334.

Horton, Donald, and R. Richard Wohl. "Mass Communication and Para-social Interaction: Observations on Intimacy at a Distance." *Psychiatry* 19 (1956): 215–229.

Isotalus, Pekka. "Friendship Through Screen. Review of Parasocial Relationship." *Nordicom Review* (1995): 59–64.

McClanahan, Amanda M. "Must Marry TV: The Role of the Heterosexual Imaginary in *The Bachelor.*" *Critical Thinking about Sex, Love, and Romance in the Mass Media: Media Literacy Applications.* Ed. Mary-Lou Galician and Debra L. Merskin. Mahwah, NJ: Erlbaum, 2007. 303–318.

Norlund, Jan-Erik. "Media Interaction." *Communication Research* 5 (1978): 150–175.

Perse, Elizabeth M., and Alan M. Rubin. "Audience Activity and Satisfaction with Favorite Television Soap Opera." *Journalism Quarterly* 65 (1988): 368–375.

Punyanunt-Carter, Narissra Maria. "Love on Television: Reality Perception Differences Between Males and Females." *North American Journal on Psychology* 8 (2006): 269–278.

Rehkoff, Raiza. "Romantic TV and Emotional Satisfaction: Does Romantic Belief Moderate the Relationship Between Satisfaction and Parasocial Relationship Strength." Conference Paper Presented at the International Communication Association Annual Meeting, New York, NY, 2005. 1–39 (39 pages, 3 charts, 1 graph; AN 18655665).

Rubin, Alan M. "Television Uses and Gratifications: The Interactions of Viewing Patterns and Motivations." *Journal of Broadcasting* 27 (1983): 37–51.

_____, and Michael McHugh. "Development of Parasocial Interaction Relationships." *Journal of Broadcasting and Electronic Media* 31 (1987): 279–292.

_____, and Elizabeth M. Perse. "Audience Activity and Soap Opera Involvement: A Uses and Effects Investigation." *Human Communication Research* 14 (1987): 246–268.

Schiappa, Edward, Peter B. Gregg, and Dean E. Hewes. "The Parasocial Contact Hypothesis." *Communication Monographs* 72 (2005): 92–115.

Segrin, Chris, and Robin Nabi. "Does Television Viewing Cultivate Unrealistic Expectations About Marriage?" *Journal of Communication* 52 (2002): 247–262.

Zurbriggen, Eileen, and Elizabeth M. Morgan. "Who Wants to Marry a Millionaire? Reality Dating Television Programs, Attitudes Toward Sex, and Sexual Behaviors." *Sex Roles* 54 (2006): 1–17.

6

Average Joe and the
Not So Average Jane

JUDITH LANCIONI

Most dating shows follow the same paradigm. An attractive man or woman is given the power to choose among a panoply of pretty faces until, by a process of elimination, he or she has found the perfect partner. In these shows, replete with hot tubs, cruises, and gourmet meals set in opulent surroundings, the dating process is romanticized and idealized. The dates are spectacular and so are the faces that fill the screen.

NBC's *Average Joe* claimed to challenge that paradigm by selecting contestants who were not unusually attractive, thereby offering a twist on the typical dating show in which handsome men court handsome women, or vice versa. Instead the series paired "a stunning beauty queen" with sixteen suitors "with great hearts, but admittedly average looks" (*Average Joe* Home page).

Executive producers Stuart Krasnow and Andrew Glassman had a definite physical ideal in mind when they chose contestants. They didn't want guys who were "hot" or who could date a cheerleader. "But to call them average is unfair," insisted Krasnow (Huff 6), which leads one to wonder what it means to be rated average. Textual analysis of *Average Joe* and *Average Joe: Hawaii* and the discourse they generated raises interesting questions about how the term average is constructed and how that construction operates as a "provoker and circulator of meanings" that relates to "dominant cultural norms" (Fiske 1). This analysis will focus on the premier of both shows, since their opening sequences establish the parameters of both series.

The premise of *Average Joe* is that Melana Scantlin, former NFL cheerleader and beauty queen, will find her true love among sixteen ordinary-looking men. A fairytale motif was established on the official website and on the show itself, portraying Scantlin as a princess who could transform these ordinary men into princes. For example, in the opening sequence a graphic — "Do fairytales come true?" — is followed by a shot of a female about to kiss the frog she holds in her hand, an obvious reference to the fairytale about the princess whose kiss transformed a frog into a prince. In the next shot, a frog lands on the O of the logo AVERAGE JOE, which casts the Joes as frogs who need transforming. Is this what it means to be average? This princess and the frog metaphor portends a polysemic discourse on what average means.

The premier begins with a shot of a beautiful blonde jogging down the beach. Her appearance is idealized through the use of soft focus. The voiceover identifies her as Melana, a "former NFL cheerleader and beauty queen" in search of "the perfect guy." This sequence ends with a facial close-up which emphasizes her beauty. As befits a princess, the narrator reveals, Melana will live "in a multimillion dollar mansion set high on a hill." She is expecting "16 modern-day prince charmings," who will compete "to win her heart." Melana herself says she feels like she's in "a fairytale." There is a soft focus close-up of Melana as the voiceover confides that this fairytale will be "beauty and the geeks." This statement clearly articulates the series' juxtaposition of the beautiful with the average, while the use of "geeks" foreshadows the negative way in which the average Joes will be portrayed.

That the sixteen contestants are not exactly princely-looking is established through mise-en-scene and editing. In fact, the opening sequence links the phrase "average Joe" with a parade of beer bellies and a shot of one of the heftier contestants cannon-balling into the swimming pool while another of the big men has booze poured down his throat in the best *Animal House* tradition.

Contrast this with Melana posing in a form-fitting strapless gown, princess-like, on a terrace. The camera cuts to a montage of "the geeks" edited to showcase their less-than-princely qualities. Dennis L. is shown gyrating in a hula-hoop while one of the men executes a pirouette and another breathes fire. Dennis admits people consider him a geek. Joe, decked out in a flowered Hawaiian shirt, admits he's "not a small guy." Marc points out how short he is (5' 4"). His admission is followed by a shot of him shaking hands with Craig, one of the big, tall men. The sharp contrast between their heights makes both look abnormal. Then Joe reappears, admitting he's "not a ripped guy," followed by a repeat shot of him cannon-balling into the pool, and then a cut back to the interview. "I am who I am," proclaims Joe. A statement which could sound confident has been re-contextualized by prefacing it with the pool shot. Even the earlier admission that he's "not ripped" is ridiculed as gross understatement, given that pool shot.

The self-evaluating continues. "I am a total geek," says a smiling John. Adam admits he's "a dork." Jay says he doesn't care that people call him "fat and bald." Walter admits he's usually the "friend rather than the boyfriend." Are these the qualities that make men average?

The next series of shots suggests an even less flattering picture of what it means to be average. Once again mis-en-scene and editing are used to show the contestants at their worst. A group shot of the men is accompanied by a voice-over that proclaims them average Joes. Meanwhile, the camera cuts to a quick montage that apparently illustrates what the adjective means. Denis L, racket in hand, is hit in the back by a tennis ball. Zach pushes one of his fellow contestants into the pool. Adam sports a food-smeared face. Jerry, with drink in hand, gesticulates comically as Jay looks on. The narrator proclaims that this group is different from other TV bachelors. His statement is illustrated by another fast-paced montage. One of the contestants swings inexpertly at a golf ball. Brad admits he's had little sexual experience, a remark followed by a cut to Marc, whose quizzical expression would seem to be a reaction to Brad's revelation. The concept of average is definitely being ridiculed.

As soft music plays, Melana reappears, wearing another elegantly sexy dress. The camera pulls back as the narrator speculates on Melana's initial reaction to the contestants. The latter half of his statement is accompanied by a cut to the former swim suit model, bikini-clad, proclaiming that the perfect guy will have "an amazing smile." Her words are accompanied by yet another montage — Marc, Adam, Craig, all turning to present not so amazing smiles to the camera. This juxtaposition of her words and their images belittles the Joes.

A montage of not-so-average future dates, future kisses, and future conflicts follow, accompanied by remarks about how "gorgeous" Melana is. One contestant proclaims that he can picture himself with Melana and another remarks that "it feels like love." Of all the statements available, why use these? In terms of looks, Melana is above average, yet these average Joes think they have a chance with her. Is this meant to rally support for the contestants as underdogs, or to ridicule them? In fact, one fan labeled them "a disgrace" because they fawned over Melana, who wouldn't have given them a second look in the real world (Howard Marshall).

The text toys with viewers' expectations, providing both positive and negative portrayals. Viewers see a montage of Melana hugging an assortment of contestants as the narrator promises that "a new type of leading man finally has his chance." Brad proclaims that he gives all geeks "hope" because sometimes he does "get the girl." The camera cuts to John serenading Melana.

As the narrator promises that this is the beginning of a "new kind of love story," viewers see, in quick succession, shots of Tareq and Melana walking through a field; Melana giving Jerry a peck on the cheek; John telling Dennis that Melana kissed him and he kissed back, followed by a shot of the event and a shot of a laughing John shaking hands with a smiling Dennis. As the narrator speculates on whether or not the Joes will have their hearts broken, viewers see Dennis L. and Craig, both teary-eyed, then a serious John lamenting, "It hurts to be the guy who loses all the time." Is losing a characteristic of the average guy, especially when he sets out to win the heart of the above-average girl? Are these average Joes "pathetic losers"? (Shales CO1). In other words, the dating sequence raises hopes for the Joes, while the subsequent sequence and the subsequent appearance of the hunks dash those hopes.

The introductory segment ends with two shots that illustrate this manipulation of viewers' conception of the contestants. In the first, a shot of Melana, clad in a bathing suit and a smile, is juxtaposed with a shot of the contestants in swim trunks. The camera pans a selection of geeky-looking, scrawny, or overweight men. The second is a silhouette of a svelte man and woman embracing on a sunset-washed beach. The narrator asks if an average Joe can ever find happiness with "a beauty"? Is the traditionally romantic silhouette meant to imply a negative answer to that question, given the less than impressive physiques of the Joes? But the text keeps playing with viewers' expectations. "Is this a new type of love story?" the narrator asks.

As if in response to Melana's announcement that she wants to find "the perfect guy," the camera records the contestants' arrival, editing together shots that foreground their idiosyncrasies and insecurities. Dennis L. arrives carrying a suitcase and hula hoops. He talks about how he's always felt like an "outcast" and a loser because of his appearance. He feels the show will give him the chance to "show America" that a guy like him can "get the girl." Marc explains that his diminutive height works against him; short guys on dating shows never win. He's sure, however, that his personality will prevail. Craig talks about his "big guy" status. To emphasize the disparity in their size (and perhaps to make both of them look below average), Marc and Craig, the shortest and the tallest, are shown together in a brief shot.

Next comes a brief scene with Melana, poolside, pondering what it will be like to meet the contestants. Of course, viewers have already been provided with ample opportunity to anticipate the shock of that meeting. Cut back to the contestants moving in. Gerry points out that he's bright, good looking and has a great job. In the middle of this confident self-appraisal he knocks over his luggage. Is this meant to be endearing, mocking, or both? Once again the sequence offers viewers an opportunity to look, listen, and speculate on what it means to be average.

The next sequence of shots explicitly raises that issue. Zach addresses the camera and ponders whether he wants to be "the best of the average," implying not only that he is above average, but also that there is something tainted about the term.* John announces he's proud of his dorkiness as well as his "charisma" and "charm," thus implying that personality can trump an average appearance, a claim which other contestants (and fans) supported. For example, Dennis S. admits his averageness but points out that people are attracted to him because he likes to have a good time. Joe acknowledges that he's overweight and out of shape but insists that any woman who really engages with him would see past his physique. Some viewers might see these men as endearing, others as delusional, but at least these shots do not directly mock their physical features. Their personalities come through, and so does the suggestion that there is a spectrum of averageness, as Zach's admittedly haughty comment implies.

The next sequence of shots resumes the humiliation of this "bunch of misfits," as Jay describes them. As Melana talks about the importance of "chemistry" in establishing a relationship, the music, which has played softly in the background, takes on a "Jaws" menace. The camera pans the contestants decked out in bathing suits that are far from flattering. Bellies abound and the camera makes the most of them.

Kathy Griffin arrives to explain the premise of the show. She asserts that this dating game is not about "pretty boys" with six-packs and coiffed hair. Her comments clearly divide males into two categories based on appearance — the handsome and the average. As she speaks, the camera continues to pan this group of not-so-pretty boys. Griffin avers that they were selected to represent the "real men" of America, love handles and all. She tells them that Melana is hoping to meet her "soul-mate" and that personality is what she will base her selection on. "Use your wits," she exhorts them, and "your charm." They are there to show America that an average Joe can get the girl. Heartening advice, but why does it have to be delivered poolside, with the contestants looking their worst? Why does an average, or a "real," man have to be equated with an unattractive appearance?

The next segment continues to hone in on the show's central theme: what does it mean to be average. The contestants are subjected to the usual

---

*Off screen Brian Worth (Average Joe: Hawaii) admitted that when he saw his competitors he considered bowing out of the competition. "I don't consider myself a 10, but I'm not a 3 either," he explained (Ryan). Brad (Average Joe) didn't see himself as part of the group (Belcher).

undercutting. They get to voice their insecurities, which might make them endearing, but they also are shown being boorish, creating a mixed message and a polysemic text.

Next viewers see a bikini-clad Melana frolicking in the surf. She's not expecting "perfection," she explains, while displaying her own near-perfect body. She wants a man who will make a good father, one with whom she can spend her life. The shots which follow invite viewers to estimate her chances of success. In the first, Jerry admits that initially he felt like he was in a movie like *Revenge of the Nerds*. This remark is followed by illustrative shots — Dennis L. gyrating with his hoola hoop and Jay announcing that he sleeps naked. The shots which follow in quick succession show various contestants behaving immaturely.

A bathing suit clad Melana is seen jogging along the seashore, then sitting contemplatively by a fountain. Her voiceover enumerates the qualities she's looking for in a man, none of which involves looks. If there's "chemistry," she'll give the relationship "a chance." Her words are followed by an unflattering montage of the contestants at play, shots that were already used in the introductory sequence: Joe cannon-balling into the pool, Adam with a food-smeared face, Craig blowing fire. Repeating them reinforces viewers' awareness of the contestants' less than exemplary behavior. Positioning implies that the qualities Melana is looking for are not to be found among this bunch.

Then the contestants start critiquing each other and speculating on their chances. The discussion is punctuated by a shot of Walter, poolside, pouring booze down Craig's gullet — another shot repeated from the introduction. John points out the obvious — that they weren't chosen for their looks. Marc argues that they're "normal" guys. The audience is given a chance to reflect on what's normal.

The next scene shows Melana on tiptoe in anticipation of meeting her "Prince Charmings." The wording provides a subtle reminder that these contestants are far from princely. The narrator speculates on how she will react when she discovers her princes are average Joes. Here is another instance in which the term "average" is undermined. "What am I getting myself into?" asks Melana over the series logo. The graphic Average Joe is projected on a sunset beach. The O encloses a couple kissing. The shot is artfully ambiguous. The setting and the embracing couple are romantic stereotypes typical of conventional dating shows. Locating the couple within the O of *Average Joe* invites viewers to try and integrate these stereotypically romantic images with the concept of an average Joe, sans six-pack, winning the beauty.

As the contestants' bus pulls up for the first meeting, Melana tries to hold on to her smile and contain her nervousness. The first to emerge is Marc. Melana frowns but quickly recovers. As he goes in she laughingly says to the camera, "Someone's messing with my head," which of course is true. After meeting Joe, one of the super-sized contestants, she says laughingly, "This is so bad."

Hidden camera shots show an agitated Melana questioning why she agreed to this. Shots of the contestants getting off the bus are intercut with her dialogue. These men are average, she says in an insert, but they've got "great personalities" and great heart, qualities which are more important than looks. But the scene casts doubt on the worth of the Joes, since the clips shown thus far haven't revealed compelling personalities.

The plan for each contestant to get alone-time with Melana is provided by an old-fashioned photo booth. Each gets his picture taken with the beauty queen. But even as the snapshots call attention to discrepancies in the looks department, viewers are given a sermon on the unimportance of looks. Another clip from a later interview is inserted. Melana continues her discussion of interpersonal chemistry, which does not depend on looks. Chemistry, she says, should not be ignored. Ultimately Melana felt the strongest chemistry with hunk Jason Peoples, leaving the audience to wonder what chemistry the average man has.

Viewers got to revisit the issue on *Average Joe: Hawaii*, which follows the same formula as its predecessor. In the premier, viewers see shots of bachelorette Larissa Meek — artist, former beauty queen, and model — in a bathing suit then another of her gazing pensively at a gorgeous sunset from the terrace of yet another mansion. She's come to Hawaii to find "Mr. Right," the narrator explains. Just in case viewers missed the first series, the narrator warns that she's in for a first date she will never forget.

This is followed by a preview of what will happen next. Donato and Phuc, two of the largest men in the group, step off the bus, as does Chris, with his long sideburns, and David with his distinctive locks. Cut to Larissa mounting the stairs and muttering, "This has got to be a joke." Rubinoff reports that off camera she fumed, "Did you take these guys and primp them so they'd look even more dorky?" (C4).

As if in answer to her question, the camera pans a line-up of lei-bedecked contestants, "what we call average Joes," asserts the narrator. The pan takes on lightning speed then cuts to a shot of Donato. Slowly the camera pans up his ample belly and pendulous breasts. David stands beside him, arms crossed on his chest, looking serene and proud and, in contrast to Donato, woefully puny. This is followed by a collage of the contestants describing themselves as nerds, dateless, and doomed. Their words are accom-

panied by a series of shots showing rowdy behavior. The most bizarre includes
Phuc proudly opening beer bottles with his teeth. Once again viewers are
treated to shots of some contestants in unflattering swim trunks while the
narrator announces that they are a "new breed of bachelor" who will risk
"their hearts" to attain the beauty queen.

Then something different happens. Viewers are introduced to the hunks
who will challenge the average Joes. Hunks had played a destructive role in
the first series, but they were introduced into the action when there were only
four contestants left. Although the first Joes had been disheartened by the new
competitors, the hunks' introduction was not nearly as confrontational as in
Average Joe: Hawaii, where they arrive in a sleek speed boat and confidently
confront the Joes. The camera pans the sexy hunks lined up on deck then cuts
to a shot of Pete warning that they are like "a torpedo in the water" that
will demolish the Joes. As if to confirm this and emphasize the difference
between the two groups, the camera cuts to a shot of the Joes grouped together
in the water. The composition of the shot, and its placement, give the
contestants an extremely vulnerable look. As the narrator predicts "trouble in
paradise," viewers see shots of the Joes looking extremely dejected.

Pete reappears, bare-chested and sporting an admirable six-pack, to
proclaim that the hunks are "just a little bit better" than the Joes. Given his
attire, it's fairly certain that his statement was made in the context of the
gym competition in which the Joes were annihilated. Placed here it smacks
of smugness and over-weaning pride. To further emphasize the contrast
between the hunks and the Joes, viewers are shown a series of quick shots
of the Joes trying to surf. Being athletically challenged is apparently another
characteristic of averageness. In both series, injecting the hunks into the
competition foregrounds the difference between average and above average
and advances the discussion of what it means to be average.

In sum, the premiere of *Average Joe: Hawaii* follows the same pattern
as its predecessor. Shots of Larissa in various gowns and bathing suits that
display her beauty are linked with shots that highlight the contestants' less
than hunky appearance, their faults and their awkwardness. It's clear that
each has packed faults and idiosyncrasies among his shirts and underwear.
Inevitably there are more bathing suit shots, just to remind viewers that these
are not hunks, but rather, as one fan described them, "dorks, dweebs, flabbies,
and some uggos" who are "over-the-top homely" (Inflatable). In fact, executive producers Krasnow and Glassman pleaded guilty to "stacking the deck,"
especially in *Average Joe: Hawaii*. Speaking of the average Joes in the second
series, Krasnow said, "I think they might make the first group look like
Adonises" (Kaplan).

Discussion

Average Joe and its successor exemplify what Roland Barthes calls "readerly" texts (6). Both shows are constituted through audience analysis grounded in that structure which is the potential text, in experience with similar texts, in personal and social experiences, and in socio-cultural practices that impact the interpretation of the text (Barthes 6–10). These variables enable fans to fill in the gaps created by editing and commercial breaks, thus engaging in the process of signification that actualizes the text's potential meanings. As Fiske observes, "Viewers and television interact," providing a polysemic text open to many readings (19). Moreover, "gaps" in a text, says Wolfgang Iser, prod the viewer "into filling the blanks with projections," thus amplifying a text's meaning (168).

The interaction of these variables is evident in a sampling of fan comments. Some viewers denied that the contestants represented the majority of men in the world (Fast Eddie; Howard Marshall; Wendiness). Others argued that the men were made to look below-average, that the shows' producers contrived to show them at their worst (Montana). One fan was outraged at the way the show humiliated "nice average guys" (Susanj12). Another alleged that producers had inserted a humiliating sound effect as Craig, one of the super-sized guys, stepped off the bus on the first night of *Average Joe* (Plain Crazy). Others countered that the guys *were* typical of the average male (Tiger Lilly; Montana). Their difference of opinion can be attributed to personal and sociocultural experiences, as well as their knowledge of the genre.

Many indicated that rating a particular male "average" was complex. One suggested that the contestants represented a spectrum ranging from below to above average and proceeded to locate each contestant on the spectrum (Blow-by-Blow). Another contended that the contestants were average if you judged them by criteria other than appearance, occupation for example (Bebo). Two fans agreed, adding that intelligence and personality must also be factored in. Even the hunks might be rated average if you considered personality and occupation (Averagejane; Sugarlady). Many fans concurred, pointing out that a hunk with a bad personality could be classified as an average Joe (Leviathon).* Rating is contextual, and the hunks became part of the equation in calculating what "average" means.

The range of these comments attest to the polysemy of these texts. Excess contributes to this polysemy. Excess can operate as hyperbole or as

---

*In fact, Melana, defending her choice of hunk Jason Peoples, insisted he was an average Joe whom she chose because he was "a good listener" (Smolowe, Rodriquez, and Ehrich 109).

semiotic excess. Hyperbole is achieved through exaggeration, especially "camp' (Fiske 90). It contains "both the dominant ideology and a simultaneous critique of it" (91). For example, these shows' extensive use of bathing suit shots for both the beauty queens and the contestants constitutes hyperbole. The overt idealization of the women's shots and the mockery of the men's constitute semiotic excess. They are over-determined as signs of the extraordinary and the ordinary in terms of appearance. These shots support the differentiation between above average and average (or below average). Excess also invites viewers to create their own meanings based on textual, personal, social, and cultural experience. Excesses in the construction of "average" stimulate viewers to question that construction and construct their own conception of average. Through excess the text ridicules the emphasis which society places on appearance while it simultaneously invokes that emphasis.

To sum up, a text is an open system that viewers interpret, within parameters constructed by its creators, based on their personal and socio-cultural experience. In other words, viewers bring to their experience of the text their own knowledge of and experience with both the rating process and the experience of what it means to be average.

Conclusion

The preceding remarks center on the role of personal and socio/cultural experience in interpreting a text. The contention is that *Average Joe* and *Average Joe: Hawaii* constitute a polysemic text on the rating of average and, by extension, on the rating process in general. However, if one considers the role of generic knowledge in interpreting a text, it becomes clear that these two shows can be read as parodies of the dating show and its ideological underpinnings. The physical attractiveness of the bachelorettes, the opulence of the setting, the elaborateness of the dates, the elimination ritual all fit the generic model of the dating show.

However, deviations from the generic norm suggest that *Average Joe* can be read as parody. Parody functions by appropriating then ridiculing, thus creating what Roscoe and Hight describe as an ambiguous and polysemic "double-edged" structure that promises then reneges (30). First, *Average Joe* and its successor promise to be a different kind of dating show in which contestants are ordinary rather than extraordinary. Instead they select contestants who, as David Bianculli put it, are "less than what you might call traditionally handsome" (80) and foreground their physical defects and their idiosyncrasies.* The shows portray their "average" contestants as "life's puny misfits, fat guys and nearsighted nerds" (McDonough); "paunchy, balding slobs" (Bawden E01); "dumpy schlemiels" and "freaks" (Shales C01).

Ridiculing contestants is not new. *Joe Millionaire* (Fox), *Cupid* (ABC), and *Looking for Love: Bachelorettes in Alaska* (Fox) portray female contestants as greedy, catty, and two-faced. (Melana and Larissa are pilloried through the use of a hidden camera). *Blind Date* (syndicated) ridicules its contestants based on appearance, personality, class, etc. (DeRose, Fürsich, and Haskins). *Average Joe* and *Average Joe: Hawaii* go farther by invoking a category representative of a substantial proportion of the population and then ridiculing that category.

Second, the two shows attack their own premise by introducing the hunks, a failing which fans noted and denounced (Lambkins; K1W1; Annray; a_canuck_01). The hunks, too, are subjected to group ridicule. Although the hunks were more handsome and out-performed the Joes, they were portrayed as more stupid and less sensitive, and considerably more arrogant. The hunks might have interests and jobs, but their primary focus was on themselves and "their hotness," Glassman suggested (Porter). Matthew Gilbert of *The Boston Globe* was even more damning, describing Gill (*Average Joe: Hawaii*) as an expressionless, "dull, pent-up dude with the magnetism of a piece of wood" (Gilbert E1). In other words, the hunks, too, are subjected to group ridicule. *Average Joe* and *Average Joe: Hawaii* lampoon the two groups they set in competition with each other.

Parody "makes its target a significant part of itself" (Roscoe and Hight 30) and in *Average Joe* and *Average Joe: Hawaii* the reality dating show they purport to represent itself becomes a target. Both shows adopt then reject the staples of their genre and its cultural norms. Roscoe and Hight assert parody goes beyond the mocking of a genre to critique the sociocultural norms instantiated in that genre. Thus "parody always situates itself in opposition to "normative discourse" (29), in this case the social norms that underlie the rating of oneself and others. Plantagina agrees, theorizing that parody and satire function as "imitation of and ironic commentary on another discourse" (qtd. in Roscoe and Hight 30). The discourse which *Average Joe* adopts is that of the traditional dating show and the rating process which underlies that discourse, which it mocks through exaggeration and excess.

The treatment of contestants on these shows deserves study. Roscoe and Hight note that American reality television ignores the rights of its participants in order to construct a "dramatic and emotional" text. They ignore the traditional ethic of the documentary genre to which they are distantly related (137). For a discussion of the ethical problems inherent in reality television, see Lancioni, "Survivor in the Vast Wasteland," in Desperately Seeking Ethics, ed. Howard Good (Lanham, MD: Scarecrow Press, 2003), 145–160.

Roscoe and Hight argue that parody situates viewers so they can be critical of a text and the social norms it embodies, thus constructing "a new focus on how we represent the social world..." (31). In other words, the personal and social factors discussed earlier, combined with a knowledge of the genre, facilitate the interpretation of *Average Joe* and its successor as a parody of both a genre and a cultural practice. Both shows question as well as support sociocultural norms through the aesthetic structure of parody. As Roscoe and Hight contend, parody is ambivalent towards its subject. It creates expectations only to dash them, nevertheless providing "opportunities for humour, anger and critical reflection" and managing to both "reinforce" and critique its object. Thus parody personifies "ambivalence and ambiguity" (Roscoe and Hight 31), characteristics which these shows exhibit towards their "average" contestants, ridiculing them much of the time but occasionally soliciting sympathy for them.

Average Joe and its sequel can be analyzed as parody. The selection of competitors, the exaggerated nature of the editing and the mis-en-scene suggest that the genre and the rating process it embodies are being mocked. The use of parody as an ideological tool in *Average Joe* and other reality television genres is certainly worth exploring.

BIBLIOGRAPHY

a_canuck_01. "A Social Experiment We Already Know the Answer." Online posting. 26 Nov. 2003. Fans of Reality TV. 30 Nov. 2003 <fansofrealitytv.com/forums/showthread. php?t=20059>.

Annray. "A Social Experiment We Already Know the Answer." Online posting. 26 Nov. 2003. Fans of Reality TV. 30 Nov. 2003 <fansofrealitytv.com/forums/showthread. php?t=20059>.

Average Joe. Co-exec. prod. Stuart Krasnow and Andrew Glassman. NBC. Premiere 3 Nov. 2003.

Average Joe: Hawaii. Co-exec. prod. Stuart Krasnow and Andrew Glassman. NBC. Premiere 5 Jan 2004.

Average Joe Home Page. 3 Nov. 2003 <http://www.nbc.com/Average_Joe/about/index. html>.

Averagejane. "The Definition of Average?" Online posting. 2 Dec. 2003. Fans of Reality TV. 1 Feb. 2004 <http://www.fansofrealitytv.com/forums/showthread.php?t= 21312>.

Barthes, Roland. *S/Z. An Essay.* Trans. Chard Miller. Pref. Richard Howard. New York: Hill & Wang, 1974.

Bawden, Jim. "Meet *Average Joe's* Gal." *Toronto Star* 23 Feb. 2004, Ontario Ed.: E01.

Bebo. "What Average Means." Online posting. 12 Nov. 2003. Community Reality TV World. DCForumID58. Thread No. 65. 14 Nov. 2003 <http://community.reality tvworld.com/bo>.

Belcher, Walt. "Beauty and the Geeks." *Tampa Tribune* 3 Nov. 2003, final ed.: baylife 1.

Bianculli, David. "In Reality, This 'Joe' Is Gentler." *New York Daily News* 3 Nov. 2003, sports final ed.: 80.

Blow by Blow. "What Average Means." Online posting. 12 Nov. 2003. Community Reality TV World. DCForumID58. Thread No. 65. 14 Nov. 2003 <http://community. realitytvworld.com/boards/cgi-bin/dcboard.cgi?>.

DeRose, Justin, Elfriede Fürsich, and Ekaterina V. Haskins. "Pop (up) Goes the *Blind Date*: Supertextual Constraints on 'Reality' Television." *Journal of Communication Inquiry* 27 (April 2003): 171–89.

Fast Eddie. "What 'Average' Means." Online posting. 12 Nov. 2003. Community Reality TV World. Forum: DCForumID58. Thread No. 65. 14 Nov. 2003 <http:// community.realitytvworld.com/boards/cgi-bin/dcboard.cgi?>.

Fiske, John. *Television Culture.* London: Routledge, 1987.

Gilbert, Matthew. "'Average' Eastie Guy Finds Looks Win the Women." *Boston Globe* 2 March 2004: E1.

Howardmarshal. "Sorry to Get on My Soapbox — But???" Online posting. 4 Nov. 2003. Fans of Reality TV. 14 Nov. 2003 <http://www.fansofrealitytv.com/forums/show thread.php?t=20057>.

Huff, Richard. "Below Average? New Show's Cast Not Exactly 'Hot.'" *New York Daily News,* 3 Nov. 2003, star ed.: 6.

Inflatable_Monk. "Thing." Online posting. 13 Dec. 2003. Everything2. 10Aug. 2008 <http://everything2.com/index.pl?node_id=68821&displaytype>.

Iser, Wolfgang. *The Act of Reading. A Theory of Aesthetic Response.* Baltimore: Johns Hopkins University Press, 1978.

Kaplan, Don. "Next Average Joe Done Before Girls Catch On." *New York Post* 26 Nov. 2003: 111.

KIWI. "A Social Experiment We Already Know the Answer." Online posting. 26 Nov. 2003. Fans of Reality TV. 30 Nov. 2003 <fansofrealitytv.com/forums/showthread. php?t=20059>.

Lambkins. "A Social Experiment We Already Know the Answer." Online posting. 26 Nov. 2003. Fans of Reality TV. 30 Nov. 2003 <fansofrealitytv.com/forums/showthread. php?t=20059>.

Leviathon. "Sorry to Get on My Soapbox — But???" Online Posting. 4 Nov. 2003. Fans of Reality TV. 14 Nov. 2003 <fansofrealitytv.com/forums/showthread.php?t=20057>.

McDonough, Kevin. "NBC Reality Show Painful to Watch." *Charleston Daily Mail* [West Virginia] 3 Nov. 2003: P5D.

Montana. "Sorry to Get on My Soapbox — But???" Online Posting. 4 Nov. 2003. Fans of Reality TV. 14 Nov. 2003 <http://www.fansofrealitytv.com/forums/showthread. php?t=20057>.

Plain Crazy. "Poor Craig. Why the Fat Guy Jokes?" Online Posting. 4 Nov. 2003. Community Reality TV World. Forum: DCForumID58. Thread Num. 26. 14 Nov. 2003 <http://community.realitytvworld.com/boards/cgi-bin/dcboard.cgi?>.

Porter, Rick. "*Average Joe* Ups the Ante in Hawaii." Online posting. 1 Jan. 2004. Friends of Reality TV. 1 Feb. 2004 <http://www.fansofrealitytv.com/forums/showthread.php?>.

Roscoe, Jane, and Craig Hight. *Faking It. Mock-documentary and the Subversion of Factuality.* Manchester: Manchester University Press, 2001.

Rubinoff, Joel. "Let's Hear It for the *Average Joe,* A Class Act." *The Record* [Kitchener-Waterloo, Ontario] 10 Jan. 2004: C4.

Ryan, Suzanne C. "Are Boston Men More 'Average' Than Others?" *The Boston Globe.* Posted by John. 2 Jan. 2004. Fans of Reality TV. 1 Feb. 2004 <http://www.fansof realitytv.com/forums/printthread.php?t=22456>.

Shales, Tom. "Average Joe Viewers: Real Losers." *Washington Post* 3 Nov. 2003, final ed.: C01.

Smolowe, Jill, Brenda Rodriguez, and Kathy Ehrich. "Goodbye Joe, Hello Love." *People* 22 Dec. 2003: 108–110.

Sugarlady. "The Definition of Average?" Online posting. 2 Dec. 2003. Fans of Reality TV. 1 Feb. 2004 <http://www.fansofrealitytv.com/forums/showthread.php?t=21312>.

Susanjl2. "Cruelty to Nice Guys." Online posting. 11 Nov. 2003. Fans of Reality TV. 14 Nov. 2003 <http://www.fansofrealitytv.com/forums/showthread.php?t=20057>.

Tiger Lily. "What 'Average' Means." Online posting. 12 Nov. 2003. Community Reality TV World. Forum: DCForumID58. Thread Number 65. 14 Nov. 2003 <http://community.realitytvworld.com/boards/cgi-bin/dcboard.cgi?>.

Wendiness. "Sorry to Get on My Soapbox — But???" Online Posting. 4 Nov. 2003. Fans of Reality TV. 14 Nov. 2003 <fansofrealitytv.com/forums/showthread.php?t=20057>.

The Swan as
Sado-Ritual Syndrome?

CHRISTOPHER D. RODKEY

The Swan premiered on April 7, 2004, scheduled as a "lead-in" for Fox's enormously popular *American Idol* reality program. Part extreme makeover reality show, part beauty pageant, and even part psychology talk show, *The Swan* took a woman with self-admitted low self-esteem and transformed her over the course of three months from an "ugly duckling" — as the classic story goes — to a beautiful "swan." The three-month transformation process included a regimen of "professionals" assembled to de-duckling the contestant by means of plastic and dental cosmetic surgery, life "coaching," psychology, and fitness advice. Each program featured two contestants, one of whom was chosen (along with a "wild card" runner-up, in a surprise-rules-loop-hole) for a beauty pageant at the end of the season. The winner was awarded cash, a scholarship, more life coaching, vacations, and a 2004 Ford Taurus.

The show was enormously successful and became immediately controversial. Had reality television finally taken it too far? The *Tampa Tribune* (FL) called it "'Queen for a Day' with a scalpel" and the *Philadelphia Daily News'* Ellen Gray wrote, "*The Swan* is a show degrading to both women and birds" (Hibberd 22). The Critic's Poll by *Television Week* named it one of the worst shows of the year. The show was popular enough to return for a second season later in 2004, though the shock value of the extremity of the first season did not hold.

Academic response to *The Swan* has been fairly minimal — even for an enormously successful television program and one that so clearly deals with medical practice. One exception is Leigh Turner, a bioethicist at McGill University, who raised a number of concerns in the *British Medical Journal* almost immediately after the show's premiere. First, Turner claimed, extreme makeover shows such as *The Swan* "foster the impression that complex per-

93

sonal, psychological, and social problems can be solved through cosmetic surgery" (1208). *The Swan* presents a world where an extreme makeover offers a medical solution to marital and psychological problems.

More troublesome, however, according to Turner, is the show's banal treatment of cosmetic surgical procedures. For example, beyond nervous phone calls to husbands and boyfriends before surgery, no mention of the risks involved with surgeries — sometimes involving up to nine procedures — is presented by the show (Dliagas 51). "Possible complications of cosmetic surgery are ignored," Turner says, and "reservations of family members and friends of program participants are dismissed." Beyond these basic elements of medical ethics that are not entertained within the show's content, Turner further suggests that the questionable ethics is a concern of social justice. "The very language of 'makeover' suggests that undergoing multiple surgical procedures is just like wearing cosmetics," she said, referring to the flippancy of the doctors' initial "Swan Plans" (Turner 1208). The way in which the medical professionals immediately begin to profile the "problems" of each woman's face at the opening of each show after seemingly seeing her picture for only a few seconds is often stunning. In one early episode, a doctor blurts out, "This nose has gotta go!" Rhinoplasty is discussed with the ease of a cosmetologist selling eyeliner.

The psychologist's role in the show is somewhat prominent, though not nearly as much as the medical professionals' roles. The mental health professional often interrupts the medical doctor's legitimizing of the experimentation on their female subjects. Even the show's host, while emceeing the first season's pageant, said that although the transformation of the Swans' attitudes and world views were most important evaluation criteria, "Let's face it, they're smokin'!" Kristen Johnson wrote in *Dialog* shortly after *The Swan* went off the air that while the show pays "lip-service to broader definitions of 'inner beauty,'" we must "be honest: No one turns on the TV to see someone become more confident, but to see an A cup transformed to a D — well now, that's something worth watching!" (Johnson 5).

Johnson's hyperbolic comment is revealing. The women on *The Swan* are being sexually exploited by a television show that deepens the symptomatic exploitation that the women have already suffered. The show plays on the exploitative environment in which its audience resides, the contemporary patriarchal United States, where women choose to undergo surgery for the entertainment of men — both on- and off-screen. The women on the show are prisoners in a system that has dictated that their own bodies are prisons; the liberation from this prison is the knife. As experimental specimens, the Swans have been unjustly coerced by a woman-hating society to provide examples, consumer samples, to a public which is both unable to afford the medical procedures and searching for new ways to technologically reiterate its fundamental hatred of women.

Medical Experimentation

To this end, I wish to draw a comparison of the Swans to prisoners who are subjects of medical experimentation. The problem of medical research on prisoners is so multi-sided that one is required to be multi-ocular in any approach to sift through the ethical puzzles. In this author's interpretation, the primary ethical dilemma is whether or not those who are incarcerated have the ability to volunteer autonomously (Verdun-Jones, Weisstub, and Arboleda-Florez 506). Following this issue is whether the rewards offered to prisoners for participating in medical research constitute coercion. Second, a question of justice arises, namely, whether volunteering for medical experiments should be seen as contributing a criminal debt to society.

First, it is not clear whether prisoners have the ability to freely volunteer for high-risk medical experiments. At what point do rewards given for experimentation "render consent involuntary" by the subject (Freedman 206)? Prisoners agree to participate in medical research for a variety of reasons; some of these include hope for early release or parole, a chance for better living conditions, a change of pace against otherwise mundane prison life or boredom, financial needs in prison, financial needs of family members outside of prison, opportunities for better job training, better health care, and even altruism. In the 1976 hearings of the Congressional Commission on Medical Experimentation on Prisoners, the most common reason why prisoners volunteered for research was "a continuing need for money" (U.S. Congress 37).

At the Maryland State House of Corrections in Jessup, Maryland, for example, in the late 1960s and 1970s, research subjects were paid $2 per day for participating in one research experiment, against prison jobs that paid only pennies per day (Verdun-Jones). Understandably, prisoners there would try to be on as many experiments at once as possible as a means of financial gain (U.S. Congress 37–38). The economic contexts of prisoners position them to be exploited by any gain from medical research, which is not entirely unlike the economic contexts of those living in below-average economic conditions outside of prison (Meyer 6; Visscher 63). Similarly, prisoners' decisions to participate in research must be examined in the context of the lack of quality medical care available inside of prisons, as well as the economic conditions of most prisoners prior to incarceration. When a prisoner volunteers to be a research subject, the decision is made within the context of the reality that most prisoners did not have access to quality or attentive medical care ever, and volunteering for experimentation may be seen as an opportunity for something that is normative or indicative of a higher economic class (Noah 241).

Second, the philosophical question: Is justice served by subjecting — or even just allowing — prisoners to take the burden of medical testing for society must be raised. Further, is justice served by directly or indirectly, rightly or wrongly, positioning prisoners to believe that volunteering as subjects in medical experiments is a means to pay back a criminal debt to society and is a legitimate form of punishment? To answer these questions requires one to again make judgments of value regarding the life of a criminal and adequate punishment for certain crimes. To be sure, these judgments of value are typically issued by courts, which on their own are very subjective toward race, class, and gender, but are later judged with fewer restrictions when parole or even pardon becomes possible.

One trend in assessing the value of the life and punishment of criminals is to equate purity or a notion of purification in correctional activities. In a discussion of the idea of purification in formal criminal punishment, one begins with *Gorgias*, the dialogue in which Plato wrote in a discussion between Polus and Socrates that the process of punishing criminals is the "release from evils, namely wickedness" (Ezorsky 37). In other words, incarceration is primarily an act of purification. This paradigm of criminal justice is called "reparative justice," that is, when criminals are punished, the consequences of why individuals do what they do is not as important as what criminal behavior was performed, and the punishment by the *polis* or state is "an act of reparation for previous crimes" (Branson 46). It is from this position toward punishment that an activity with such a high personal risk attached to it is deemed appropriate for the prison population.

As a result of this general reparative understanding of punishment, the medical profession of the United States is permitted to use prisoners as test subjects by a largely indifferent public because the experimentation is "carried on under the guide of disciplinary action" (Visscher 60–61). But is medical testing really punishment, or is it an opportunity for inclusion of under-represented groups in medical experimentation? Women, for example, have traditionally been under-represented in phase-one pharmaceutical testing, which leads to inadequate testing for a product or procedure's safety. Beyond this, is medical experimentation a privilege that should only be allowed for the middle and upper classes of the United States? This restructuring of test populations would be only fair, because the upper and middle classes directly and disproportionately benefit from medical experimentation on prisoners, especially through non-therapeutic testing, far more than the vulnerable populations who are typically research subjects. Reparative punishment, in its obsession with purification in the form of medical experimentation on prisoners, suggests that the unstated social goal of this medical research is an instant gratification of the rich against the suffering of the poor, and assumes that reparative punishment in a sense "pays a debt to society," specifically the rich society, against which most criminal acts of the poor are believed to be directed. Reparative justice in the form of medical experimentation is understood, then, as one of many easy answers to the more complicated philosophical and practical problems of how to punish criminals adequately and cost effectively.

The Sado-Ritual Syndrome

Reparative social surgery, like that on *The Swan*, is a kind of medical experimentation to repair women's bodies broken by the same system that, in many cases, broke the women's bodies in the first place or convinced the women that they were broken. Just as experimentation on prisoners may be economically, socially, and even ethically legitimated by our culture, the gynocide, as a kind of genocide, implicit in this culture suggests that television shows like *The Swan* are indicative of deeper cultural problems than shady medical practices. Use of the feminist term gynocide as a kind of genocide is not intended to obscure other, more widespread genocides and holocausts that occur on a daily basis throughout the world. Gynocide is intended to interpret the means by which a vulnerable population is exploited and suffers by the psychic and physical domination of a ruling class or population. The genocide becomes more poisonous when the power exerted or taken is gendered. Using feminist philosopher Mary Daly's model of "Sado-Ritual Syndrome" for identifying gynocide, the intention is to demonstrate that *The Swan* is a symptom indicative of a spiritually and philosophically sick society.

In her primary feminist ethics text, *Gyn/Ecology*, Mary Daly traces the history of genocide as a gynocide that always targets women at the center of human atrocities throughout history, including Chinese foot-binding practices, Indian *suttee* rituals, European witch burnings, American gynecological medicine, and Nazi medical experiments. The model she uses to explain these gynocides is Sado-Ritual Syndrome. The syndrome's symptoms are (1) a "fixation on purity"; (2) an "erasure of male responsibility" or "total erasure of responsibility" for the act; (3) "an inherent tendency to catch on and spread," often in a situation where the richer classes exploit the poor; (4) women used as scapegoats and "token torturers"; (5) "compulsive orderliness, obsessive repetitiveness, and fixation upon minute details, which divert attention from the horror"; (6) "behavior which at other times and places is unacceptable becomes acceptable and even normative as a consequence of conditioning through the ritual atrocity"; and (7) a "[l]egitimation of the ritual by the rituals of 'objective' scholarship — despite appearances of disapproval" (Daly 132–136).

Citing Nietzsche's *Genealogy of Morals*, Mary Daly explains that for those with social power, memory is created through pain. "Whenever man has thought it necessary to create a memory for himself," Nietzsche observed, "one of the most enduring psychological axioms ... his effort has been attended with torture, blood, sacrifice" (192–193). Daly writes that this is the process of "meaning-making" around physical memory: "the 'thing' that is impressed/branded on the memory is forced into the mind by some violent and painful means, by pressing/cutting/invading. This is the mind rape that accompanies male myth creation." Not just a singular rape, being done in large numbers, the Sado-Ritual Syndrome is "gang rape.... Done over and over again" (Daly 109–110). The Sado-Ritual Syndrome is the means by which those with power maintain their power — and this social mechanism of power maintenance is often largely unspoken and even unknown by those who participate in it.

First, Daly says, the Sado-Ritual Syndrome is obsessed with purity. Those who were tortured through medical practices in Nazi concentration camps, for example, were regarded as "criminals," and bizarre experimentation was acted out as the norm for the criminal prisoner population. The Nuremberg Trials, which addressed the genocide of the Nazi Holocaust, focused on the horrors of the concentration camps as an issue specifically associated with prisoners. The drive for the extermination of Jews and other "undesirables" was a racist cultural belief fueled by a need to purify the country of its tainted, dirty, and undesirable populations. Similarly, reparative justice paradigms for criminal punishment has as its center a belief that criminals need to be purified for their criminal behavior — that their wickedness may be removed by a process that is initiated in prison settings. In *The Swan*, the purification process is the painful process the Swans experience.

The opening sequence of the first episode of *The Swan* describes the three-month program of the show's contestants as a "brutal ... program" that "requires discipline, sacrifice, and pain." The exercise sequences are reminiscent of boot-camp montages from daytime talk shows, where a disrespectful or promiscuous adolescent is shipped away to a prison or military institution to be scared into knowing her place with the parents upon return, except the mouthy adolescent is replaced in *The Swan* by a socially unattractive woman who needs "fixing." Marital problems discussed by contestants are only mentioned later as "issues that are being worked out" later in the show; troubled marriages appear to be healed by plastic surgery during the final pageant. Contestants claim that they have learned to demand more from themselves than they had previously, but take the role of finding the right combination of social attractiveness and relational passivity in their own descriptions of themselves. Again and again, the Swans testify throughout the show that they have learned to accept themselves and that they are "stronger" people. No one stops to observe that to finally accept oneself by means of adherence to societal beauty standards requires no existential courage, yet the triumph of the show surrounds the Swans' willingness, perhaps unknowingly, to sacrifice their own lives.

Lorrie Arias, a contestant on the show, wrote about her experiences on an internet message board sponsored by the Fox Network. She said that when it came to close relationships "we didn't really have time to think" about how their actions would affect those around her. These are all cases of the female selves being exorcised and manipulated by the memory-creating mechanisms of medical practice. This exorcism of the female self through the cutting of female flesh is an act of purification.

Second, the Sado-Ritual Syndrome always has an erasure of responsibility, especially male responsibility. The role of men, especially in the first season of *The Swan*, is fairly minimal, with the exception of the medical and fitness professionals, who are usually thanked in the same breath as God in a continual mantra of praise at the end of each show. Beyond the professionals, the husbands and boyfriends are in the background, being supportive of their partners — checking in like they would with a car mechanic. Occasionally the significant other avoids the contestant, perhaps enveloped by guilt over the situation or, as one admits, fears that his partner will leave him now that she is more sexually attractive. She, of course, at least in the show, stood by her man, and a great triumph seems to be achieved when the Swan devalues her new commodity for the sake of maintaining her marriage. Throughout the show, the series' host, Amanda Byram, is given the stature of leading discussions with doctors, describing the medical procedures, and even announcing changes of rules. The only other men are two models who open the doors for the ladies when ordered by Byram. *The Swan* is designed to look like a woman's game controlled primarily by women for the benefit of women in general.

Third, according to Daly, the Sado-Ritual Syndrome has a tendency to spread. Even after numerous strict policies, Congressional hearings, and some public outrage, prisoner research is constantly evolving into new forms to avoid regulations and laws, often involving the guise of academia, so that an illusion is manufactured whereby pharmaceutical research by universities is performed for humanitarian reasons and not for profit. While it is unknown how much prisoner experimentation is happening today, it in fact does continue, though often in a hidden and silent manner. Similarly, extreme makeover shows, such as *The Swan*, have given the American public a sense that cosmetic surgery is normalized medical practice for "normal" people; a new demand for plastic surgery has emerged in recent years. Lorrie Arias notes on the Fox internet bulletin board that in her hometown, plastic surgery was not common or publically discussed before *The Swan*. In fact, she writes, "One of my friends got breast implants while I was on the inside," that is, while Arias was still in her "Swan Plan." To this, a regular board participant replied: "Wow! Looks like the plastic desire ended up being contagious!" Although *The Swan* is no longer on the air, cosmetic surgery shows — both "reality" and intentionally "fictional" — have proliferated. Two years after *The Swan*'s final season, it was still viewed in fifty countries (Weber 290).

Fourth, women are used as scapegoats for the torture. Some feminists' outcry for more equality in phase-one pharmaceutical testing obscures the exploitation and "research abuse" present in risky tests, and fails to recognize the fact that a feminist pushing for more representation among research subjects will only lead to a higher percentage of women of color, lower economic status, and the incarcerated population participating in these tests (Noah 25ff). The illusion that *The Swan* creates is that the women's problems, from dentistry to relationships, are solipsistic or individualized. While American audiences surely appreciate rugged individualism, an individual taking responsibility for themselves, the contextual problems of body image, family, education, race, and economic status are never addressed. The woman is dealing with her problem alone, and she believes that she can change her reality by changing her body's sexual value. This is the symptom of the Sado-Ritual Syndrome at its most powerful.

Fifth, as with all gynocide/genocide, in Sado-Ritual Syndrome there is an obsession with attention to detail, obsessive repetitiveness that directs attention away from the horror of the torture. The real danger and risk which prisoners face in many of their experimentations, as well as the coercive living conditions of prisoners in the U.S., are obscured by some ethical issues, such as naive claims that the possibility for altruistic voluntariness justifies the availability of medical research opportunities to prisoners. Almost every comprehensive study of prisoner experimentation has noted one way or another that the physicians, corporations, and institutions involved in it are universally silent. As such, the medical community, specifically physicians, as legal commentator Benjamin Meier writes, "Facilitate human rights violations through [their] silence" (430). As discussed earlier, the problems and risks of cosmetic surgery are silently obscured and ignored on *The Swan*, and any concerns that are raised are portrayed as indicative of the contestant's weaknesses or a medical side-consequence. It is not uncommon for the liposuctionist to predict that "this one's gonna be depressed," which is "typical" or "normal" for similar women undergoing cosmetic surgery.

Sixth, unethical or immoral behavior is justified in the Sado-Ritual Syndrome under the claim of normalcy. *The Swan* mixes reality show competition with a makeover show and beauty pageant — three interrelated kinds of television entertainment at least understood by the general television-watching public. Even though the show generated bad reviews and negative press, it was still watched by millions of Americans. The feminist publication *Lilith* even observed a lack of outrage about *The Swan* among feminists, likely because the show wasn't as sophisticated or compelling as *Sex and the City*, which generated more discussion among feminists (Ofman 9). *The Swan* was reality television inevitably doing what reality television does, that is, confusing realities. Assuming that reality itself is a primary text to be interpreted and that fictions are a secondary text which have meaning when they intersect with the *logos* between primary reality, reality television does what only religious "classics" claim to do: present reality in a normative way. It is much more difficult to criticize *Sex and the City* and its confusions about women than a show where "normal" women get to share their experiences. To challenge their own worlds is to challenge religious values and paradigms — which are just assumed to be reality. As such, the banal nature of the show's events also plays into the commonplace attitudes reflected by the public about cosmetic surgery; it is all just part of the reality of the contemporary medical establishment. Realities are manufactured, confused, commodified, rated, and built upon if there is enough demand for consumption.

Finally, scholars "re-enact the original rites by erasing their memory and by effacing those" who have the courage to speak against genocide. By withholding information from the public and having policies of silence regarding the actual risks of cosmetic surgery, *The Swan* hides behind the guises of what is real and what is reality. Contestant Lorrie Arias' words both disclose and seek to erase her *Swan* transformation; on the Fox internet bulletin board she defends the superiority of *The Swan* over *Dr. 90210*, another "extreme makeover" show, claiming that *The Swan* provided women with the "'Super Woman' makeover"—clearly naming the makeover as super, empowering, ontologically superior. She also indicates that *The Swan* required a high level of psychological endurance, especially when compared to other reality shows. Another board participant asked Arias directly what she feels the difference between *The Swan* and *Pimp My Ride* is, since in the latter a (usually male) contestant's old car is revamped. This question points at the complex layering of reality at work in *The Swan*. Arias responds, "You have no idea how HARD we worked for what we got!!" *Swan* contestants surely made sacrifices, namely their bodies and selves, which at least initially reduces the differences between themselves being "fixed" and a car being "pimped"—the difference is that the Swan is a living person. While Arias later warns her readers to not regard surgery as a "cure," and that those thinking about doing the same should get "[l]ots of therapy to repair the inside," she refers to her "outside" as being "fixed" in another board conversation. The psychologist's role is seen as curing a sickness; the "inside" is referred to as being something in need of repair, rather than as empowered, encouraged, respected, and loved.

The comparison of a car being pimped with a Swan being transformed is telling. In the first season of the show, one contestant told her story as part of a montage legitimizing her impending transformation. "I used to have the perfect body and I used to be pretty and I used to be able to walk down the street and have guys chasing me," she lamented. She said she was talked into doing some modeling as a teenager and loved the attention. But then her life was ruined by "the wrong guy," and two abusive marriages. Now, she says, "When I look in the mirror, I see a big fat cow," she explains. "My dream for myself is to learn to know that I deserve for someone to treat me good." Her surgical program is, then, to restore her purity, like a reclaiming of virginity. The invasion of the knife into her flesh is redemptive, baptismally washing away the sins of her world. The kind of man she attracted in her "former life" didn't work out, but she longs for the commodification of strangers. And when that commodification disappeared, so did her self-value, because her own value was skin deep. Yet she longs for it. She is, of course, right in wishing for a respectful partner, but her words suggest the cycle of being sick with the Sado-Ritual Syndrome, and living in a society sick with it, too.

Hers is a seemingly hopeless situation, corrected by a team of professionals and a beauty pageant. Even through all of the Swans' sincerity, did any of them really think the show would solve their problems? *People* magazine followed up with the first season's contestants. One Swan reports that her husband will now allow himself to be seen in public with her. Another, now preparing to be a police officer ("Don't let the boobs fool you," she remarks), brags that other men hit on her in front of her husband. Two others laments that the show did not offer adequate maintenance instructions for their new bodies, including a lack of follow-up "life coaching." Another even reports that her transformation backfired: people used to give her insulting names because of her looks, and now she is called "Miss Fake." "It's the same Kelly," she admits, "just more perfect" (Gliatto 84–88).

As objects for a viewing audience's consumption, *The Swan*'s contestants are societal prison experiments offered by a medical establishment that wishes to convince us that we need our bodies to be homogenized. They want to convince us that we need to consume their ultimate product: a life that is not ours and redemption for the problems imposed on us individually by a socially and spiritually sick society. As members of the audience, we participate in the experimentation by consuming the show as a product and recasting its implicit values and medical assumptions onto the world. Given the ease and positive outcome of the show, even the most skeptical could even be convinced to justify *The Swan*'s treatment for women who are burn victims or harshly abused by their husbands. This was the foundation for the second season of *The Swan*, which did not attain nearly the same ratings as the first. Only when playing within the parameters of the ridiculous does the morality implicit of *The Swan* appeal to its viewing public. The reality reflected by this "reality television" program is not a literal reality, but a spiritual one that points to the deep sicknesses, the ritualized sadism, implicit in our culture.

BIBLIOGRAPHY

Arias, Lorrie. "Comments on *Fox Reality* Internet Bulletin Board." 9 Dec. 2007. 19 Jan. 2009. <http://www.foxreality.com/community/viewtopic.php?t=5864>

Branson, Roy. "Philosophical Perspectives on Experimentation with Prisoners." *Research Involving Prisoners: Appendix to Report and Recommendations.* Prep. The National Commission for the Protection of Human Subjects of Biomedical and Behavioral Research. DHEW pub. (OS) 76–132. Washington, D.C.: U.S. Department of Health, Education, and Welfare, 1976. 1:1–1:46.

Daly, Mary. *Gyn/Ecology: The Metaethics of Radical Feminism.* Boston: Beacon, 1978.

Dliagas, Linda. "Can Ugly Ducklings Become Beautiful Swans?" *Hispanic* 17.9 (2004): 50–52.

Freedman, Benjamin. "A Moral Theory of Informed Consent." *Ethical and Regulatory Aspects of Clinical Research: Readings and Commentary.* Ed. Ezekiel Emanuel, et al. Baltimore: Johns Hopkins University Press, 2003. 203–207. Org. pub. *Hastings Center Reports* 5.4 (1975): 32–39.

Gliatto, Tom, et al. "Life after *The Swan*." *People* 62.5 (2 Aug. 2004): 84–88.

Hibberd, James. "'Swan' Song? Critics Hope for Reality Show's Demise." *Television Week* 24.1 (3 Jan. 2005): 22.

Johnson, Kristen. "I've Had It with Reality TV!" *Dialog* 44.1 (2005): 5.

Meier, Benjamin. "International Criminal Prosecution of Physicians: A Critique of Professors Annas and Grodin's Proposed International Medical Tribunal." *American Journal of Law & Medicine* 30 (2004): 419–452.

Meyer, Peter. *Drug Experiments on Prisoners: Ethical, Economic, or Exploitative?* Lexington, Mass.: Lexington, 1976.

Nietzsche, Friedrich. *The Geneology of Morals*. Trans. Francis Golffing. Rpt. in *The Birth of Tragedy and the Genealogy of Morals*. Garden City, NY: Doubleday, 1956.

Noah, Barbara. "Participation of Underrepresented Minorities in Clinical Research." *American Journal of Law & Medicine* 29 (2003): 221–245.

Nuremberg Military Tribunal, *U.S. v. Karl Brandt, et al.* "The Nuremberg Code." *Ethical and Regulatory Aspects of Clinical Research: Readings and Commentary*. Ed. Ezekiel Emanuel, et al. Baltimore: Johns Hopkins University Press, 2003. 29.

Ofman, Kaitlin. "Is It Just a T.V. Show?" *Lilith* 29.4 (2005): 9.

Plato. "Punishment as Cure." *Gorgias. Philosophical Perspectives on Punishment*. Ed. Gertrude Ezorsky. Albany: SUNY University Press, 1972.

The Swan: The Complete Series. DVD. Xenon, 2006.

Turner, Leigh. "Cosmetic Surgery: The New Face of Reality TV." *British Medical Journal* 328.7449 (15 May 2004): 1208.

U.S. Congress, Committee on the Judiciary. *Hearings Before the Subcommittee on Courts, Civil Liberties, and the Administration of Justice, First Session on H.R. 3603*. Ser. 31. Washington, D.C.: U.S. Government Printing Office, 1976.

Verdun-Jones, Simon, David Weisstub, and Julio Arboleda-Florez. "Prisoners as Subjects of Biomedical Experimentation: Examining the Arguments For and Against a Total Ban." *Research on Human Subjects: Ethics, Laws, and Social Polity*. Ed. David Weisstub. Oxford, UK: Pergamon, 1998. 503–530.

Visscher, Maurice. *Ethical Constraints and Imperatives in Medical Research*. American Lectures, vol. 985. Ser. ed. Ralph Slovenko. Springfield, IL: Charles Thomas, 1975.

Weber, Brenda. "What Makes the Man? Television Makeovers, Made-Over Masculinity, and Male Body Image." *International Journal of Men's Health* 5.3 (2006): 287–307.

The Boob Tube

Authority, Resistance, and Dr. 90210

SHANA HEINRICY

She picked such a tiny little implant, it almost breaks my heart. It'll barely be a little bee-sting, barely, barely, barely rise. Wow, it's really little, but there's nothing else I can do.
— Dr. Rey, *Dr. 90210*, "Is Bigger Better?" 2004

Dr. Rey is the lead character on the hit plastic surgery reality show *Dr. 90210*, which airs on E! The show follows the lives of several cosmetic surgeons, including the personal as well the professional, but focuses on Dr. Robert (Roberto) Rey.

The above statement was said by Dr. Rey about the unconscious Ana during her breast augmentation surgery. She desired B-cup implants to replace the implants she previously had removed in order to breastfeed. Ana's resistance to Dr. Rey's wishes regarding her breast size serves to highlight the ways in which Dr. Rey authorizes particular forms of a narrowly defined beauty standard. Note that Ana's defiance, though heavily disciplined throughout the show, is still within the realm of acceptable beauty practices. She is thin, stereotypically beautiful, and chooses to have breast implants. Even so, her small deviation from accepted practices (choosing a smaller implant) warrants the activation of authorial measures.

Dr. 90210 portrays cosmetic surgery as a personal choice. Dr. Rey and his patients are shown discussing possible options and jointly coming up with the "best solution" to their wayward bodies, as assessed by Dr. Rey's standards. As with all makeover reality shows, someone must rate and assess the "quality" of the individual's looks and suggest areas for improvement.

However, Ana helps to highlight that the "options" from which they chose are limited, and must be authorized by Dr. Rey.

In this essay, I will show how that authorial voice is constructed on television. I argue that television itself is an authority figure which lends its authority to those appearing on it. Appearing on television renders Dr. Rey an expert on beauty and medicine, regardless of his credentials, allowing him to judge others' bodies and act on them. While all reality television makeover shows use authority to justify particular beauty norms, I focus specifically on a cosmetic surgery program to explore the ways medical authority and beauty authority intersect and reinforce each other. Specifically, I will show how *Dr. 90210* is different from other shows featuring cosmetic surgery, such as *The Swan* and *Extreme Makeover*, because of the way Dr. Rey's stardom is cultivated, adding to his authorial voice.

I explore the ways the stardom of beauty "experts" is crafted on makeover shows, especially the stardom of Dr. Rey, thus allowing stardom to override credentials as a way of authorizing particular looks. Next, I examine the intersection of beauty authority and medical authority. Combined with stardom, this creates a nexus of discipline, presenting only a few, narrowly defined bodily choices as acceptable. Finally, I analyze the case of Ana, who destabilizes the discourse of personal choice and draws attention to some of the ways in which particular aesthetics are authorized while people are shamed for others.

Beauty, Authority, and Celebrity

Television not only presents ideals of beauty, but also serves as an authorial voice on beauty. The plethora of makeover shows, such as *What Not to Wear*, *The Swan*, *Extreme Makeover*, *10 Years Younger*, *Cover Shot*, and *The Biggest Loser*, coupled with a flow of advertisements of beauty products, present a relatively singular view of beauty, shaming those who do not adhere to those standards and then transforming them into human beings who are better able to contribute to society. Individuals in these programs are portrayed as making a "personal choice" about their bodies and beauty. While this is true, the possibilities from which they may chose are severely limited by the authorial voice of the program.

Media images serve to reinforce the need for beauty products, through the visual depictions of beautiful women, narratives in which less-than-beautiful women are undesirable, literally indicating a beauty-need fulfilled by a product through advertising, and through the illustration of beauty processes by experts, such as makeovers. In these ways, television itself serves as a sort of authority on beauty. Founded on a commercial model dedicated to selling products and lifestyles, television in the United States sells beauty and all of the rewards that supposedly come with beauty. Televisual images authorize particular aesthetic styles, especially when combined with celebrity. Images which appear on television are authorized as acceptable, simply by the fact of appearing on television.

While television can present subversive and non-normative beauty ideals as acceptable, such as in the tattoo show *Miami Ink*, that is not happening in makeover television. The narrative arc of makeover television constructs authorities on beauty, in order to authorize normative looks as acceptable, and all others as worthy of shame. One way they do this is through the creation of celebrity. Despite lack of credentials, the very act of being on television, looking attractive, and telling others how to look more attractive warrants the cast members as legitimate authorities on beauty. Simply being on television warrants these people as experts, as television itself serves as an authorial voice in culture. This is inherently necessary for the success and salience of makeover television. For the narrative of shame, transformation, and redemption to be salient, an adequate judge needs to be constructed.

Makeover television allows star experts to authorize some looks and chastise others. Gledhill defines stars as those who are such an object of public fascination that their off-screen lives begin to surpass their acting ability in importance. In a way this applies to reality television, since acting ability is supposedly of no importance. These stars are defined as non-actors. Despite the staged and rehearsed nature of reality television, it cultivates an aesthetic of the un-staged, and becomes defined by the inclusion of non-actors. Dr. Rey destabilizes this notion slightly by noting that he had his Screen Actors Guild card long before his medical license (Singer 1). But his "previous" career as an actor is not discussed within the show. Nonetheless, the on- and off-screen personas of the hosts of numerous makeover television shows are objects of fascination for the public. I argue that the personas of expert-oriented reality television stars such as Stacy and Clinton of *What Not to Wear* and Dr. Rey of *Dr. 90210* not only surpass their acting ability in importance, but more importantly surpass their credentials and expertise in importance.

Participants on makeover shows have committed some "sin" of appearance, which requires the intervention of star experts. Their expertise often stems from presumed training in hair, makeup, nutrition, exercise, or style, although their credentials are rarely stated. For example, on TLC's *What Not to Wear*, hosts Stacy London and Clinton Kelly never have any sort of credentials stated to present them as authorities on fashion. The official website of the show provides some, although limited, background information. They have both, in fact, worked at several fashion magazines, but this information is not provided on the show (*What Not to Wear*). Similarly, Nick Arrojo and single-named Carmindy, the respective hairstylist and makeup artist of the show, never have their credentials stated either. Presumably being on television cutting and dyeing someone's hair means that the person is not only qualified to do so, but also qualified to override any decisions the individual has made about her or his own hair. All of the cast members veto the beauty decisions made by the individual on the show, shame the individual for making bad choices in the first place, and strongly encourage them to adapt the look authorized by the cast. Ultimately, as with all of the makeover shows, everyone made-over on the program ends up looking very similar, with traces of their individual style erased.

On the *What Not to Wear* website, one of the most important credentials stated is the names of celebrities the individual cast members have worked on. The beauty of the various other stars functions as evidence of the beauty workers' expertise, and therefore bolsters the stardom of the beauty worker. In this way, celebrity infects those who come into contact with a star and spreads to others, carrying with it a presumed expertise.

Credentials are often stated of medical staff such as cosmetic surgeons, such as on *Extreme Makeover*. However, the credentials are brief and vague, not as important in showing expertise as the act of being positioned as an expert on television. The fact that they are on television performing cosmetic procedures and looking attractive appears to render them authorities on the subject. This helps to illustrate how television itself is an authority on beauty. Simply appearing on television in a beautiful fashion that corresponds to the ideals appearing on other televisual bodies gives the individual authority. Apparently, a televisual homogeneity (looking like other accepted televison stars) lends authority. After appearing on a show, these often unknown beauty industry workers gain fame and fortune, regardless of their credentials. The act of appearing on television renders these people experts through the authority of television.

Dr. Rey's Celebrity

According to *The New York Times*, Dr. Rey on *Dr. 90210* is not a board certified cosmetic surgeon. Yet his appearance in his own television series made him "perhaps the best-known cosmetic surgeon in America" with a patient waitlist "as long as Sunset Boulevard" and 38 million viewers (Singer 1). His stardom is somewhat contradictory. He serves as an expert on cosmetic surgery for *The Today Show, Dr. Phil, The Early Show,* and *The View* and also as a commentator for the Oscars, Emmys, and Golden Globes. His expertise is as much on science as it is on beauty and the two become inseparable.

Adding to his bravado on the show, Dr. Rey is a black belt in Tae Kwon Do and continually practices his moves for the camera. Although not on camera, in superheroic fashion, he subdued and restrained an agitated octogenarian on a plane with the help of a fellow passenger. He attributed his success to Tae Kwon Do, which apparently is necessary for two physically-fit men to subdue an 80-year-old. The headlines further bolstered his ultimate act of the good citizen ("'Dr. 90210' and Fellow Passenger Restrain Man on Flight"; "Plastic Surgeon Caught up in Mid-Air Terrorist Scare").

Dr. Rey functions as a Latino crossover star. Beltran notes that a crossover star can be anyone who appeals to an additional audience, but the term is generally used to apply to non–White stars appealing to a White audience. However, the tensions produced by his non–White status must be negotiated. Dyer explains that the stardom of Paul Robeson, a singer and Black film star in the 1920s through 1940s, was negotiated to appeal to a White audience. This occurred through the inclusion of White perceptions of Blackness in Robeson's star image. Similarly, Rey is presented as a model minority through his achievements, being saved from poverty in Brazil by White missionaries and "working hard" for his success, which shows adherence to White standards of model citizenry, including a denial of racism inherent in cultural systems. Rey's story serves as an example to bolster claims that equality has been achieved, thus relieving White guilt. In addition, in a way that lessens his Latino status, he removed the telltale "o" from his given name of Roberto, even "Whitening" and eliminating any threat of his name.

Nonetheless, White stereotypical notions of "Latino" culture (which is a White construction in and of itself) embed themselves in his star portrayal, particularly in a certain sort of machismo. The combination of his televisual stardom and medical authority has been criticized by some. Other surgeons have criticized his interaction with patients as inappropriate, such as telling a patient she looks "hot" after a breast augmentation surgery, hugging and touching his patients in non-criminal but inappropriate ways, his pre-surgery behavior of doing pull-ups, which can cause muscle fatigue and tremors during surgery, altering his surgical scrubs to show more arm muscles, and wearing a stethoscope, which cosmetic surgeons rarely use, around his suit collar when doing patient consultations (Singer 1). His physical prowess and sexual bravado are emphasized, thus stressing his embodiment, while simultaneously allowing his achievements to grant him authority over the beauty of women. Portraying Rey as an expert over a traditionally feminine realm feminizes him, thus lessening some of the threat of this Latin body.

The cameras linger on his multi-million dollar house and beautiful cars, as they do on his other coveted possessions, his wife and children. He married an extremely thin (down to 88 pounds in one episode), blonde, White woman with breast implants. She is a full-time stay-at-home mother to their daughter and new son and appears to be extremely loving and interested in their family. Within the show he is an exemplar of the ideal family and ideal life, a model citizen for others to emulate. Thus, he is able to assist others in achieving similar ideals.

All of these aspects together help to establish Dr. Rey as an authority on beauty. He is not simply altering patients' physical appearance, but also intervening in psychological problems. Cosmetic procedures are not simply supposed to change how a person looks, but also how a person thinks, feels, and what a person can achieve. Because medicine requires doctors to "do no harm," cutting into a healthy body, via cosmetic surgery, is justified as treatment for an ailing mind or sense of self (Gilman 7). These procedures supposedly enable people to form "better" relationships and achieve more in their careers. Dr. Rey's stardom, established through his presence on television, positions him as an expert on beauty who can authorize the various beauty looks of others.

Medicine and Beauty

Dr. Rey is both surgeon and artist, rendering his view of the beautiful, primarily feminine and White, body on women throughout the globe. Dr. Rey stresses that most of his clientele are women, and 88 percent of plastic surgery patients were women and 77 percent were White in the United States in 2005, according to the American Society of Plastic Surgeons. Unlike an artist, his medium has more serious potential material effects. Individuals with healthy bodies die from cosmetic surgeries, or can potentially be left paralyzed, deformed, or with a variety of infections or illnesses. Nevertheless, Dr. Rey's status as a celebrity intersects with his medical authority, making his judgment on beauty more difficult to resist.

Until the advent of cosmetic surgery, beauty products may have had serious health effects which required medical intervention, such as the lead-based skin bleaches used by African Americans (Peiss 212), but doctors were authorities on health, not beauty. Often the interests of health and beauty were in competition with each other, with medical authorities prevailing on the side of health.

The mixing of medical authority and beauty authority creates a powerful force due to its ties to the discourse of science. As Nandy explains, there is a strong incongruity between the claims of science and the ability to evaluate those claims, which is held only by the few with expertise in the arena of science. While the discourse of science circulates, affiliating science with knowledge, reason, and objectivity, which are culturally prized, it is difficult for the average citizen to dispute the claims of science without appearing ignorant and unreasonable, thus encouraging the mass acceptance of scientific claims. Scientists may encourage disputation of claims for the advancement of science. However, because few people have the expertise to do so in a valuable manner, the discourse of science, in opposition to actual scientific practices, functions in a hegemonic manner to secure the agreement of the masses.

Because beauty and science are tied to the expertise of the cosmetic surgeon, it is difficult for individuals to question the doctor's authority. Treichler notes:

> The problem of traditional childbirth for women is rooted not in "medicalization" per se, but in monopoly: monopoly of professional authority, of material resources, and of what may be called linguistic capital — the power to establish and enforce a particular definition of childbirth [Treichler 116].

Plastic surgeons similarly monopolize the authority, resources, and linguistic capital associated with many aspects of beauty, as plastic surgeons must authorize particular procedures, have sole access to the resources necessary for the procedures, and define what beauty is through their procedures. It is not that everyone should have access to a scalpel or Botox to perform medical procedures on each other, but that people should be cognizant of the distribution of power in the beauty economy.

Medicine has not viewed women's bodies in the most positive light, which means that women perhaps should be more questioning of medical claims. Bordo writes that the body, merely by being female, is constituted as diseased. Balsamo notes that within medicine the female body is reduced to its reproductive capabilities (or incapabilities) and discourse on technological innovations for women's bodies dwell on the womb. In addition, medical technology serves to better write gender upon the body, in attempts to create a "perfectly" female and feminine body, thus furthering gendered and sexed dichotomies.

Martin argues that female bodily processes are deemed "failures" by medicine. For example, menstruation and menopause are discussed as outcomes of the failure of the female body to conceive. Male processes such as sperm production are rarely discussed as failures, even though all of the sperm will likely die. She states:

> Clearly, just as conceptualizing menopause as a kind of failure of the authority structure in the body contributes to our negative view of it, so does the construction of menstruation as failed production contribute to our negative view of that process [Martin 75].

This "failure of the authority structure in the body" is justification for the medical intervention on the body by those who are greater authorities. A similar justification is used for the medical intervention of cosmetic surgery, as the individual has failed to properly discipline the body, thus necessitating intervention. Gilman explains that the cutting into of a healthy body for cosmetic purposes is justified as an intervention on a wayward character. The individual's character has failed somehow, as evidenced by a wayward body. This does not simply apply to processes purportedly under one's control, such as weight, but also in physical features such as the nose or brow. Cosmetic surgery is never simply a medical choice, as it also exists in the nexus of a culture of consumption, self-presentation, and sexist and racist ideologies (Haiken 12).

Resisting Authority

Within the narrative of *Dr. 90210*, patients rarely resist the authority of any of the doctors on the show. Usually, the patients welcome the advice and recommendations of the lauded doctors and appear to come to the surgeon's office encouraging any guidance through this medical process from the doctors. Patients are told what is possible for them to achieve and what the doctor deems to be the most desired outcome.

However, options are rarely provided that are not Dr. Rey's personal beauty preference or which do not bring him economic gain. I have never heard him say, "Perhaps you should go with a smaller implant" or "I think your nose looks fine as it is." His job, and the job of the program, is to encourage the consumption of cosmetic surgery and thus the view of the body as a commodity. Audience members are trained in assessing minor "defects" in a face or body through the visual positioning of the patients in "before" and "after" photos and through viewing repeated consultations. *Dr. 90210* helps to create the need for cosmetic surgery by creating a population more apt to judge the ways their own bodies and others can be altered through cosmetic surgery.

Also, the risks of such procedures are not discussed on the program, such as the real possibility of death anytime someone undergoes anesthesia or the risk of partial paralysis from a facelift. Presuming that Dr. Rey is a competent surgeon, he likely does discuss the risks of the procedures with his patients, but if this does occur it is lost during editing. This helps to further the need and desire for transformation, without a discussion of the material effects of the procedures on bodies.

Within the first season episode of "Is Bigger Better?" Ana does resist Dr. Rey's personal preference for her breast size. I note that this is a "personal" preference, because there is no medical reason why Ana needs implants at all, let alone larger implants. The medical authority of the doctor becomes conflated with authority on beauty.

This is an interesting site of analysis because it is the only case of resistance of Dr. Rey's recommendations in the series so far. This resistance helps to highlight the authorial structures present in the show which are used to seek Ana's compliance. Ana, who wants "tiny" implants, as Dr. Rey said, was contrasted with Jackie, who desired larger implants.

With Ana's implants removed, her small breasts visibly sagged and appeared "deflated," according to Dr. Rey. She stood topless for the camera to give the audience the full effect of her "deflated" breasts and to fully objectify her breasts. However, the photos were taken in the clinical context of having photos of her breasts taken for her doctor, despite millions of viewers watching. This context served to comfort the viewer and reduce the exploitative meanings of Ana's naked performance for the camera.

Ana expressed concern about working with Dr. Rey when she first saw him, stating, "I was looking through his pictures [of patients before and after breast implants]. I was really concerned because all of them were, you know, too big. I was looking at the before pictures and going, 'God, that's nice'" (Is Bigger Better?).

This comment, expressed in a direct-to-camera interview, sets the stage for Ana resisting Dr. Rey's choice of breast size. She already disagreed with his judgment that the women in the "before" pictures needed implants and that the "after" pictures were indeed more aesthetically pleasing. This destabilized the "need" for cosmetic surgery, if the authority of the surgeon did not necessarily yield a more beautiful result.

Ana expressed that she only wanted a B cup, which would simply fill the loose skin of her breasts caused by the destruction of breast tissue from the implants. She said, in another direct-to-camera interview, "He was very honest about the fact that people love breasts and he liked them large. For my breasts, I would like to be a B. He definitely would prefer for me to be a full C or more, but I don't want to go there" (Is Bigger Better?).

Ana says "people" love breasts. It is unclear who she is referring to, but it is clear that Dr. Rey prefers large implants. Therefore, choosing to have breast implants become a way of pleasing the medical establishment through pleasing one's surgeon. Choosing smaller breasts rebukes that medical authority.

Ana was repeatedly verbally disciplined for her refusal of Dr. Rey's standards. Ana was shown standing topless, with Dr. Rey kneeling in front of her taking implants out of a box. The following conversation took place:

> REY: Here are your implants. They're very, very, very, very petite. I can't really remember the last time I used such small implants here in Beverly Hills.
>
> ANA: Well, to me as long they can fill my skin, I'm happy. I don't want anything else.
>
> REY: [Cutting Ana off while she's speaking] These will barely fill your skin. I'm talking barely. Remember the smaller you go the wider the cleavage [because smaller implants will sit farther apart on the chest]. I just want you to know that your cleavage is not gonna be the best. [Cutting to a direct-to-camera interview with Dr. Rey] Nothing uglier than a wide cleavage. As a matter of fact, my reputation rides on that cleavage. If they're very far apart, horrendous, they look terrible.

The cut to the interview segment with Dr. Rey was incredibly revealing. He indicated an ownership over his patients' bodies. His reputation, and therefore his celebrity, was materially attached to his patient's cleavage. Thus, his stake in surgery was not simply giving the patients the outcomes they desired, but in crafting a reputation for himself through the public display of his creation of the perfect breast. These women's bodies further his celebrity and therefore his beauty authority. In addition, he desired a certain sort of breast, perhaps a branded breast, to represent his authority over the female body, one which is large and fills the entire chest.

Second, he explained that non-surgically altered breasts are "horrendous," as few unaltered breasts touch each other in the mid-sternum without the aid of a bra. According to his ideal, breasts need implants in order to look attractive. In another direct-to-camera interview in this episode Dr. Rey stated, "Women are working out so hard nowadays. Everyone is on a diet. That little bit of fat they have they're losing. So we made a generation of breastless women." The show then cuts to a direct-to-camera interview with Dr. Robert Kotler, another surgeon featured occasionally on Dr. 90210, who explained, "How does a real thin lady have generous breasts? Only by having artificial breasts inserted." According to these doctors, breast implants are required on beautiful women and it is thus a duty of women to get breast implants if they want to be beautiful. Due to the medical expertise of these doctors, this is not simply a statement of opinion, but an expert opinion which authorizes particular bodies as beautiful (ones that are thin with surgically implanted breasts) and negates the potential of beauty in others.

Dr. Rey not only disciplined and attempted to override Ana's choice to her personally, but continued to discipline her while she was unconscious. During the surgery, Rey continually lamented the "tiny" implants, while visually cutting and tearing her flesh. First, he disciplined her decision to have breast implants and then have them removed, stating, "I don't know what kind of scarring she has in here. It could be a nightmare" (Is Bigger Better?). This focuses on his labor. The "nightmare" is presumably the large amount of work he will have to do to correct her wayward breasts, not the pain or suffering that Ana may experience. Many other plastic surgery shows operate with a similar trope, such as *Extreme Makeover* and *The Swan,* of the doctors lamenting the extreme difficulty of making over such an ugly patient, focusing the show on the doctors' labor of transformation, rather than the labor of the patient's suffering.

After the aforementioned comment, Dr. Rey inserted the implants, while saying the opening words of this article: "She picked such a tiny little implant, it almost breaks my heart. It'll barely be a little bee sting, barely, barely, barely rise. Wow, it's really little, but there's nothing else I can do." He disciplined her choice a final time, indicating an emotional and personal involvement by saying that it almost breaks his heart. He constituted his discipline as being from the heart and in her best interest, such as the criticism from a family member rather than from a doctor. He then distanced himself professionally from the outcome of her breasts, no longer accepting ownership over her cleavage. Her body is clearly not one on which he wants his reputation riding.

Conclusions

The authorial voice on makeover television reaches a large audience, standardizing norms for beauty by creating a narrow spectrum of acceptable possibilities and clearly demarcating the unacceptable ones. Bodies are disciplined through their visual display and evaluation by "experts." Subjecting oneself to such scrutiny is a way of redeeming a wayward character and transforming one's body into an acceptable product of society.

Television serves as an authority on beauty, lending expertise and celebrity to those appearing on it. The authority of makeover television is specifically televisual, created and cultivated through the spectacle of television. Simply by the act of appearing and monopolizing appearance, things are rendered good (Debord), such as images on television. Appearing on television can make someone an authority on all sorts of things (see Oprah, for example). Because television is intrinsically about appearance, about literally appearing on the television, it creates authorities on proper appearance simply as a matter of being on television. Appearing in an acceptable manner is what television is, thus making appearance its proper realm.

Televisual authority, along with medical authority and that of celebrity, intersect to create a nexus of control in makeover television. This nexus of discipline is difficult to resist and even more difficult to question, given that the very standards of beauty and judgment are created by it. Not only does televisual authority allow the beauty of participants to be judged, it also makes it acceptable for viewers to judge others by the standards expressed on the show.

BIBLIOGRAPHY

American Society of Cosmetic Surgeons. *2005 Gender Quick Facts: Cosmetic Plastic Surgery*. 2005 <www.plasticsurgery.org>.

Balsamo, Anne. *Technologies of the Gendered Body: Reading Cyborg Women*. Durham: Duke University Press, 1996.

Beltran, Mary C. "The Hollywood Latina Body as Site of Social Struggle: Media Constructions of Stardom and Jennifer Lopez's Crossover Butt." *Quarterly Review of Film & Video* 19 (2002): 71–86.

Bordo, Susan. *Unbearable Weight: Feminism, Western Culture, and the Body*. 10th anniversary ed. Berkeley: University of California Press, 2003.

Debord, Guy. "The Commodity as Spectacle." *Media and Cultural Studies: Key Works*. Ed. Meenakshi Gigi Durham and Douglas M. Kellner. Malden, MA: Blackwell, 1977/2001. 139–43.

Dr. 90210. E! Exec. prod. Donald Bull. 11 July 2004–.

"'Dr. 90210' and Fellow Passenger Restrain Man on Flight." *Associated Press* 23 May 2006.

Dyer, Richard. *Heavenly Bodies: Film Stars and Society*. London: Macmillan Press, 1986.

Gilman, Sander L. *Creating Beauty to Cure the Soul: Race and Psychology in the Shaping of Aesthetic Surgery*. Durham: Duke University Press, 1998.

Gledhill, Christine. "Introduction." *Stardom: Industry of Desire*. Ed. Christine Gledhill. London: Routledge, 1991. xiii–xx.

Haiken, Elizabeth. *Venus Envy: A History of Cosmetic Surgery*. Baltimore: Johns Hopkins University Press, 1997.

Martin, Emily. "Science and Women's Bodies: Forms of Anthropological Knowledge." *Body/Politics: Women and the Discourse of Science*. Ed. Mary Jacobus, Evelyn Fox Keller, and Sally Shuttleworth. New York: Routledge, 1990.

Nandy, Ashis. "Science as the Reason for the State." *Internationalizing Cultural Studies: An Anthology.* Ed. Ackbar Abbas and John Nguyet Erni. Malden, MA: Blackwell, 2005. 21–29.

Peiss, Kathy. *Hope in a Jar: The Making of America's Beauty Culture.* New York: Henry Holt, 1998.

"Plastic Surgeon Caught Up in Mid-Air Terrorist Scare." WENN Entertainment News Service, Los Angeles. 23 May 2006.

Singer, Natasha. "A Doctor? He Is One on TV." *New York Times* 16 Mar. 2006, late ed.: G1.

Treichler, Paula A. "Feminism, Medicine, and the Meaning of Childbirth." *Body/Politics: Women and the Discourse of Science.* Ed. Mary Jacobus, Evelyn Fox Keller, and Sally Shuttleworth. New York: Routledge, 1990.

What Not to Wear. TLC. Discovery Communications, New York. 5 May 2006 <http://tlc.discovery.com/fansites/whatnottowear/whatnottowear.html>.

Revising Bodily Texts to the Dominant Standard

A Feminist Rhetorical Criticism of the Makeover Episode of America's Next Top Model

JULIE-ANN SCOTT

"Thirteen beautiful girls stand before me, but only twelve will continue on in hopes of becoming America's Next Top Model ... the girl whose name I do not call will need to go back to the loft, pack her bags, and leave."

Each week one young, tall, thin female is eliminated. Over the course of weeks the audience members come to know the women and are happy or sad to see them go. Each week one woman sadly says goodbye to the remaining contestants, looks into the camera, and reminisces on the past weeks and her future as a model once the show ends. Next, previews of the coming weeks flash on the screen as the remaining contestants continue to improve their bodies and performances in order to avoid elimination. First Kathy the housepainter is eliminated; followed by Wendy, whose family lost everything in Hurricane Katrina; followed by Kari, whom the judges told needed to lose weight in her face to make it as a lingerie model; Gina, who never managed to take a good picture but had "great cheekbones"; Mollie Sue, who was deemed too reserved to stand out amongst her competitors; Leslie, who always posed like a "man's magazine model"; Brooke, whose face was beautiful, except she "looked like a trout" and never learned to "work her best angles"; Nnenna, who wanted to be a role model for other African women; Furonda, who couldn't "take consistently good pictures"; Sarah, who wasn't progressing in her photos enough to stay in the race; Jade, who just couldn't take criticism; and Joanie, who just took the runner-up position despite her

118

beautiful portfolio; leaving the one winner, Danielle, who tearfully looks in to the camera to say, "I'm a cover girl, Mommy!"

Carole Counihan equates a woman's body to a "form of currency," in that a woman's appearance becomes her "economic value"; her level of physical attractiveness correlates with her perceived worth in society, and she is compensated or awarded based on her level of attractiveness (19). Beginning in 2003, the reality television show *America's Next Top Model* (*ANTM*) created a context for the general society to view women grooming their bodies to compete in hopes to literally enact Counihan's metaphor, in that one of fourteen young women between the ages of 18 and 27, is presumed to have a potential annual worth of $100,000, plus the additional financial benefits of a contract with one of the top world fashion modeling agencies, *Ford Models Inc.*

The reward and compensation for ability is not a phenomenon unique to the modeling world; when one is on any payroll it is usually assumed that the person is offering a talent, service, or creating a product that others see as worthy of purchasing. In many cases, including, but not limited to, the entertainment industry, one's level of attractiveness and sex appeal is figured into one's marketability. However, arguably in the U.S. culture, fashion models are considered to embody the standard to which other women aspire. They are valued first and foremost (and arguably entirely) for their appearances, so that the selection and grooming of women into a supermodel functions rhetorically as a means for the general population to gain knowledge of how one embodies the standards of the dominant beauty discourses in U.S. culture. The show's executive producer and lead judge, Tyra Banks, in an interview about *ANTM*, explains that she created the show to give viewers an authentic, inside look into what it takes to make it in the modeling world through the documented journey of fourteen hopeful models.

This research will show that *ANTM*'s documented journey of the field of modeling is in essence an authentic inside look at how the women who have the capacity to be the most beautiful in U.S. culture are chosen, and how they mold their bodies to achieve this status, and set a cultural standard for ideal beauty. In addition, I will argue that the authentic, inside look into the process of becoming a supermodel which *ANTM* provides reifies dominant discourses that to be beautiful and successful, one must embody White, middle- to upper-class standards of beauty, particularly as related to one's hair, teeth, and facial features. If one cannot potentially accomplish this through bodily revisions, they are excluded from this category of privilege.

Of the thousands of applicants to the show, thirteen are selected. All contestants must be 5 foot 7, between the ages of 18 and 27, and have the ability to walk and pose as deemed necessary by those in the modeling world. These criteria exclude many people based on age, height, and physical ability, though this analysis will focusing on racial and socioeconomic prejudices alone. The Black women selected to compete all have features that resemble and can be molded to White standards of beauty through treatments administered throughout the duration of the show. This selection process ultimately reinforces White, middle- to upper-class standards of beauty and privilege, veiled as diverse and universal, unbiased criteria for a super model. To attain White, middle- to upper-class standards of beauty, Black and working class bodies are conditioned to conform to these standards through costly beauty regimens that are not affordable to the majority of the population but essential to achieve the high standards of beauty expected of models. As a result, the beauty discourses reified in *ANTM* function as a hegemonic force so those of minority and working-class status are considered less valuable and attractive than those who already hold the monetary, social, and political power in society.

Enacting Criticism from a Marked Body: The Potentials for Social Change

As a 25-year-old White, physically disabled woman from a working-class background currently undergoing graduate work in communication studies, I viewed the fifth season of *ANTM* and enact this criticism. I approach this text as a critical postmodernist. I believe that social understandings and realities are not natural or innate but emergent from within culture, which I define as the interaction of people in a construction of practices, shared understandings, beliefs, and values that are subject to change in any given context. I recognize that I am a member of a society in which certain members are oppressed and privileged through societal discourses and the texts our society produces (See Johnson; McIntosh; Shome). Our bodies are marked and categorized by gender, social class, age, race and appearance among others. My interpretations and understandings of this dynamic emerge in part from my own experiences, which stem from my given characteristics and contexts and are embedded within the same cultural discourses in which we all operate. Despite the characteristics of our individual identities, as members of a culture, we cannot escape participation on some level (including resistance) to our shared cultural discourses from which meanings emerge. I also believe that it is through the coordination and resistance of societal members that oppression associated with the status quo is challenged, potentially dismantled, and replaced with new meanings.

I consider both my status as a woman and a disabled person to be marginalized identities within a patriarchal culture that values male, able bodies. In regard to my social status, though I am from a working-class background, my education has allowed me access to a middle-class lifestyle. In regard to racial identity (the primary discourses I will be examining in relation to *ANTM*), I occupy a privileged place in the U.S. culture. Despite the privileged status my body occupies because of my White skin, I do recognize how easily "racial logistics inflect and infect my view of the world, and are therefore worthy of examination" (Nakayama and Krizkek 109). I concur with Thomas Nakayama and Robert Krizkek in their concerns surrounding the "White social practice of not discussing whiteness" and other privileged identities within U.S. culture and the need for academics to continue to resist this recurring practice in mainstream societal discourses. For those who are placed in the position of instructing the next generations of educated professionals who have a potential to hold positions of social, political, and economic power in society, it is important to engage with each other and our students in the interrogation of power relations in society.

All discourses are influenced by power relations that in turn "influence communication research and our everyday lives," and it is important for us to examine these discourses and their implications for human interaction, not simply internalize them as reality, if our nation's history of oppression is to be challenged in the present and future and generations of our country (Woodward 304–305). Radhika Gajjala uses "...the term *negotiation* to refer to our everyday transactions of meaning-making from within hierarchies and power structures" (83). As critical scholars, we need to "interrogate the taken for granteds of nationalistic and colonial discourses in our society" and the criteria for the modeling industry, which sets standards for beauty in our society, is arguably one of these discourses (Hasian 80).

BODIES FUNCTIONING AS ERASED AND/OR REVISED TEXTS

To examine *ANTM* as text from within the dominant discourses of beauty and attractiveness in U.S. society, I will investigate the process by which the women's bodies are "made-over" to be more marketable within the makeover sessions of the show, and how the changes to the women's bodies required by Banks can be traced back to White, middle- to upper-middle-class standards of attractiveness. In this case, I will seek to demonstrate how the makeover changes to the bodies function as revisions of texts to make the women more valuable in society. Black women with broad facial features common to their racial heritage are excluded from the competition, and by their absence function rhetorically within U.S. culture as a representation of bodies that do not have the potential to be beautiful.

Regina Spellers argues that rather than focusing on human beings' spoken and written words, one should examine the bodies themselves as "discursive texts" through which power structures are created and reinforced (240). This concept becomes particularly pertinent when examining discourses surrounding beauty and their rhetorical power within society. The texts that emerge from the discourses of beauty and fashion in society are largely visual images, and many are not accompanied by words. The images of fashion models become familiar and equated with beauty standards; their bodies become the texts to be read and used to evaluate the bodies of the broader society, so individuals negotiate these images related to their own bodily identities and personal experiences (Reaves et al.). The standards set by the dominant discourses of beauty are not limited to the modeling world but can also be traced throughout our daily lives in discourses surrounding professionalism, respect, and power within U.S. culture.

Beauty Descriptors in American Culture

ANTM goes beyond granting access to the lives of ordinary people in different circumstances, such as *MTV's The Real World*, by providing access to the fashion world once only granted to those on the "inside" such as photographers, runway experts, editors, and models. Tyra Banks is famous for being the first Black model to grace the cover of *Sports Illustrated Magazine*, afterward appearing in countless advertisements and magazine covers for more than a decade (*ANTM*). Banks is given authority within the context of *ANTM* due to her success in the difficult industry, and her assessments of the women's bodies and performances go unchallenged throughout the duration of the show. The other judges (an esteemed runway coach, another former successful model, and a professional photographer, along with a weekly guest judge deemed an expert in the fashion and modeling industry) also weigh in with their opinion of which of the remaining contestants should be sent home each week. Women resisting the makeovers that enable them to embody Whiter, upper-class beauty standards are considered grounds for elimination or dismissal. In the fourth season of *ANTM* Cassandra was not allowed to continue with a photo shoot and opted to go home rather than have her hair cut any shorter, she was portrayed as not realizing the importance of following Banks' directions without question, and therefore was not cut out to be a model. The contestants must agree to the makeovers or risk elimination as a result. Helene Shugart asserts,

> It is hardly news that the mainstream media function ideologically insofar as they promote dominant, privileged perspectives relative to race, [gender] and class; nor is it news that disenfranchised members of society are rendered invisible, silenced or marginalized in a variety of ways by the media [84].

In this way, observations made regarding the privileging of White, middle- to upper-middle-class contestants on *ANTM* are not unique. According to Sheila Reaves et al, the effects of the media on women's self image has been "aggressively investigated in the past decade" and exposure to the media's thin ideals leads to reduced body satisfaction and self esteem and increased self-consciousness regarding appearance (Reaves et al. 58). Many scholars also study how media representations of people of color affect societal understandings of minority groups (Valdivia; Dates and Barlow). In short, the rhetorical function of media portrayals of different groups in society and of cultural beliefs is not unexplored territory in academia. Reality shows, while a relatively new genre of television, also receive much attention from media scholars.

Over fifty reality shows have aired in the United States since 2000, *ANTM* included. Although initially media experts were skeptical of the public's reception to such shows, they have become a popular genre (Andrejevic; Deery). A show marketed to viewers as reality television, through the use of the descriptive "reality" claims an authentic, rather than contrived-for-entertainment experience (Andrejevic; Deery). Through the naming of this genre of entertainment, viewers are encouraged to respond to the situation and characters not as representations of reality, but as the actual realities of individuals that would be closed to them if it were not for the context of the program. When marketed as "reality television" the standards for beauty demanded of contestants are assumed as the "real criteria" for the modeling industry, not the fictional reality of a sitcom author's imagination. The woman who wins the competition receives an actual modeling contract and is featured in media and print advertisements and on fashion runways after the show. This apparent, real success arguably gives validity to the standards of beauty set within the episodes for the contestants to reach.

Beauty Discourse as Bodily Performance in ANTM

In each episode of *ANTM*, one model is eliminated until only the winner remains. Throughout the show, the young female contestants learn how to condition their bodies to be more model-like. This conditioning involves what kinds of foods to eat and exercises to perform in addition to how to hold their bodies to take the most aesthetic photos and master complicated catwalks in restrictive clothing and abnormally high heels. These skills are considered essential to modeling, allowing them to be chosen as contestants. At the beginning of the show, Banks comments the women would not have been chosen to participate if they had not been beautiful. The term beautiful is not defined but assumed. As the audience, we are expected to already be familiar with the discourses of beauty within the U.S. culture.

THE WHITE AESTHETIC

From the colonial era there has been documentation of White European settlers dedicated to preserving the *lovely White* aesthetic through the oppression and ostracizing of Black people and discouraging interracial marriage and children (Harding). Navita James, a member of the baby boom generation, recalls, "When I was a child I secretly yearned for a Black Miss America: To me that would have been a sign that our culture was learning to value Black women — that we could be viewed as beautiful, smart, and virtuous" (65). In U.S. society today, from James' perspective, her dream is a reality. She notes that "in the course of my daughters' childhoods, Black women have finally been crowned Miss America" (65). In addition to Black Miss Americas, in the fashion industry, women such as Tyra Banks and Naomi Campbell are known as beautiful Black supermodels. However, it is important to recognize, the Black women who have become mainstream beauty icons in the media and fashion industries, with their sleek straight hair and small noses and only moderately full lips arguably have bodies which adhere to White standards of beauty. The coarse, curly texture of the contestants of color's natural hair and broad features commonly associated with Black people are erased from the Black bodies celebrated as beautiful within our culture either through exclusion (i.e., not chosen as icons of beauty) or revision (i.e., the makeovers on *ANTM*).

Within the United States the argument for an innate, natural beauty has been claimed from a scientific standpoint. "Symmetry has been scientifically proven to be inherently physically attractive to the human eye.

[Beauty] has been defined not with proportions, but rather with similarity between the left and right sides of the face" (Feng). In addition to symmetry scientists go on to articulate that "males in Western cultures" generally prefer females with "slight jaws, small noses, large eyes and defined cheekbones" (Feng). The scientific explanation for this preference is that these particular features "indicate youth, and a high estrogen level associated with reproduction." These preferred features, however, arguably occur together most often in a White face. Sandra Harding argues that Western Culture has used science as a justification for exalting the White race over others for centuries in areas of intelligence, self-restraint and hygiene. The deemed "scientific" standards of beauty put forward by biological and psychological health professional's studies are no exception.

White female faces are arguably more likely to have all three of the facial attributes deemed attractive by Western men (slight jaws, large eyes, and defined cheekbones) than other ethnic groups. People of African descent are more likely to have larger, stronger noses rather than small ones, Asian people stereotypically have small hooded eyes rather than large eyes, and Native Americans are often stereotyped as having prominent jaws and foreheads, not small ones.

Multicultural White Beauty

The privileging of White beauty could explain why two thirds of the contestants at the beginning of *ANTM* are White, and the women of color selected to compete all have facial features that resemble those of the White woman ideal in that they have smaller noses, prominent cheekbones, and tall waif-like frames. During the third episode of each season, the twelve remaining young women undergo makeovers to enhance their appearance and bring out what Banks describes as "their full potential."

The one contestant who has been eliminated thus far is White. At this point in the show, six White women, four Black women, one Latina woman, and one Chinese contestant remain.* The women are a mixture of middle- and working-class backgrounds. At first glance, if one were to simply count the numbers of people from varying social and ethnic backgrounds, it would appear that *ANTM* is a diverse, multicultural representation of U.S. society. However, even media programs that appear resistant to

---

*One of the women whom I describe as White has olive skin, long curly hair and a prominent nose. Her ethnicity is never discussed on the series, and she is eliminated at the end of the makeover episode. Her heritage could be Italian American or South Asian, since it is not named within the series, and White people are usually those who are left uncategorized, I am assuming she is of White European descent.

dominant discourses may actually be reifying and preserving them. The makeover session shows that those of lower socioeconomic and minority racial classes are expected to embody a middle- to upper-middle-class White standard of beauty if they are to be accepted as worthy of entering the modeling world.

White Beauty: A Description of the Makeovers of ANTM

The makeovers largely apply to the contestants' hair lengths, colors, and textures because they already undergo make-up, fashion, diet, and fitness training from week to week. The three blonde contestants, Sarah, Kari, and Joanie, each have their hair lightened a few shades and styled. The red haired woman, Molly Sue, who already has shorter hair, receives a pixie cut with an intensified shade, while the three women with dark, but not African hair, Wendy, Leslie, and Gina, have layers added for body and fullness. The changes in the color and texture of the women who are not Black are not dramatic, but rather updated versions of their current hairstyles, colors, and textures. This is not the case for the African American women.

Three of the Black women, Nnenna, Furonda, and Danielle have short, chemically straightened Black hair, while the last, Jade, has naturally tight curls. For their makeovers, two of these women, Furonda and Danielle, receive long, straight weaves which have the texture most commonly associated with White people's hair. Another Black woman, Nnenna, has her head shaved, and the other, Jade, has her hair cut short, relaxed and dyed blond. This is a common trend for the makeover sessions of *ANTM.** The Black contestants, after the makeover scene, either have no hair at all, or extensions added to give them longer, more Caucasian-like hair. In addition, two of the women from lower-class backgrounds that have imperfect teeth are sent to the dentist to get them fixed; otherwise, according to Banks, they have no chance of becoming America's Next Top Model. Because these makeovers are supposed to make these women more aesthetically pleasing and model-like, the choice to alter the Black women's hair to White people's hair color or texture or remove the hair entirely, and to also require all the women to have the straight perfect teeth that those from the middle and upper social classes can afford to possess, despite their genetics, exemplifies

*The trend of the makeovers of the Black contestants involving eliminating hair altogether or adding extensions/weaves can be traced through all five episodes of ANTM; for series summaries see the UPN official website, http://www.upn.com/shows/top_model.

that within the United States, the discourse of beauty emerges from a White middle to upper-middle-class standard.

Hair, Skin, Teeth and Class: An Interpretation of Rewards in Reality Television

Regina Spellers argues that "Black women's ideas about beauty and femininity are largely shaped through a discursive understanding of hierarchies based on hair texture and skin tone" (223). This could explain why Banks focuses primarily on the women's hair when deciding how they should be made-over. Angharad Valdivia says, "Hair is a big indicator of social class and ethnicity," and that women of color are often featured with "bigger, coifed curly hair" to emphasize the contrast between the more demure, refined hair of caucasian women with whom she is contrasted in various films. Banks explains to the women that their marketability depends on their versatility, and as a result instructs the Black contestants to change their hair to meet the universal standards for feminine beauty, because the natural texture of African hair would limit them in the fashion industry. The hair texture of minorities, like that of actress Rosie Perez for example, can restrict them to the margins of modeling rather than the status of top models, which the program aspires to condition them to achieve.

Banks often uses her own experiences and observations within the modeling world to justify how she directs the contestants in their appearances, mannerisms, and poses throughout the show. Her famed success as a supermodel grants her expertise, and explains her decisions, but as Rona Halualani et al. argue, "Experience is not inherently explanatory; it is constituted historically and politically by systems of language and representation, governmental and class ideologies and concrete social interaction" (5).

The beauty standard for modeling, rather than being based on natural, objective and universal criteria, can be viewed as the product of a society in which being Black is seen as unattractive and therefore should be transformed to mimic White beauty standards. Black women who are considered to be the most beautiful are those whose bodies can adhere to the standards of White beauty, and receive the benefits that come with beautiful status. Regina Spellers explains that when we "deconstruct and reconstruct" the dominant discourses of Black woman's beauty we often "reveal a culture's oppressive aesthetic values. Through this approach we also see the anguish that emerges in women's lives as a result of trying to live up to externally defined standards" (226).

Regina Spellers interviewed Black mothers and daughters about their beliefs and experiences surrounding their hair. One younger woman explained that in high school one of her close male friends chastised her for having short hair with natural African texture. She responded by "getting a perm quick" to relax her hair and make it appear longer. One mother cited how her family criticized her for attempting to put her daughter's hair in dreadlocks because her daughter was thought to have attractive facial features, and therefore her appearance should not be ruined by leaving her hair in its natural state. African American women who can pass for White beauty standards can have access to more privileges, and their Black peers expect them to take advantage of these potential privileges.

PASSING FOR WHITE BEAUTY

The process of a Black woman transforming her body to meet White standards can be termed "passing." According to Moon passing occurs when individuals seek to transcend their oppressed and/or marginalized identities, in relation to race, physical ability, education, and social class. "Passing practices [are] used to gain entry into neighborhoods of desirability, cultural spaces inhabited by those with greater amounts of privilege. These spaces are not necessarily geographic; instead, they are frequently metaphorical locations in which one may feel at home and safe" (Moon 227). The makeover episode increased the confidence of some of the Black models in their ability to become fashion models.

Danielle and Furonda, the two contestants who received weaves that resembled White women's hair, expressed an increased confidence in the competition. Their new hair allowed them to more effectively embody the White standards of physical attractiveness, to pass for beautiful, and as a result possess a greater chance of passing for members of, and feeling at home in, the modeling industry. Jade and Nnenna, two other Black contestants, neither of which received weaves, expressed concern over their new hairstyles. Both commented at different points throughout the series that they did not have their hair to hide behind or rely on, and wished they had also been given what they saw as classic model hair, long and either straight or slightly wavy. The feeling of belonging Danielle and Furonda expressed would most likely not have been possible for these women outside the context of the reality show, given both are from low socioeconomic backgrounds

TEETH AND CLASS

Danielle and Joanie (a White contestant) were the two women from the lowest socioeconomic backgrounds, and from families who could not afford to have their teeth straightened. As the show progressed, Banks told them that there was no way they would be able to be top models with gaps and extra "snaggle" teeth. Joanie cried with joy at the opportunity to have her teeth straightened and the extra "snaggle tooth" removed. Danielle first resisted the idea of having the gap in her teeth fixed, calling it her "signature gap," but after a phone call to her mother and some insisting on the part of Banks ("Do you really think you will be a Cover Girl with that gap? All they will see is a gap, not the cosmetic") she decided that the opportunity to enter the modeling industry was worth the sacrifice of losing what she first saw as a unique piece of her identity.

Danielle was also instructed to take voice lessons because her Arkansas accent is considered unmarketable on a national level. As each young woman follows Bank's advice, the odds of her dream of modeling coming true increase. "Fairy tales can come true" was the slogan for the fifth season of *ANTM*. Only in this fairy tale setting could Furonda and Danielle afford the professional weaves (in addition to the teeth whitening, hair, and makeup styling sessions) facilitated by *ANTM*. Likewise, Danielle and Joanie's parents could not afford the cosmetic work on their teeth during adolescence, which is provided on *ANTM* once Banks deems it necessary for them to enter the modeling world.

One is rewarded, given acceptance and a sense of security when she adopts the dominant societal standards. According to Michel Foucault, the object of discipline is to "produce subjected and practiced bodies, 'docile' bodies" that uphold the status quo and (138). If we were not rewarded for disciplining our bodies, through diet, exercise, grooming, and self-restraint in expected situations, for example, we would be less motivated to subject ourselves to this control.

The Black women whom Regina Spellers interviewed commented that conditioning their hair and bodies to meet White standards of beauty came with the rewards of esteem and respect from their peers. Contestants on *ANTM* who complain or question Banks' decisions or instructions are chastised and portrayed negatively, as not really wanting the reward of a modeling contract. The women who are obedient to Banks and able to successfully follow her instruction are rewarded from week to week as the most worthy contestants. Those who are not deemed agreeable are singled out and confronted over whether or not a modeling contract is truly their dream come true. Not living up to one's full potential is grounds for elimination.

The theme of fairy tale dreams coming true for those who hold minority positions in society in the context of a television series is recurrent in reality programming, and could arguably be seen as part of "the American dream," in which America is seen as the Land of Opportunity, classless and color blind. Alison Graham-Bertolini argues that many reality programs in which women compete for prizes such as husbands, makeovers, or money depict the female body as "an item of value to be bartered"; she equates women's roles to that of "fairy tale characters" who functioned as rewards and prizes for the heroes of the story (343). In a fairy tale context, a woman's dream is to be chosen as a wife by a powerful man. In reality television shows, such as *The Bachelor* and *Joe Millionaire*, women who are depicted as virtuous, virginal, and obedient to societal standards are often rewarded with a man's favor.

In the context of *ANTM*, a reward of Banks' favor results in the reward of a modeling contract and the esteemed identity as a top high fashion model. The winner, Danielle, tells another rags-to-riches fairy tale story:

> My mother's going to be so happy right now. It hasn't always been easy, and we've had struggles, we've had ups and downs. Right now it ... doesn't seem real to me, because I've had so many struggles. I've had a hard-knock life. Everything happens for a reason, and I know God blessed me with this opportunity. And we don't have to struggle anymore. I'm a Cover Girl, Mommy ... I'm a Cover Girl!

The idea of individuals from lower social and/or minority classes accessing some form of the idealized, fairy tale American dream is showcased in other reality programs as well. For example, Helene Shugart asserts that reality court shows present the American dream of wealth, freedom, and respect as "available to members of the working and poverty classes and people of color only to the extent that they adopt the conventional, middle class, conservative, and largely white sensibilities and hallmark of success" (96). This involves two-parent homes, conservative clothing, eloquent speech, and higher education. In *ANTM*, these White, middle class, conservative sensibilities include women who are sexy, yet conservative enough not to be deemed "trashy" by Banks, with subdued, classy make-up and modeling poses that resemble high fashion, not pornography (according to Banks' standards). Women from all ethic and social backgrounds are given access to the modeling world, but only if they diminish their accents, fix their teeth, style their hair, and condition their bodies to meet mainstream middle- to upper-class standards of modeling beauty.

Those who choose to resist the dominant societal standards in appearance and or behavior are punished by being ostracized from society, while those who conform are rewarded with affection, admiration, and esteem (Foucault). The makeover sessions and transformations of lower-class and/or minority women into fashion models in the reality television series *ANTM*, reiterate the dominant discourses emerging in many reality television shows: that embodying White, middle to upper-class standards, from morals to appearance, comes with rewards, respect, and esteem.

The Cultural Implications of Beauty Standards in Competing for Love, Fame, and Money

One may ask Black and/or lower-class women why they would adhere to, rather than resist, societal expectations. The same questions could also be asked of any woman who runs the risks of complications during elective plastic surgery, goes into debt to buy expensive cosmetics and clothing and undergoes beauty treatments, or engages in excessive dieting to meet dominant standards. I would argue that conforming to societal standards comes with rewards for individuals (even as it reinforces the status quo, and arguably increases oppression) and is the personal choice of any woman.

It should be noted that those who may be categorized as "the standard" still struggle with beauty standards. Even on *ANTM*, two of the contestants who were most unhappy with their new looks, Sarah and Keri, were tall and blonde with blue eyes, the look that has often been assumed to be a stereotypical, Aryan ideal (Harding). Sarah, a law student who was found by modeling scouts while walking through the mall, was unhappy with her lighter, more trendy haircut (which includes a light "skunk" stripe) and called her boyfriend for consolation. The other contestants resented Sarah's inclusion on the show, arguing that a woman pursuing a law degree should not be allowed to win a prize of which all the others had dreamed and pursued as their highest goal. Keri was hesitant about her blonde extensions, calling them Malibu Barbie-like, before crinkling her forehead with skepticism over the judges' choices. The fact that beauty in and of itself, especially in female bodies, is so valued, reinforces the objectification and domination of women in a patriarchal society, but this does not erase the perceived benefits that come to women who embody the standards of beauty (Bordo; Counihan).

In reality television, particularly dating and makeover shows, the idea that there is a perfect female form, and if one achieves it, she should be rewarded, often serves as a premise of the show. Rewards range from a modeling contract, newfound self-esteem, monetary prizes, or a "perfect mate" (one who treats her according to her worth, which has dramatically increased with the improvements offered within the context of the show). To resist the expectations of the show whether it be a chaste, conservative, yet sexy femininity or the teeth and hair that are thought to be aesthetically pleasing, means she has failed the audience, her loved ones, and herself.

The young women in the Women's Studies class which I teach are enraptured with *ANTM*, and as a result this show served as an excellent example of how we "revise" bodies of color to meet our standards. The more aware we are of this practice, the more aware, as cultural members and consumers of the media, we can become of the fact that those rejected on dating and makeover television shows have not failed us, but perhaps we have failed them.

BIBLIOGRAPHY

America's Next Top Model. UPN. Exec. prod. Anthony Dominici, Ken Monk, Tyra Banks. 20 Sept. 2006–.

"America's Next Top Model: The Official Site." UPN. 30 May 2006 <http://www.cwtv.com/shows/americas-next-top-model11>

Andrejevic, Mark. "Reality TV: The Work of Being Watched." *Critical Media Studies: Institutions, Politics and Culture.* Lanham: Rowman & Littlefield, 2004.

Bordo, Susan. *Feminism, Western Culture and the Body.* Berkeley: The University of California Press, 1995.

Counihan, Carole. *Anthropology of Food and the Body: Gender Meaning and Power.* New York: Routledge, 1999.

Dates, Jannette L., and William Barlow. *Split-Image: African Americans in the Mass Media.* Washington, D.C.: Howard University Press, 1993.

Deery, June. "Reality TV as Advertisement." *Popular Communications* 2.1 (2004): 1–20.

Feng, Charles. "Looking Good: The Psychology and Biology of Beauty." *Journal of Young Investigators* 6 (2002).

Foucault, Michel. *Discipline and Punish: The Birth of the Prison.* Trans. Alan Sheridan. New York: Vintage, 1995/1977.

Gajjala, Radhika. "Negotiating Cyberspace/Negotiating RL." *Our Voices: Essays in Culture, Ethnicity, and Communication.* Ed. Alberto González, Marsha Houston, and Victoria Chen. 4th ed. Los Angeles: Roxbury, 2004.

Graham-Bertolini, Alison. "Joe Millionaire as Fairy Tale: A Feminist Critique." *Feminist Media Studies* 4.3 (2004): 341–43.

Halualani, Rona, et al. "Between the Structural and the Personal: Situated Sense-Makings of 'Race.'" *Communication and Critical/Cultural Studies* 3.1 (2006): 70–93.

Harding, Sandra. *The Racial Economy of Science: Toward a Democratic Future.* Bloomington: Indiana University Press, 1993.

Hasian, Marouf, Jr. (2001). "When Rhetorical Theory and Practice Encounter Postcolonialism: Rethinking the Meaning of Farrakhan and the Million Man March Address." *Constituting Cultural Difference Through Discourse.* Ed. Mary Jane Collier. Thousand Oaks: Sage, 2002. 77–106.

James, Navita Cummings. "When Miss America Was Always White." *Our Voices: Essays in Culture, Ethnicity, and Communication.* Ed. Alberto González, Marsha Houston, and Victoria Chen. 4th ed. Los Angeles: Roxbury, 2004.

Johnson, Allan. *Privilege, Power and Difference.* 2nd ed. Boston: McGraw Hill, 2006.

McIntosh, Peggy. "White Privilege: Unpacking the Invisible Knapsack." *Independent School*. Wellsley: Independent School, 1990. 31–36.

Moon, Dreama. "Interclass Travel, Cultural Adaptation, and 'Passing' as a Disjunctive Inter/Cultural Practice." *Constituting Cultural Difference through Discourse*. Ed. Mary Jane Collier. International and Intercultural Annual. Thousand Oaks: Sage, 2001. 215–40.

Nakayama, Thomas, and Robert Krizek. "Whiteness: A Strategic Rhetoric." *Quarterly Journal of Speech* 81.3 (1995): 291–309.

Reaves, Shiela, et al. "If Looks Could Kill, Digital Manipulation of Fashion Models." *Journal of Mass Media Ethics* 19.1 (2004): 56–71.

Shome, Raka. "Outing Whiteness." *Critical Studies in Media Communication* 17.3 (2000): 366–71.

Shugart, Helene. "Ruling Class. Disciplining Class, Race, and Ethnicity in Television Reality Court Shows." *Howard Journal of Communication* 17.2 (2006): 79–100.

Spellers, Regina. "Kink Factor: A Womanist Discourse Analysis of African American Mother/Daughter Perspectives on Negotiating Black Hair/Body Politics." *Understanding African American Rhetoric: Classical Origins to Contemporary Innovations*. Ed. Elaine Jackson and Ronald Richardson. New York: Routledge, 2003. 223–44.

Valdivia, Angharad. "Big Hair and Bigger Hoops: Rosie Perez Goes to Hollywood." *Readings in Cultural Contexts*. Ed. Judith N. Martin, Thomas K. Nakayama and Lisa A. Flores. Mountain View: Mayfield, 1998. 243–249.

Woodward, Jeffrey Lyn. "Africological Theory and Criticism: Reconceptualizing Communication Constructs." *Understanding African American Rhetoric: Classical Origins to Contemporary Innovations*. Ed. Ronald Jackson and Elaine Richardson. New York: Routledge, 2003. 133–54.

Tyra Banks' Top Model
Makeover in Reality Television

Frank H. Wallis

As the most complex makeover television show in the reality TV (RTV) genre, *America's Next Top Model* (*ANTM* 2003) offers rich opportunities for interpretation. As an artifact of makeover television, how do we interpret this program where contestants vie for a lucrative modeling contract? One must examine how persons and even institutions interpret their roles in it, or present themselves. Research questions along this line of inquiry include (1) How do the contestants interpret their assigned roles on photo shoots? How are they presented in the narrative arc? (2) How do photographers interpret themes assigned to them? (3) How do Tyra Banks and her panel of judges interpret and present the candidates and place them in a gradually narrowing rank order? (5) How do producers and the network present the show to attract a large target audience for advertisers, who pay close attention to a show's success, measured in ratings? Makeover TV is the re-interpretation of the individual, and *ANTM* as makeover television presents interpretation of the self as a contest to be judged and rated to attract high ratings in a very competitive industry.

I examine *ANTM* primarily as an example of a successful makeover show. *ANTM* is almost a program in a genre unto itself. In fact, *ANTM* replicated itself in several local versions throughout the world, for example *Canada's Next Top Model*. A few versions have been broadcast on American television, such as *Britain's Next Top Model*. Copycat shows were broadcast, including *The Shot* (VH1 2007), a spin-off with a fashion photography premise, and *Make Me A Supermodel* (Bravo 2006), in which 24 men and women compete in challenges "designed to test their professional modeling potential" (Make Me a Supermodel).

What is makeover TV? Among the numerous sub-genres of reality TV,

Nabi, Stitt, Halford, and Finnerty have identified romance, crime, informational, reality-drama, competition/game, and the talent show. Leone, Peek, and Bissell posited only three: the docu-soap, the contest, and the dating show. Confusingly, the term "lifestyle television" is sometimes used in Britain to denote "makeover television," the genre in which real people seek style guidance and personal transformation as in *What Not to Wear* (Palmer).

For an industry-inspired elucidation of "makeover" one may consult the schedule of the Style Network on cable television, which might properly be dubbed the Makeover Network. Jointly owned by Comcast and E! Entertainment, its 2007 schedule included several examples of the sub-genre. *The Biggest Loser* had overweight contestants compete for $250,000 through diet and exercise. Style promoted it as being for people who aspired to a healthier lifestyle (*Style* 2007a). *Clean House* helped families with interior design. Experts decided "what stays and what goes" for a home makeover (*Style* 2007b). *Dr. 90210* featured Beverly Hills plastic surgeons and their clients: "Some seek beauty and happiness, others strive for success and power — and others simply need to be healed" (*Style* 2007c). *Dress My Nest* helped a woman create interior design based on a favorite outfit: "Now you can feel as sexy and stylish in your home as you do when you wear your favorite clothes!" (*Style* 2007d). *Extreme Makeover* "pushes the limits of what's possible in personal transformation" as a team of plastic surgeons, dermatologists, nutritionists, cosmetic dentists, trainers, and stylists changed the appearance of the weekly subject (*Style* 2007e). *How Do I Look?* presented a "fashion-impaired victim" receiving a makeover from two close friends and an expert stylist, resulting in a transformation and newly found confidence (*Style* 2007f). *Style Her Famous* showcased a makeover candidate who desired the look of her favorite celebrity. Experts revealed the "professional secrets of high-end hair and makeup" before the final transformation with new clothes and accessories (*Style* 2007g). The common denominator for every one of these makeover shows is "the reveal," in which the subject is shown transformed and improved in some inner way, to match the obvious external transformation (Palmer 174).

Discussion

ANTM was a commercial television show in the sub-genre of Makeover TV, and separated from others in the category by making transformation a professional objective of multiple candidates on every episode. A reveal took place multiple times every week, compressing the makeover schedule that

professional models might experience. When it first aired in the winter of
2003 it was a unique hybrid with a premise featuring young women who
aspired to become fashion models, subjected to numerous challenges; one
contestant was eliminated at a judgment panel week by week. As a hybrid,
it shared ideas from the history of television: documentary, soap opera, game
show, talent search, makeover. Documentary aspects included the use of
hand-held cameras, personal interviews, and surveillance cameras. When
combined with soap opera drama (seemingly irrelevant and incessant "cat
fights" among women) the sub-genre becomes a docusoap, soap-doc, or real-
ity-soap, which first appeared on British TV in the 1990s, and which was
concerned about self-display in a character-driven format, with priority of
entertainment over social analysis (Hill 451). The game show element (e.g.,
Jeopardy) is related only to competition for a prize: unlike all game shows,
ANTM candidates are not quizzed for memorization or trivia skills. Talent
is an element, judged each episode after photo shoots or other model-specific
challenges. The makeover element is prominent. Candidates must be made
over for each shoot with distinct hair, makeup, and clothing according to
predetermined themes, and Banks has each woman undertake (or suffer) a
makeover to obtain a signature look for the entire cycle (season). Candidates,
especially cycle winners, express the feeling of being transformed by the
ANTM experience into more confident women, ready to take on the world.

ANTM's most famous progenitor was also a hybrid, the Miss America
Pageant, one of the first televised beauty contests. Miss America employed
talent competition, modeling, and news-style topicality in a live broadcast.
Wide shots of the venue suggested impartial surveillance found later in RTV.
Drama came in the form of contestant elimination, after a suitable momentous pause before the dreaded or hoped-for announcement. Interviews
with contestants were done in the manner of broadcast news segments.
Miss America's target audience was avowedly women, with advertisements
and product placements heavily skewed towards this demographic. Pageant
conventions included: preparation, judging, coronation (Corsbie-Massay).
A ghoulish update of this format was Fox's *The Swan*, in which numerous women submitted to plastic surgery before appearing in a beauty contest.

Tyra Banks, a former supermodel, designed *ANTM* as an advertising
vehicle to reach women between the ages of 18 and 34. Banks was creator
and euhemerus, the only female auteur in RTV: she also edited, promoted,
and marketed her show. The presentation of Tyra as mythic forebear for
aspiring models was inescapable: "Tyra Mail" was used to announce challenges; photographs of Tyra were part of Model House decor; Tyra fashion

photos introduced each judgment panel segment; Tyra served as mentor, teacher, exemplar, and final judge. She dismissed mentees week after week, after having her creative acolytes test them in challenges. As threshold guardian, Tyra set up tasks for candidates to perform, challenging them to transform themselves. Banks sought a winner able to project a fierce persona, a woman able to make consumers buy things just by the look in her eyes. The top model was not the most beautiful: she had a personality that the whole world could relate to. As Banks said in 2003 before the airing of Cycle 1, her winner would have a beauty that was not intimidating, a fun personality, and the ability to speak well and represent products (Christian). Banks calculated rightly that viewers would prefer to watch "nasty" before "nice," and made it challenging for candidates on her "dramality" show, because "I've got to sell a TV show." In 2005, *ANTM* ratings ranked behind only one show, *American Idol,* among women younger than 35 (Blakeley).

Although unscripted, *ANTM* did not lack a narrative arc, sense of drama, climax, and resolution of crisis. In RTV "unscripted" does not mean an absence of story, for instead of script writers, *ANTM* producers employed story editors who culled useable clips from hundreds of hours of video to fashion each episode's story line (Dehnart). As RTV characters, the candidates were not trained actors performing dialogue from a script. This meets the RTV criteria of unscripted television, but the women still had to live under continual camera surveillance and turn on the personality during photo shoot challenges and judgment panel. They were also placed in stressful situations designed to elicit soap opera drama and perhaps viewer anxiety over what might happen to their favorite candidates. Unlike other makeover shows in which the subjects only need to portray themselves, their authentic personalities, the subjects in *ANTM* had to alter their personalities and engage in role playing before photographers, and sometimes adopt a character for life in Model House. This could have confusing consequences. Ebony (Cycle 9) was disappointed with her experience, feeling that she had to project a persona that was not authentic to herself. She found it annoying to be filmed 24/7, but also tried to create a personality for *ANTM* to make her more valuable. Ebony thought the show needed a drama queen, so she created one, but was confronted by Banks on this trope at judgment panel. She vowed to reform and not to perform, but it may have been too late. She wished she had stayed true to herself throughout the competition (Rocchio).

Candidates presented themselves in everyday life as a performance. Behavioralists say that people in situations such as these are cognizant of their audience. Social interactions involve going back and forth between cynicism and sincerity, performing self and true self. RTV viewers see this and judge authenticity according to what appears natural, true to the situation portrayed, and true to the self portrayed. Assessment moves back and forth between suspicion and trust, as Goffman predicted, and audiences are keen to detect signs of fake behavior in RTV subjects, as are contestants of each other (Goffman 31, 203; Hill 2005b, 459–462). Runner-up Melrose in Cycle 7 believed *ANTM* was about stress manipulation among women: "I really did put my real stuff out there, and it hurts to be called fake" [by some of the contestants] "and it hurts to be called a 'bitch,' because I'm not those things" (Melrose).

With a view towards performance, candidates may have been cast for convention potential. Viewers noted a trend in *ANTM* personality tropes, not confined to RTV alone (FORT): (1) Hardened Black Girl: Camille C2, Tiffany C4, Bianca C9; (2) Diva: Robin C1, Eva C3, Jade C6; (3) Androgynous Girl: Nicole C3, Kim C5, Mollie Sue C6, Megan C7; (4) Ill Girl, highlighted for an ailment: Mercedes C2, CariDee C7, Heather C9; (5) Hippie: Brittany C4, Jael C8; (6) Jolly Plus-size: Tocarra C3, Whitney C8, Sarah C9; (7) Shy Girl: Kahlen C4, Sarah C6, Samantha C8; (8) Outsider: Mel Rose C7, Renee C8.

But against convention, creator Banks cast each cycle with an ethnic and background diversity beyond then current standards of network programming, representing Banks' own notion of an ideal model society. In C1, there were three Black women, one Hispanic woman, and six White women (Christian). Half of the winners of the first eight cycles of *ANTM* were minorities: Adrienne (White); Yoanna (White); Eva (Black); Naima (Black); Nicole (White); Danielle (Black); CariDee (White); Jaslene (Hispanic).

Candidates were required to pose for photo themes and accept makeovers not of their choosing, but they were also given freedom to bring unique personality to their presentation of assigned characters, much as actors in fictional productions. This unity of free interpretation and imposed theme gave candidate performance an artistic and innovative nature, especially brought into focus by the guest photographers, who themselves had to interpret model and theme. The correlations in this creative equation are complex, beginning with the producer searching for photo themes, creative personnel finding them, models posing, photographers shooting, editors tweaking photographs, and story editors weaving the results into each episode. The resulting work became part of the narrative arc, used in panel deliberations as criteria for advancement of candidates.

Photo themes were therefore a critical element in the presentation of self on *ANTM*, and television story editing allowed one to see both on-stage interpretation of character, and the off-stage presentation of the individual as she ruminated on her performance in relation to her competitors. Space limits will not allow discussion of examples for all photo themes, but conventions are apparent. The *beauty shot* offered an added element of stress, such as posing with snakes (C1.3), without make-up (C3.3), and with a tarantula (C3.8). The *suspension shot* increased stress, such as being suspended over a giant hole (C2.3), posing as a flying super-heroine (C5.1), and a mermaid caught in a net (C6.9), inside a sky-diving simulator (C7.9), and on rock-climbing wall (C9.3). *Implied nude shots* existed in all cycles. The *water hazard shot* have the contestants underwater in a glass tank (C2.5), posing as gas station workers in rain (C4.6), balancing on an unsteady boat (C6.12), and on a catwalk suspended over water (C7.4). The *dynamic shot* included dancing on Tyra's music video (C2.7), on roller skates (C3.5), dancing with South African men (C4.11), falling down and looking good (C6.4),and interpreting aboriginal dance (C8.12).

Dual stressers are present and visually indicated through editing in all photo themes: inner anxiety over presentation of the self, and outer anxiety induced by the contrived situation. The built-in opportunity for drama and cliff-hanging was too good to pass up, and allowed story editors to find suitable breaks for the mandatory commercial breaks (see below).

Perhaps with intended irony, Banks never let a cycle pass without testing the models' interpretation abilities in photo themes centered on stereotypes, many of them self-referential to fashion and celebrity. Examples included celebrity impersonations, male and female (C2.4); ethnicity switching, in which models portrayed an ethnicity other than their own (C4.5); plastic surgery *faux pas* (C5.4); 1940's Vargas pin-ups (C5.6); career women (C6.5); and model stereotypes (C7.2). Candidates were not only visually transformed in these professional makeovers, but were called upon to transform their personalities to give life to each theme.

For the interpretation of stereotypes Cycle 8 was without peer. Episode 8.2 featured controversial issues such as pro/anti veganism, pro/anti gun control, pro/anti gay marriage, pro-choice/pro-life, death penalty, pro/anti fur. Episode 8.3 had high school personality types, including valedictorian, cheerleader, bad girl, jock, bookworm, mean girl, teacher's pet, and class clown. Episode 8.6 had the models pose as masculine tropes: outdoorsman, collegian, rapper, rocker, yachtsman, bohemian, movie star. Episode 8.8 was the most ironic, with interpretations of previous cycle candidates, such as twins Amanda and Michelle (C7), Kim's lesbian kiss (C5), Rebecca's fainting at panel (C4), stolen granola bar incident with Bre (C5), Michelle's impetigo (C4), Joanie's tooth removal (C6), and Shannon's refusal to do a nude shoot (C1). Playing with a binary opposition in image morality, Episode 8.11 required sensual poses for a women's magazine and sexy poses for a men's magazine. Some candidates had an easier time representing the latter, which drew reprimands from Judge Banks, exemplifying the sometimes fine and false line in fashion photography between art and sleaze, and the bewildering commandment to models on *ANTM* shoots to be sexy but not porno. More than any other theme, this one highlighted the difference of creative mindset required for the two principal markets for photography of women.

The most controversial theme in Cycle 8 was that of death. Episode 8.5 in March 2007 had photographer Mike Rosenthal interpret violent death in a cinematography context, a theme which suggested itself to producers upon review of a print in his portfolio of a woman gazing blankly. Rosenthal, whose early career had been in Hollywood cinematography, relied on his experience to transform each candidate into a crime scene victim (Rosenthal). In a private email to this author, Rosenthal wrote that Goya's work on the French invasion of Spain circa 1800 was disturbing but beautiful; art did not need to fit the expected, and should be polarizing; the theme was about role play and fantasy, taking dark concepts and interpreting them. But for some feminists, this theme provided a cornucopia of ideological ammunition: "The most brazen bit of ad-industry misogyny ever to grace the reality TV genre" (Pozner). *ANTM* was therefore part of a heterosexist cabal meant to dehumanize and objectify women. The New York chapter of the National Organization for Women issued a press release condemning *ANTM*, adding some institutional feminist ire (Pozner). The incident was hyped on feminist blogs and entered the mainstream news media for a day or two, encouraging some to believe that *ANTM* provided a good opportunity to influence public opinion and stop the backlash against women, and to increase the struggle against silencing of women by the mass media.

Some of the women who worked on the death scene did not agree with feminist outrage. In later interviews Brittany said, "My favorite shoot was the crime scene. I loved the artistic direction" (Trotter-James). Felicia said, "I was excited to do the death scene. Like the whole nasty, gaudy makeup they put on us was very cool. I was confident throughout the whole thing. I wasn't nervous, or scared, or doubting myself at all" (FORT Felicia). Jael said it was too soon after her friend's death to be enthusiastic, but she was happy to have "pulled through and did my best" (FORT Jael). Whitney said her favorite shoot was the "Crime Scene photo shoot — the makeup was fierce" (FORT Whitney).

Ratings Depend on Ranking

It is common in all commercial television to present a crisis just before an advertising break (e.g., before the judgment panel on *ANTM*). Commercial television depends on advertisers for revenue. Critical in this dependency is the factor of audience ratings, the currency used to buy and sell media and advertising. Advertisers buy audiences and networks sell them. It cannot be overemphasized that the client of a network is the advertiser, not the viewer. This means advertisers buy the highest ratings for a targeted market, and in television the annual outlay on adverts is about $75 billion (Webster 11, 14). Banks and co-producer Ken Mok proposed *ANTM* as an excellent advertising vehicle and revenue generator first for UPN in 2003 and then its successor CW in 2006. One cannot study *ANTM* or any example of the RTV genre without reference to its *raison d'etre* of attracting an audience that will not run away from adverts, which are part of the product, inserted at regular commercial interval points, pods, or breaks. Few shows in RTV had such finely honed integration of products and cross-platform promotions as did *ANTM*.

As one example, on Episode 9.6 (aired 24 Oct. 2007 in the New York city market) advertisers included several multi-billion dollar corporations seeking the young women's demographic: GEICO automobile insurance; Bluefly Inc., an internet retailer; Church & Dwight's First Response pregnancy test; S. C. Johnson's Glade and Oust air fresheners; Electronic Arts' *SIMS 2: Castaway* video game; Warner Chilcott's Loestrin 24 Fe oral contraceptive; Pontiac automobiles; Microsoft's careerbuilder.com; Target department stores; Allstate automobile insurance; Ford automobiles; Verizon Wireless; Sprint; Abbott Laboratories' NutriPals; Quiznos fast food; Kohl's department stores; Honda Civic; Hasbro toys; Reckitt Benckiser's Lysol disinfectant; Johnson & Johnson's Aveeno lotion; and Carrie Underwood's music CD cross-promoted by Target.

More importantly, *ANTM* was absorbed into the Procter & Gamble (P&G) branding machine in C3, debuting September 2004, transforming itself into an advertising platform for CoverGirl, the largest cosmetics maker in the U.S.A. This had momentous implications for the creative direction and meaning of the show. The grand prize was no longer just a lucrative modeling contract. It also included work as a CoverGirl spokeswoman. In effect, *ANTM* became America's Next CoverGirl. In one example P&G used *ANTM* to advertise Clairol, Swiffer, Pantene, and Secret deodorant in commercial pods, but P&G also placed CoverGirl products in almost every episode, and had models work on CoverGirl photo shoots and television spots in the show itself. The dramatic final episode in each cycle after C2 required the winner to do very well in a CoverGirl video shoot. P&G invented the idea of building brand equity, converting products into brands, or positive stereotypes, to give consumers a reason to purchase CoverGirl in preference to competitors. Brand requires benefits: (1) product benefit, or what's in it for the consumer? (2) emotional benefit that results from product benefit; (3) product differentiated from competitors in special methods of action, features, ingredients. "Any area of strategic distinctiveness, done well over time, becomes a brand equity" (P&G). *ANTM* was one element in the P&G strategy of marketing its brands, and one could claim that *ANTM*'s ratings success proved its own brand equity.

CW and P&G used *ANTM* in cross-platform marketing with Cover-Girl in an intertextual commercial television strategy. In the CoverGirl of the Week contest, viewers voted online for their favorite candidate of the week. Voters could enter a sweepstakes to win a trip to New York to meet the season's winner. Meanwhile, website visitors could chat online, where "CoverGirl Beauty Consultants will help you find the makeup and shades just right for you" (CoverGirl). CW published an online *ANTM* forum, featuring 900 web pages of fan responses to numerous polls and contests with an *ANTM* theme (CWTV). In 2007, cell phone text messaging was exploited in an *ANTM* trivia sweepstakes under the aegis of CBS Interactive and the CW network, with a prize of $10,000 (CWTV Trivia).

Conclusion

In keeping with the editorial design of this collection of essays, a few words about rating and ranking need to be said. Gramscian ideas about hegemony (*Television Studies* 117) might include rank ordering of face and figure, and *ANTM* provides some evidence of ranking, but whether there is enough correlation to prove hegemonic ideology is open to debate, and has not been the focus of this article. The criteria for judgment (ranking of candidates) each week rested on the effective presentation of personality, performance of a character, interpretation of a photo theme, and not on great looks or adherence to a specific body type. Each episode had a rank order in the judgment panel call-out, with the best candidate of the week called forward first. And such rank ordering had some bearing on the final outcome of judgment, for only two women were in the bottom two each episode, and one was eliminated after a suitable emotional buildup and climax when the week's loser (lowest rated) was dismissed. The most important judgment in each cycle was almost an anti-climax, as the final two candidates in the last episode heard the final ranking verdict resulting in top model status, what everyone had been waiting for all these episodes, announced by the appearance of the winner's portrait on a video screen. Tyra the Judge exited. Enter Tyra the spectator and well-wisher. Oddly enough, until that last reveal, the most valuable candidate to the story line was not first, but last, because she was the answer and resolution to the crisis of every episode, the climax and last element in the dramatic arc.

Rating things is part of life, voting, buying a car, grading students. In *Reality TV: Audiences and Popular Factual Television,* Hill observes that in RTV the most important audience factor is perceived authentic presentation of the self, which viewers rate in a critical manner. But the most important factor for a network and the producers of any given show is audience ratings, the lack of which means the death of text (the program). *ANTM* was in one sense rated on the basis of advertiser commitment, using a successful formula to attract an audience, demonstrating that makeover television is more about advertisers than viewers. Carefully targeted advertisements for *ANTM* concentrated mostly on women's products and made an obvious dovetail with cultural assumptions. The fact that the show featured women exclusively and depended on assumptions about beauty and attractiveness echoed larger cultural stereotypes in America (i.e., that some people may rank or rate women solely on these criteria). But *ANTM* was about more than beauty ranking. Tyra Banks had to get an audience hooked to generate income from interested major ad clients, and promoting beauty alone would not have been as effective. The show would have been nothing without a bit of drama, usually coming from candidate anxiety over performance in photo shoots and challenges, and pressure over presentation of the self, whether it was genuine or tailored for television consumption.

BIBLIOGRAPHY

America's Next Top Model. UPN. Exec. prod. Anthony Dominici, Ken Monk, Tyra Banks. 20 Sept. 2006–.

Blakeley, Kiri. "Tyra Banks On It." *Forbes* 178 (3 July 2006): NA. *Expanded Academic ASAP.* Gale, 11 Oct. 2007: Gale Doc. A147228101.

Christian, Margena A. "Tyra Banks: Says 'It's a Lot More Than Just Looks' to Become America's Next Top Model." *Jet* 26 May 2003: 56(5). *General OneFile.* Gale14 Oct. 2007: Gale Doc. A102453160.

Corner, John. "Performing the Real." *Television and New Media* 3 (2002): 255–70.

Corsbie-Massay, Charisse. "Television Conventions and Beauty Pageant Ideology." Paper presented at Pacific Sociological Association, Universal City, CA, 2006. 22 Nov. 2007. <http://themediamademecrazy.com/papers- projects/usc-critical-studies/tv-and-bp>

CoverGirl. Website. Procter & Gamble. 25 Oct. 2007. <http://www.covergirl.com/ANTM/cycle9/index.jsp>.

CWTV. "*ANTM* Forum." The CW Television Network. 1 Nov. 2007. <http://lounge.cwtv.com>.

_____. "*ANTM* Total Trivia Sweepstakes." The CW Television Network. 27 Nov. 2007. <http://www.cwtv.com/page/contest/*ANTM*-sweeps-rules.html>.

Dehnart, Andy. "Reality TV Is Unscripted — Mostly." MSNBC.com. 12 Nov. 2007. 14 Nov. 2007. <http://www.msnbc.msn.com/id/21741803/>.

FORT. "Conventions Thread." Fans of Reality TV Website. 13 Nov. 2007. 27 Nov. 2007. <http://www.fansofrealitytv.com/forums/america-s-next-top-model-9/69469-conventions-stereotypes-*ANTM*.html>.

_____. "Felicia Interview. Fans of Reality TV Website." 22 March 2007. 12 Oct. 2007. <http://www.fansofrealitytv.com/forums/americas-next-top-model-9/62287-americas-next-top-model-8-interview-felicia-3-22-07-a.html>.

_____. "Jael Interview." Fans of Reality TV Website. 23 April 2007. 12 Oct. 2007. <http://www.fansofrealitytv.com/forums/americas-next-top-model-9/63173-america-s-next-top-model-8-interview-jael-4-19-07-a.html>.

_____. "Whitney Interview." Fans of Reality TV Website. 12 April 2007. 12 Oct. 2007. <http://www.fansofrealitytv.com/forums/official-articles/62995-america-s-next-top-model-8-interview-whitney-4-12-07-a.html>.

Goffman, Erving. *The Presentation of Self in Everyday Life.* New York: Doubleday Anchor, 1959.

Griffen-Foley, B. "From Tit-Bits to Brother. A Century of Audience Participation in the Media." *Media, Culture & Society* 26 (2004): 533–548.

Hartley, John. "The Infotainment Debate." *The Television Genre Book.* Ed. C. Creeber. London: BFI, 2001. 118–21.

Hill, Annette. *Reality TV: Audiences and Popular Factual Television.* London: Routledge, 2005.

_____. "Reality TV: Performance, Authenticity, and Television Audiences." A *Companion to Television.* Ed. Janet Wasko. London: Blackwell, 2005. 449–67.

Leone, Ron, Wendy Chapman Peek, and Kimberly L. Bissell. "Reality Television and Third-Person Perception." *Journal of Broadcasting & Electronic Media* 50 (June 2006): 253–270(17). *General OneFile.* Gale. 15 Oct. 2007: Gale Doc. A154756996.

Make Me a Supermodel Website. Bravo. 25 Jan. 2007. <http://www.bravotv.com/ Make_Me_A_Supermodel/season/1/about/index.php>.

Melrose. "Interview with Melrose." Fans of Reality TV Website. 9 Dec. 2006. 26 Oct. 2007. <http://www.fansofrealitytv.com/forums/americas-next-top-model-9/59671-*ANTM7*-interview-melrose-i-dont-really-feel-like-i-lost.html>.

Nabi, Robin L. "Determining Dimensions of Reality." *Journal of Broadcasting & Electronic Media* 51 (June 2007): 371–389. *General OneFile.* 15 Nov. 2007: Gale Doc. A167695500.

_____, C. Stitt, J. Halford, and K. Finnerty. "Emotional and Cognitive Predictors of the Enjoyment of Reality-Based and Fictional Television Programming." *Media Psychology* 8 (2006): 421–447.

Palmer, Gareth. "The New You: Class and Transformation in Lifestyle Television." *Understanding Reality Television.* Ed. Su Holmes and Deborah Jermyn. New York: Routledge, 2004. 173–90.

Papacharissi, Zizi, and Andrew L. Mendelson. "An Exploratory Study of Reality Appeal: Uses and Gratifications of Reality TV Shows." *Journal of Broadcasting & Electronic*

Media 51 (June 2007): 355–371. *General OneFile.* Gale. 15 Oct. 2007: Gale Doc. A167695499.

Pozner, Jennifer L. "Top Model Looks Ugly to the Blogosphere & the Media — Thanks for Rolling With Our Outrage!" WIMN's Voices. 27 March 2007. 12 Oct. 2007. <http://www.wimnonline.org/WIMNsVoicesBlog/?p=467>.

Procter & Gamble. "Building Brand Equity." 25 Nov. 2007. <http://www.pg.com/jobs/consumer_is_boss/building_brand.jhtml>.

Rocchio, Christopher. "Top Model Quitter Ebony Morgan: I was so Over the Whole Reality Thing." Reality TV World. 26 Oct. 2007. 11 Nov. 2007. <http://www.realitytvworld.com/news/top-model-quitter-ebony-morgan-i-was-so-over-whole-reality-thing-5994.php>.

Rosenthal, Mike. Website. 1 Nov. 2007. <http://www.mikerosenthal.net>

Style Network. (2007a). E! Entertainment Television, Inc. 24 Oct. 2007 <http://www.stylenetwork.com/ssms-site/style.do?showId=6323>.

_____. (2007b). E! Entertainment Television, Inc. 24 Oct. 2007 <http://www.stylenetwork.com/ssms-site/style.do?showId=6266>.

_____. (2007c). E! Entertainment Television, Inc. 24 Oct. 2007 <http://www.stylenetwork.com/ssms-site/style.do?showId=6157>.

_____. (2007d). E! Entertainment Television, Inc. 24 Oct. 2007 <http://www.stylenetwork.com/ssms-site/style.do?showId=6286>.

_____. (2007e). E! Entertainment Television, Inc. 24 Oct. 2007 <http://www.stylenetwork.com/ssms-site/style.do?showId=6266>.

_____. (2007f). E! Entertainment Television, Inc. 24 Oct. 2007 <http://www.stylenetwork.com/ssms-site/style.do?showId=6143>.

_____. (2007g). E! Entertainment Television, Inc. 24 Oct. 2007 <http://www.stylenetwork.com/ssms-site/style.do?showId=6273>.

Television Studies: The Key Concepts. Ed. Bernadette Casey, Neil Casey, Ben Calvert, Liam French, and Justin Lewis. London: Routledge, 2002.

Trotter-James, Belinda. "Brittany Hatch Talks About Her 'Top Model' Experience." Reality TV World. 7 May 2007. 10 Oct. 2007. <http://www.realitytvworld.com/news/interview-brittany-hatch-talks-about-her-top-model-experience-5149.php>.

Turner, Graeme. "Genre, Format, and Live TV." *The Television Genre Book.* Ed. C. Creeber. London: BFI, 2000. 6–7.

Understanding Reality Television. Ed. Su Holmes and Deborah Jermyn. New York: Routledge, 2004.

Wasko, Janet (ed.). *A Companion to Television.* London: Blackwell, 2005.

Webster, James G., Patricia F. Phalen, and Lawrence W. Lichty. *Ratings Analysis.* 3rd ed. Mahwah, NJ: Erlbaum, 2006.

11

"She Just Called You a Metro"
Rating Masculinity on Reality Television

Matthew Johnson

When Mark Simpson introduced the term "metrosexual" in 1994, he pinpointed a new trend among heterosexual men. Metrosexual referred to the scores of heterosexual men that Simpson saw in urban spaces whose lifestyle and appearance resembled those of stereotypical homosexual men — well-dressed and well-groomed. The emergence of metrosexuality as an alternative idea of masculinity owes much of its resonance among men to the marketplace. *Queer Eye for the Straight Guy* first popularized metrosexuality in the United States, but the subsequent male makeover shows, spoofs, commercials, and companies that attempted to take advantage of its popularity are responsible for its persistence and growing audience. At the same time, the marketplace has also contributed to an important backlash against metrosexuality. Companies and television shows hoping to take advantage of men who detest metrosexuality have spurred increasing attention to a hypermasculinity that defines itself against femininity by valuing athleticism, competition, physical strength, heterosexuality, homophobia, and restricted emotions. This essay suggests that the logic of the marketplace, whether advertently or inadvertently, plays an important role in gender construction. I use certain reality television shows, advertising, and the reactions to them in popular culture as a window into the competing conversations about masculinity in the twenty-first century.

The competing notions of masculinity seen in the emerging popularity of metrosexuality and the increasing attention to traditional masculinity suggest that masculinity is in flux. As Gail Bederman and others note, gender is never stable (Bederman; Butler). Historians have referred to certain periods in American history where notions of gender were particularly unsta-

146

ble as "masculinity crises" (Cuordileone 9–17; Dubbert). The two periods in the twentieth century where historians argue that masculinity was least stable (the turn of the twentieth century and the 1950s) share a number of similarities. In both periods, demographic and social changes, war, and expanding roles for women in the public sphere sparked anxiety among men over the future of masculinity. Beginning in the 1950s, men's new role in the marketplace also sparked concern but did not create the level of anxiety seen in the current period (Osgerby). More importantly, since the mid-twentieth century, masculinity has been explicitly defined in opposition to homosexuality (Cuordileone 15; Chauncey). I argue that masculine norms are even more unstable today. While gender is constantly in flux, masculine norms now appear to be especially unstable. The overt connection between the masculine style of metrosexuality and homosexuality helps explain why so many Americans perceive gender roles to be in flux. Metrosexuality challenges the way Americans currently invest sexuality into their ideas about gender. At stake in these discussions is where homosexuality fits into the changing ideas about male identity. There is, of course, a spectrum of homosexual identities. The very definition of metrosexuality, which connects clothing style and grooming with homosexual men, frames the way Americans talk and think about homosexuality in this essay. Rather than acknowledging the various lifestyles and appearances of gay men, the popularization of metrosexuality gives the stereotype of the limp-wristed, effeminate, and well-dressed homosexual more weight and visibility in American culture.

Makeover Shows

In this essay I analyze two makeover shows: *Queer Eye for the Straight Guy* and *What Not to Wear*. *Queer Eye for the Straight Guy* features five hosts, referred to as the Fab 5, each responsible for a different aspect of metrosexuality: fashion, food and wine, culture, design, and grooming. Carson, Ted, Jai, Thom, and Kyan help a straight man in each episode develop a new wardrobe, pick out new furniture, learn grooming techniques, social manners, and basic cooking skills. Like *Queer Eye for the Straight Guy*, *What Not to Wear* hosts Stacy London and Clinton Kelly help straight men (and women) develop a new wardrobe and teach them grooming skills. Each participant receives $5,000, a trip to New York, and the hosts' advice. But unlike *Queer Eye*, *What Not to Wear* is far more limited in scope, focusing on dress and appearance.

While there are differences between the shows, both *Queer Eye* and

What Not to Wear teach men how to lead a metrosexual lifestyle — a lifestyle that takes great concern with one's appearance — emphasizing the central importance of clothing, skin care, and grooming in a heterosexual man's daily life. Most of the participants on the show express little concern about their appearance, seeing nothing wrong with poorly groomed facial hair, white socks with dress shoes, and pleated dress pants. By the end of the show the hosts provide the participants with the skills to dress and groom themselves in a way that resembles metrosexual style.

Charlie, a participant on *What Not to Wear*, might illustrate the show's most dramatic makeover. As a boat restorer he often wore paint-stained pants to dinner, sported long, raggedy-blonde hair, and owned a wardrobe that might serve a circus performer better than a working professional. Deeply embarrassed by his appearance on the show, Charlie passively took the advice of London and Kelly. The hosts helped him pick out a radically new wardrobe, arranged for a new haircut and taught him grooming skills. By the end of the show, the previously rugged boat restorer looked like a stereo-typical metrosexual. The show portrays metrosexuality's effect on notions of masculinity in American culture by showing men embarrassed by their appearance and passively accepting a makeover.

Another episode illuminates the anxieties that some men feel when taking on a more metrosexual style because of the link between homosexuality and metrosexuality. Carlos is a martial-arts fighter who demonstrates the hypermasculine backlash to metrosexuality, that of the physical man who rejects attempts to change his appearance and asserts his sexual preference publicly. Part of this identity is expressed in the way Carlos dressed: he consistently wore baggy pants, ripped sweatshirts, and snow caps. When the hosts Stacy London and Clinton Kelly ambushed Carlos during one of his training sessions, he immediately showed resistance to a dramatic change in his wardrobe. Pointing to Clinton's faded jeans, dress shirt, and matching jacket, Carlos yelled: "I'm not wearing that!" Carlos's girlfriend had warned the hosts before the program that he "thinks guys that are really into their style are a little too girly for him." In an interview after the ambush, Carlos immediately expressed his anxiety over the future of his masculine style. Reminding the audience about the masculinity of fighters, he worried about the effects that the makeover would have on his martial arts career: "I don't know how I'm going to fight after this. I'm going to look like a sissy." London and Kelly, although they serve as experts, are hardly imperious figures in this episode. As noted above, Carlos saw his clothing as one of the most important markers of his masculinity and sexuality. The hosts realized that Carlos's wardrobe had to reassure him of his masculinity. As a result of negotiation between participant and hosts, a compromise was reached where Clinton and Stacy simply showed him how to pick out clothes that fit. At the end of the show Clinton reassured Carlos about the clothes that he had picked out: "It's a very luxurious masculine look. You still maintained your masculinity."

While one way the hypermasculine backlash to metrosexuality is expressed is through dress, another way of expressing this backlash is through behavior. When Carlos feels most uncomfortable because of his belief that buying trendy clothes puts his sexuality into question, he responds with hypermasculine behavior that draws attention to his heterosexuality. At one store Carlos saw a beautiful young woman working behind the counter. He turned to the camera and asked, "Can I take her with us? I've got a shirt that says 'I only sleep with the best.'" In an interview during the show he further made explicit his heterosexuality: "I think I look pretty good. What's the number for girls to call when they see what they like?" In one of the most telling examples, during the shopping expedition, Carlos wrapped his arms around Stacy's waist. When she asked him to try his clothes on, he asked her where her dressing room was, making it clear to London that he was interested in her. The hypermasculine backlash to metrosexuality is an anxious response to some men's discomfort with the changing markers of heterosexuality. Appearance once offered heterosexual men the most visible way to distinguish themselves from homosexuals. Because heterosexuality is such an essential component of contemporary masculinity, some men have taken on a hypermasculine persona in response to the loss of an important gender and sexual marker.

Members of the Boston Red Sox express this anxiety on an episode of *Queer Eye for the Straight Guy*. When the Fab 5 made over five members of the Red Sox (Johnny Damon, Kevin Millar, Doug Mirabelli, Tim Wakefield, and Jason Varitek), the players constantly referred to the connection between metrosexual style and homosexuality. The players often used humor as a way to express this anxiety rather than using the form of hypermasculinity displayed by Carlos above. As Kevin Millar soaked his feet at the spa, he joked with a teammate: "Who said gay was bad? I am now gay." Later in the show Tim Wakefield turned to another player and commented, "How gay do you feel right now?" At the end of the show the players revealed their new look in front of fans at the Red Sox's spring training stadium. Kevin Millar again used humor to express his discomfort over the connection between the makeover and homosexuality by walking into the stadium with limp wrists and a wide grin. But of course the players never questioned their sexuality. As if to remind the viewers of their heterosexuality, the players' wives were always within arm's length. While the players were not as explicit as Carlos in displaying their sexuality, their wives' presence and their use of humor never left their heterosexuality in question.

Even though their sexuality was never in question, the players lacked the language to explain their experience. Some of the players looked confused and uncomfortable when discussing their manicures. Doug Mirabelli asked, "Is this gay, though?" One of the hosts quickly responded, "It's metrosexual." The term does not catch on during the show, and the players and even the hosts still work within the heterosexual-homosexual binary. Carson, possibly the most flamboyant of the Fab 5, calls the players during their makeovers "hidden homosexuals." The structure of the show offers the potential to emphasize the diverse spectrum of homosexual identities. All five hosts present different personalities on the show and several do not fit the most visible stereotype of the limp-wristed, effeminate sissy. Nevertheless, the show does not even attempt to provide a language for men to work outside of the heterosexual-homosexual binary and gives further weight to association between grooming, style, and gay men.

Though most of the players expressed discomfort through homosexual jokes, one player felt comfortable during the makeover. Johnny Damon, one of the Red Sox's most popular players and known for his long hair, brought his own stylist. As Damon received a pedicure Ted remarked, "Here we thought they were going to be like oh my god." Damon responded, "Like we're all macho like we act." For Damon, the makeover hardly challenged his masculinity or sexuality. But Damon was the exception.

The hosts of *Queer Eye for the Straight Guy* and *What Not to Wear* serve as experts on their respective shows. They offer a rating system to audiences for judging masculine style and they often embarrass participants when they do not conform to their rating system. These shows offer an important window into the anxieties over the loss of gender and sexual markers due to the rising popularity of metrosexuality. The participants might accept the advice of the hosts but their reactions to changing their lifestyle and appearance to resemble one of a homosexual sparks various reactions to make their masculinity and heterosexuality visible. In the next section I analyze examples of the backlash to metrosexuality on *MTV*. If makeover shows offer a notion of masculinity (whether accepted or not) that values a greater concern with grooming and style, attributes more closely associated in American culture with women and homosexual men, dating shows privilege a more aggressive, competitive, and hyperheterosexual masculinity.

Dating Shows

Unlike the makeover shows on *TLC*, the dating shows on *MTV* provide an environment where men often prove their masculinity through competition. Competition over women is one of the oldest tropes of masculinity and emphasizes the connection between sexuality and gender. In *Exposed*, a woman chooses between two male contestants who do not know that one of the woman's friends is sitting in a van using lie detection software to gauge their honesty. She begins the show with a soccer game. The woman sets up two goals, throws a ball on the field, and announces that the first one to score wins. If the woman's passive position as a spectator does not illuminate the differences between masculinity and femininity, she makes it more explicit when she reminds the contestants that she will not play because "I just got a pedicure." Other examples on the network illustrate this dichotomy between stylized notions of what it is to be masculine and feminine.

For example, *Next* promotes an aggressive, hypersexual style of masculinity in episodes in which a woman chooses between five male contestants who wait on a bus. Contestants compete by each going on a "date" with the woman, which she can end at any time. She just has to say, "Next." Again the hypermasculine theme is established immediately by the idea that men compete for the woman. If rejected, the contestant returns to the bus like a romantic gladiator vanquished from the field, and a new contestant comes out. In one episode, Eric, a ballet performer, attempts to present himself as aggressively heterosexual, but it is quickly evident that he does not fit in with the other contestants. If the viewer does not recognize this, the other contestants and the woman make it clear. While on the bus, the contestants exchange outrageous sexual stories. Eric tells the others that he had a threesome with another male and a woman. The other contestants laugh and show how uncomfortable they are with homosexuality, or perhaps even with any form of sexuality that diverts from traditional heterosexuality, by berating Eric for having a sexual experience with another man. Even though Eric makes it clear that he was only interested in the woman, one contestant, upon hearing the story reminds the audience of the important association between masculinity and heterosexuality by responding: "There's only one penis in my parade." When it is Eric's turn to go on a date with Portia, she is in a mock courtroom. He opens the door and leaps into the courtroom, demonstrating to Portia that he is a ballet dancer. Portia immediately yells, "Next!" When he leaves she laughs into the camera and says, "I think Frodo got lost on his way to the hobbit ballet."

In *Room Raiders* a male or a female picks their ideal date after examining three bedrooms. They are not allowed to meet the contestants before they choose their date and must make decisions simply based on the objects in their rooms. Before the contestants can clean their rooms, the producers of the show take them from their homes and place them in a van where all three contestants sit together to watch their potential date comment on their belongings, and make fun of each other. Interpretations of certain objects as masculine or feminine often play an important role in the decision-making on the show, and also surface in the way the contestants interact with each other.

For example, during one episode Rachel, with the help of her friend Layla, looks through the rooms of Tyler, Byron, and Arean. Looking for what she calls a "real man," Rachel gives insight into the gendered connotations of particular objects. Walking into Tyler's room, Rachel becomes excited when she sees a trophy that suggests that he likes cars. But as masculine as cars are, his pageant sash, lip gloss, and poems to his ex-girlfriend deter her. She turns to the camera and asks, "Are you a girly guy?" In the van Byron laughs, turns to Tyler and comments, "She just called you a metro." While makeover show hosts present metrosexuality as essential to any heterosexual attempting to attract women, and thus important to a man's masculinity, most of the *Room Raiders* episodes suggest that metrosexuality deters women and is unmasculine. Rachel especially laughs at the pageant sash: "It's just too girly to be in a pageant. Maybe guys should just stick to football." She adds that his room "was just too girly for me. I need a manly man."

Where Rachel identifies masculinity in opposition to "girly" in Tyler's room, she defines masculinity in opposition to childhood in the final two rooms. In Byron's room Rachel finds a stack of comic books in his desk. Disappointed she yells to the camera, "I don't need a child, I need a man." In the final room she has similar criticism for Arean. Finding video games and monster slippers she again appears frustrated and repeats herself: "I don't need a child, I need a man." In the end she finds important objects in Byron's room that suggest that he is more of a man than the others. Uncovering weights Rachel's friend says approvingly, "Rachel needs a strong man to take care of her."

Occasionally *Room Raiders* privileges alternative forms of masculinity. Where Rachel looks for a mature "manly man" that represents the polar opposite of a metrosexual, Cherie looks for a different style of masculinity. Searching through one of the contestant's rooms she finds a teddy bear. Instead of finding it childish and unmanly, Cherie finds it appealing. Cherie tells the contestant through the camera that the bear "shows me that you're secure with your masculinity" and Cherie adds that she likes his sentimental side.

Even the show *Next*, which usually evaluates gender through hypermasculine activities, occasionally offers criticism of aggressive masculinity. In one episode of *Next*, Preston, a hyper-heterosexual athlete rejects several girls until he meets a tall, athletic-looking woman. Preston first takes the woman to the batting cage where gender differences are emphasized. Attempting to hit balls in a short skirt, the woman looks helpless while Preston laughs in the background. Preston offers to help her and emphasizes gender differences by walking behind her and pressing himself against her, while holding the bat from behind the woman. Later in the date the two sit down and he explains his athletic history in a long monologue. When Preston asks her if she would like to go on another date she rejects that idea and instead chooses the alternative of a sum of money. Rather than approving of the hypermasculinity that many of *MTV*'s shows promote, she looks at the camera as she walks away and makes a comment about how insulting Preston was to her.

Like makeover shows, dating shows allow space for participants to challenge the dominant narrative. But participants like Cherie, who appreciates a man's sentimental side, or the woman who disapproved of Preston's hypermasculine characteristics, represent the exception rather than the norm. Most of *MTV*'s shows promote a rating system that values hypermasculinity. Aggressively heterosexual, the style of masculinity promoted in many of the episodes value heterosexuality overall and make explicit the separation between masculinity and homosexuality.

Reactions to Metrosexuality

The metrosexual lifestyle championed in the episodes of *Queer Eye for the Straight Guy* has sparked important conversations about masculinity in the media, popular forums, and in the marketplace. Its visibility on television as well as in society has produced varied reactions from Americans. A major backlash is evident among men and women who feel metrosexuality threatens masculine conventions, especially the visible markers of heterosexuality. Others accommodate certain attributes of metrosexuality in their conception of male identity. The fight over metrosexuality's place in our notions of masculinity is far from resolved but it is certain that the marketplace will be the major battlefield.

The rise of metrosexuality depends upon consumption. Joe Lee, former editor of *Vitals*, has gone so far as to suggest that Madison Avenue created the term to sell more products (Wilson). Whether the advertising industry responded to the metrosexual trend or created it, it is evident that men are consuming more products such as moisturizers than ever before. But while companies fill the market with metrosexual products, the marketplace also provides space for a backlash against metrosexuality.

Miller changed its Miller Lite commercials to target an audience resistant to metrosexuality, using the marketing company Crispin Porter & Bogusky. Alex Bogusky, chief creative officer for Crispin, justifies the advertisements by citing the ambiguousness of ideas of masculinity: "Guys are really confused about how to behave. A lot of unspoken rules are being broken, and guys are lost. Our research shows us that guys in bars are grasping for the right thing to do, the right way to act" (Howard). Miller crafted advertisements about the unwritten code for males that feature a secret society of men, including former National Football League (NFL) player Jerome Bettis, former NFL football coach Jimmy Johnson, and World Wrestling Entertainment (WWE) wrestler Triple H. According to Miller's vice president of marketing, these men are appropriate for the ad because they are "true men" (Bosman). The gimmick behind the ad campaign is that this "society" develops a set of rules they call "man laws" meant to guide men's behavior in certain situations. In the advertisements, they answer apparently troubling questions to men, such as how long must a man wait before dating his friend's ex-girlfriend, or should men put fruit in their beer (Bosman).

Even ad campaigns for certain consumer goods play into notions of sexuality. Miller recently changed its advertising campaigns after attempting to market its Miller High Life as an upscale drink. From 1998 to 2003, the company used the High Life Man in advertisements. Employing gendered branding, Miller exploited a caricature that exulted in the "joys of eating bacon grease and doughnuts with unwashed hands" (Mullman). When the company transitioned to a new Girl in the Moon emblem, which attempted to expand the beer's consumers, sales dropped for four consecutive years, including a 7.5 percent decline in early 2006. Miller has since gone back to more masculine advertising. A representative of Miller justified the change: "High Life drinkers like making fun of French bistros and froufrou stores" (Mullman).

Other companies have followed in Miller's footsteps. In 2006, after contracting the Miller's marketing firm, Burger King released a hyper-masculine commercial promoting the Texas Double Whopper. The commercial features a song that emphasizes the masculine nature of the burger. The song, which is fittingly titled "I Am Man," declares things like tofu and quiche to be "chick food." The Whopper, in contrast, is "manly." The voiceover that follows the song reaffirms its message: "Eat like a man, Man." The commercial goes further to connect the burger to aggressive masculinity by showing displays of physicality. One man breaks a cinder block with his fist, while another punches a fellow worker in the stomach. In the final scene, a man drives up to the mob of men holding burgers in a minivan and the men throw the "feminine" vehicle over a bridge. Important to note here is the appearance of the men in the advertisement; few of these men fit the metrosexual norm presented in makeover shows. Instead, most of the men sport beards, hardhats, and athletic wear ("I Am Man").

Mitchum, a company that sells deodorant for men, also relies on the backlash against metrosexuality to market its products. Deutsch Inc., Mitchum's marketing company, conducted focus groups, talking to men in their 30s, to better market the product. Kathy Delaney, chief executive officer for the company, stated that the men in the focus groups "felt metrosexuality took their masculinity away" (Stewart). In response, Deutsch created the "Mitchum Man" marketing campaign. One commercial tells viewers, "If you've ever killed a bug with a nail gun, you're a Mitchum Man" ("If You've Ever Killed a Bug"). Another commercial suggests, "If you had nothing to do with planning your wedding, you're a Mitchum Man" ("If You Had Nothing to Do"). Mitchum connects a product that might otherwise be associated with personal appearance, and thus metrosexuality, with aggressive masculinity.

The country music industry, known for its homophobic, anti-urban style of masculinity, has taken advantage of the contemporary dialogue about masculinity. The metrosexual lifestyle, with its connections to feminine and homosexual style, is a perfect target. Brad Paisley's "I'm Still a Guy" illustrates one of country music's most popular examples. Paisley is quick to connect metrosexual activities such as facials and eyebrow grooming to femininity. According to Paisley, while metrosexuals are "lining up to get neutered," he still has "a pair." Fishing and hunting are activities that "real" men pursue, while neutered men get manicures.

The popular Internet website *YouTube*, which allows members to share videos on the website, also provides an important forum to discuss contested notions of masculinity. Spoofs of *Queer Eye for the Straight Guy* that criticize metrosexuality abound on the website. These videos, many titled "Straight Eye for the Queer Guy," instruct homosexuals on heterosexual, masculine norms. In one offensive video the "Flab 5" invade a homosexual's home, replace his designer shirts with athletic tank tops and exchange his designer table for a cooler filled with beer. Another video features a diatribe on metrosexuality. The speaker instructs men to "talk in their normal tone of voice," to wear anything but pink, to watch professional sports, and not to wave with a limp wrist. He also reminds viewers that pedicures are not manly: "They're feet, they're male feet, they're not supposed to look pretty" ("Straight Eye for the Queer Guy" [b]).

Some women are joining men in their vocal distaste for metrosexuality. A *Boston Herald* columnist, Lauren Beckham Falcone, expresses her anxiety over the slow decline of what she sees as traditional masculinity. Some women might dream of metrosexual Ryan Seacrest, but her ideal men are Tony Soprano, Jack Black, and Vince Vaughn. For Falcone, Seacrest's "only hope of defending a woman's honor is to attack with his VO5 mousse and undeserved talk show contract." She explains, "It's not that we want he-men, we just don't want to share our night cream, razors or hair colorists. I get ticked off when my husband eats the last of the bologna. Can you image if he were pilfering my $50 eye cream" (Falcone)?

At the same time, public forums, such as Internet forums, provide space to attack the aggressively heterosexual style of masculinity. Many criticize *Queer Eye for the Straight Guy* for promoting a feminized version of masculinity, but others criticize shows such as *Next* in online blogs and magazines for presenting a hypermasculine idea of masculinity. Lauren Butts writes of *Next* that "in no way does this show reflect the realities of dating. For people who watch this show literally, you are receiving a false representation of gender, dating, and everything in between." Even the males on *Next* that act charming while on the mock date "march back on to the bus and into hyper masculinity mode again" (Butts). One blog depicts *Next* as an "extreme depiction of men and women in society" ("Femininity and Masculinity").

Amid discussions of neutered males, many men defend metrosexuality as essential to their heterosexual lifestyle. In an article in the *Seattle Post-Intelligencer* men interviewed about their metrosexual lifestyle said women drove them to a greater interest in style. One man explaining his sense of style said, "The girls that I'm attracted to have really nice style and taste. And I guess I can't expect to be with them if I don't pay attention to that stuff too." A former sales associate at Barneys New York told the reporter that men frequently told her, "My wife told me to come here" (Dizon).

Other men include certain characteristics of metrosexuality in their definitions of masculinity while still holding on to their homophobia. In an opinion section of the *St Louis Post-Dispatch* Bryce Chapman defends his masculinity against his wife's accusation that he is a metrosexual. His wife claims that he carries a "murse" (a man purse), owns 48 dress shirts, a Burberry tie, and is well groomed. Chapman claims his "murse" is actually a "very masculine, black messenger bag for work purposes only" and his extensive wardrobe is simply a product of his wife's shopping habit. Besides,

Chapman does not see himself as a metrosexual because he loves camping, fishing, Sonic cheeseburgers, frequently belches at the dinner table, recently installed a laminate floor in his living room and plans to "single-handedly" put "a new roof on my house." His idea of a metrosexual involves sipping fruity martinis and getting manicures (Chapman). By accommodating certain metrosexual characteristics and rejecting others, Chapman redefines metrosexuality to appear much more like a homosexual lifestyle and thus, in contrast, clearly identify himself as heterosexual. Chapman's attitudes show how men can accommodate homophobic attitudes with metrosexual norms.

Conclusion

The hotly contested conversations about masculinity suggest that men and women are searching for an appropriate rating system to judge men's masculinity. But viewers will not find a coherent and consistent set of conventions on the makeover and dating shows on television. On the contemporary minefield of gender politics no style of masculinity can survive without criticism. The hotly contested conversations about masculinity suggest that notions of gender are in flux. Since the mid-twentieth century, definitions of American masculinity have been intimately bound to heterosexuality. The popularity of the metrosexual lifestyle, explicitly connected to homosexual stereotypes by shows such as *Queer Eye for the Straight Guy*, among straight men threaten the visible differences between heterosexual and homosexual men. In contrast, dating shows such as *Next* make sexual distinctions a cornerstone of the program. Perhaps more than any time in the past one hundred years, an alternative style of gender presents a formidable challenge to the dominant notions of masculinity. The hotly contested debate in public forums should be no surprise to the American public.

Important to this conversation about masculinity is the influence of the market. Although American viewers are far from passive observers, American corporations play an important role in perpetuating the discussion and anxieties about masculinity. One only needs to open the pages of *Esquire* or *GQ* to appreciate the number of companies that take advantage of the metrosexual trend. But other companies take advantage of the backlash against metrosexuality. Corporations such as Burger King and Miller tie their products to more traditional notions of masculinity. The numerous advertisements that currently connect traditional masculinity to products suggest the market plays an important role in the conversations about gender.

While it is evident that metrosexuality provides an alternative style of masculinity, its social utility is uncertain. Michael Kimmel, a leading scholar of masculinity, paints metrosexuality as an important agent of change. Kimmel argues that metrosexuality "promotes an idea of masculinity that's premised on the collapse of homophobia among straight men" (Campbell). But as much as metrosexuality is modeled on stereotypical gay norms, it does not necessarily breed respect for homosexuals. In fact, men have accommodated certain metrosexual norms while distancing themselves from homosexuals. Bryce Chapman's article, discussed above, is an excellent example of this. Chapman redefines masculinity by accommodating certain metrosexual norms such as wearing nice clothes and carrying a "murse," but he defines himself against metrosexual norms that are more explicitly tied to homosexuality, such as pedicures and drinking martinis.

Still, the important conversations about masculinity in reality dating and makeover shows have sparked a challenge to traditional notions of masculinity. For many men, appearance has become a significant component of their male identity. More men associate with masculinity some of the lifestyle choices connected to homosexuality than ever before. But scholars and activists waiting for a style of masculinity that values and respects homosexuals will have to wait for a day when men change more than their clothing.

BIBLIOGRAPHY

Bederman, Gail. *Manliness and Civilization: A Cultural History of Gender and Race in the United States, 1880–1917.* Chicago: University of Chicago Press, 1995.

Bosman, Julie. "Beer Ads that Ditch the Bikinis, But Add Threads of Thought." *New York Times.* 1 May 2006. 1 Dec. 2007. <http://www.nytimes.com/2006/05/01/business/media/01adco.html?_r=1&oref=slogin>.

Butler, Judith. *Gender Trouble: Feminism and the Subversion of Identity.* New York: Routledge, 1990.

Butts, Lauren. "MTV Dating Show *Next's* Individuality." *The BG News.* 6 June 2007. 1 Dec. 2007.<http://media.www.bgnews.com/media/storage/paper883/news/2007/06/06/Pulse/Mtv-Dating.Show.nexts.Individuality-2911991.shtml>.

Campbell, Kim. "'Manly' Gets a Makeover." *Christian Science Monitor* 7 April 2004. 1 Dec. 2007.

Chapman, Bryce. "Manly or Metrosexual? It All Depends on Whether You Carry A Messenger Bag or A Man Purse." *St. Louis Post-Dispatch* 5 April 2006: B6.

Chauncey, George. *Gay New York: Gender, Urban Culture, and the Makings of the Gay Male World, 1890–1940.* New York: Basic Books, 1994.

Cuordileone, K.A. *Manhood and American Political Culture in the Cold War.* New York: Routledge, 2005.

Dubbert, Joe L. "Progressivism and the Masculinity Crisis." *Psychoanalytic Review* 61 (Fall 1974): 433–455.

Exposed. Prod. Dianne Martinez and Kalissa Miller. MTV 2007.

Falcone, Lauren Beckham. "Mano a Mano: Tough Guys Tackle My Heart Every Time." *Boston Herald* 22 April 2004: 65.

"Femininity and Masculinity on MTV's *Next*." Homepage. 1 Mar. 2007. 20 Nov. 2007. <http://melisthoughtswgs.blogspot.com/2007/03/femininity-and-masculinity-on-mtvs-next.html>.

Howard, Theresa. "Miller Lite Ads Celebrate Manly Men." *USA Today* 27 Nov. 2006: 9.

"I Am Man-Burger King." Advertisement. *You Tube*. 26 Jan. 2007. 1 Dec. 2007. <http://www.youtube.com/watch?v=vGLHlvb8skQ&feature=related>.

"If You Had Nothing to Do." Advertisement. 1 Dec 2007. <www.mitchumman.com>.

"If You've Ever Killed a Bug." Advertisement. 1 Dec 2007. <www.mitchumman.com>.

Mullman, Jeremy. "Miller Hails Triumphant Return of High Life Man." *Advertising Age* 78.7 (2007): 6. 2 Dec. 2007.

Next. Prod. Meg Ruggiero, Kalissa Miller, Howard Schultz, and Jacqui Pitman. MTV 2007.

Osgerby, Bill. *Playboys in Paradise: Masculinity, Youth and Leisure-style in Modern America*. Oxford: Berg, 2001.

Queer Eye for the Red Sox. DVD. Dir. Stephen Kijak, Max Makowski, Brendon Carter, Joshua Seftel, Michael Selditch. Genius Entertainment, 2005.

Room Raiders. Prod. Charles Tremayne, Mike Powers, and Tony DiSanto. MTV, 2007.

Simpson, Mark. "Here Come the Mirror Men." *The Independent* 15 November 1994: 22.

Stewart, Sara. "Beasty Boys-'Retrosexuals' Call for Return of Manly Men; Retrosexuals Rising." *New York Post* 18 July 2006: 41.

"Straight Eye for the Queer Guy." (a) *YouTube*. 16 September 2006. 1 Dec. 2007 <http://www.youtube.com/watch?v=ahEupxaI06Q>.

"Straight Eye for the Queer Guy." (b) *YouTube*. 11 Oct. 2006. 1 Dec. 2007 <http://www.youtube.com/watch?v=psjpdePcmHw>.

What Not to Wear. Prod. Dean W. Slotar, Catherine Scheinman, and Robin Berla. The Learning Channel, 2007.

Wilson, Eric. "O.K. Fellas, Let's Shop. Fellas? Fellas?" *New York Times* 2 April 2006, late ed.: Sec. 9, 1. 1 Dec. 2007.

Materialism, Disposal and Consumerism
Queer Eye *and the Commodification of Identity*

Yarma Velázquez Vargas

On July 5, 2003, the show *Queer Eye for the Straight Guy* premiered on Bravo. The show, a reality television fashion makeover show, featured five gay men and used sexuality as a selling point. The program was part of the summer lineup on Bravo, an NBC Universal Inc. Cable Network (General Electric and Vivendi) and it quickly became one of the station's most profitable shows, winning two of four Emmy nominations and bringing great recognition and commercial success to the five main characters.

The Fab Five, as they are commonly called, have been marketed by Bravo television as a sophisticated team of gay men. Most often a straight guy was selected and the five experts of *Queer Eye*—Ted Allen, Kyan Douglas, Thom Filicia, Carson Kressley and Jai Rodriguez — gave him a makeover. Each character of this makeover show has an area of specialty. Ted is the food and wine expert. On the show he illustrates the appropriate kitchen tools and how to use them; sometimes he teaches men special recipes and gives them lessons for buying and ordering wine. Thom is the decoration expert; his contributions consist of rearranging the space in which the straight guy lives. Carson is the fashion expert in charge of deciding the "appropriate" look for each character. Jai covers the area of "culture." For *Queer Eye for the Straight Guy*, "culture" translates into: lessons on public speaking, dancing and body language, mostly etiquette. However, it can also cover areas such as pet grooming and dating. In sum, the focus of the makeover will depend on the mission of the week. Finally, Kyan is the grooming specialist, as he covers issues related to skin and hair care.

The Fab Five have several items and merchandise associated with the production of the show, including DVDs, numerous music CDs and a book with general tips. Moreover, some of the main characters have additional books. For example, Carson has a children's book, Ted released a cooking book and Kyan published a grooming book for ladies.

These five characters are the self proclaimed embodiment of good taste and class. They are depicted as five super heroes traveling through the streets rescuing males from bad taste. They arrive at the "challenged" straight man's house in a black SUV, a contemporary representation of the "Batmobile." In the SUV they describe the mission of the day, reminiscent of Charlie's call when assigning missions to his angels in the series, *Charlie's Angels.* The superhero theme is also made evident in all advertising and promotion efforts. In fact, David Metzler and David Collins, the producers of the show, commented:

> When the Fab Five was born, they were superheroes in our minds — bigger-than-life gay men, armed with great fashion, good looks and bottles of eye cream. If there was a straight guy in need, they'd rush to his rescue [Allen, Douglas, Filicia, Kressley, and Rodriguez 8].

The show starts with a shot of the five characters in their areas of expertise being paged with a "QE" (*Queer Eye*) emergency. They discuss the day's mission in their SUV while driving to the straight guy's house. During that time they provide the audience with a demographic profile (age, profession, marital status, location) of that week's character and describe the mission or objective.

Once at the home of the straight guy, the Fab Five start ranking him based on style, decoration, clothing and belongings, in sum his consumption habits. Each of the five experts discusses his plan for the day and the areas he will be working on. Each Fab has some alone time with the straight guy while selecting and buying all the elements needed for the makeover. When the straight guy returns home, he admires and reviews all the day's accomplishments (new clothing, decoration, food, etc). Then he has a final meeting with each of the Queer Guys, and he is left physically alone to practice what he has learned. However, the Fab Five meet at their New York apartment and watch a video of the straight guy during the "life changing" event. They discuss the video over some glasses of wine or another alcoholic beverage and debate the success or failure of the mission. The program ends with some concluding thoughts from the *Queer Eye* guys.

During the first season, the show's audience share reached unforeseeable numbers, making *Queer Eye* the best rated show of the summer of 2003. Wayne Friedam and Richard Linnett reported that the show captured 2.8

million total viewers, out of which 2.1 million were adults age 18 to 49. In the article "Jay Leno Slated for '*Queer Eye*' Makeover," Friedman and Linnett explain that the primary target for the show was women 18 to 49, with a secondary target of gay men. By July 29, 2003, *Queer Eye's* audience numbers had reached an all-time high. *Queer Eye* quickly became Bravo's highest rated show ever.

By the end of the first season, executive producers for Scout Productions, David Collins, Michael Williams, and David Metzler, had deals for a spin-off of *Queer Eye* and franchises throughout the world. Between 2003 and 2005 the original version of the show, featuring Ted Allen, Kyan Douglas, Thom Filicia, Carson Kressley and Jai Rodriguez, was broadcast in over 100 countries including Spain, England, Turkey, Portugal and South Korea, among others. Also, the franchise was sold internationally; 13 countries (among them France, Italy, Spain, Finland, Australia and England) were licensed to produce their own versions of the show featuring a local cast (NBC Universal Media Village).

The success of the series enticed Bravo's parent network, NBC Universal, to air a compressed version of the show — from the regular hour format to a 30 minute format — on NBC that attracted 6.9 million viewers. Claire Atkinson, in her article "Comeback Trail," explains that *Queer Eye's* success with audiences impacted the way marketers used their advertising dollars. The show made media buyers look at cable as an alternative to the networks to place their ads. Moreover, Richard Linnett reported that the success of shows like NBC's *Will & Grace*, and Bravo's *Queer Eye for the Straight Guy*, was taken as evidence that gay themes were mainstream and profitable.

The show was also significant for the five main characters. Claire Atkinson and T.L. Standley's article "*Queer Eye* for Rich Guys" describes how the Fab, who were each getting $3,000 per episode during the first season, moved to $10,000 a show each for the subsequent seasons. They also received individual offers for sponsorships and commercial deals. However, the salaries of the five characters were not the only thing that changed after the first season.

The concept of the show also changed significantly during the third season. With the beginning of the third season, Bravo's president announced in June 2005 that the title of the show had been abbreviated to *Queer Eye* because producers wanted to venture into new kinds of makeovers and add more compelling narratives to the story lines. According to NBC Universal Media Village article "*Queer Eye* Charges," the changes were a response to a decline in the popularity of the show and increasing competition from the makeover show *Extreme Makeover Home Edition* ("*Queer Eye*"). However, in an interview included on the bonus video section of the *Queer Eye* website, Ted Allen mentions, "We just call the show *Queer Eye* because we want to be able to work with women, gay women, straight men and gay men." The changes during the third season included a makeover for a gay and transgendered man, thereby refining the positioning of the program. Finally, on January of 2007, Bravo announced the final season of *Queer Eye* (Serpe). The last ten episodes of the show aired in October of 2007.

The concept of the show generated great controversy in popular and academic circles. For scholars, the program created hype around issues of representation, identity politics, the use of term queer and the commodification of sexuality, sex and gender through aggressive marketing strategies. *Queer Eye for the Straight Guy* also had an enormous impact on popular culture. A year after the show premiered, *Television Week* reported that as a direct consequence of the success of the show NBC started discussing development of a series of spin-offs of the program. Indeed, in the fall of 2005, Bravo aired a spin-off of the show called *Queer Eye for the Straight Girl*, a program in which gay men conducted a makeover of a "fashion-challenged" straight woman.

The title of the show and the use of the term queer suggested the possibility of the development of a new discursive space for contested sexualities. In fact, the promotion of the show generated great appeal among gay audiences. But this excitement was short sighted because, as this thesis argues, *Queer Eye* is first and foremost a space for the reproduction of common stereotypes about the gay community. Although Paul Allatson, Robert Bateman, Mark Gallagher, Misha Kavka, Kyra Pearson and Nina M. Reich, Dana Heller, and Toby Miller have conducted studies about the show since its debut in 2003, most of the literature on *Queer Eye* centers around issues of representation of homosexuality and the use of different patterns of consumption to regulate social relations (e.g., heterosexuals and homosexuals, men and women, and characters and the audience). Thus, this paper looks at the many ways through which the program sustains structures of power and the corporate capitalist media system to promote consumerism.

Consumerism

The engine motivating *Queer Eye* is consumption. In the first few seasons, the intent of the program was to educate straight men about a specific aesthetical mode of thinking and consuming. A clear example of this is found during Episode 119. When talking about shopping Thom, the design consultant for *Queer Eye,* tells Warren, "It's like you have blindfolds when you pass through the good stuff." Later in that show, at the furniture store Ikea, they go through all the "must have items" in the store. Thom strives to educate Warren's taste and modify his perceptions. When commenting later on his new apartment, Warren explains how much he has learned and explains how much he enjoys all the things that if left alone he would never get. The program becomes a guide for consumption, one that is manipulated by the interest of the brands advertising on the show.

Queer Eye is a program that serves as a normative institution embracing consumerism and vigorously promoting a culture of consumption. Excessive and immeasurable consumption and disposal of resources are some of the ideas of capitalism reinforced in the program. Beyond the customary shopping, the Fab Five serve as normative figures within the structure of the capitalist system. It is evident in their actions that they embrace the values of a materialistic society. In many ways the show ranks and evaluates individuals to propose that consumerism is the best route to self improvement. This message is reinforced in the several themes represented on the show such as: disposable consumption and waste, consumption as a means to construct one's identity; and consumption as a desirable skill that one must learn.

Disposable Consumption and Waste a Matter of Destruction

For the Five, being wasteful is often seen as a pleasurable act. For them there is a joy that comes with the destruction of functional goods. Goods are disposed of if they don't fit a particular aesthetic form. Often, wastefulness is represented as a fun and liberating act and ironically any challenge to this form of consumptiveness is described as being careless. For example, during Episode 119, Ted suggests purchasing new glassware, because it is very inexpensive. Moreover, he argues that the glassware is so affordable that he is tempted to break it just for fun. He later makes a case to replace all functioning dinnerware, just because he prefers a different color. This type of consumption is socially irresponsible and encourages disengaged social beings. It encourages hyper-consumption and ignores all ecological consequences that might come from that.

This idea of disposable consumption is never more evident than in Episode 101, when Kyan states that the best feature of disposable razors is precisely that they are disposable. Moreover, let us reconsider the most common phrase used by the Five in Episode 120, "Out with the old and in with the new." In this episode, leaving the old behind includes breaking and smashing some planting pots, an improvised ritual that actually and symbolically kills a living organism.

When the Fab Five's consumptive ideology is contested, their power is enforced. During Episode 123, James initially resists the transformation. The Fab Five hate his brand new couch because it is cheap looking, but for James it is functional and aesthetically pleasing. Here the theme of destruction and careless consumption is reflected when the Fab Five throw food and later toss the furniture only because they dislike the fabric. During Episode 123 Ted criticizes the synthetic fabric of the furniture by attempting to stain it while Thom and Kyan tear the window treatment apart. Later on in that episode Thom and Carson throw the couch out the window and all while making fun of James (the straight guy) who complains in disbelief.

Functional goods are often discarded because they don't meet specific aesthetic guidelines. Sometimes objects are even replaced just because they are dirty. During Episode 127, Thom replaces functional but old appliances with new GE appliances in stainless steel and explains that it is easier to buy a refrigerator than to clean the existing one. In redefining the concept of what is perishable, Thom is undeniably advocating an unsustainable form of consumption in today's global society.

Moreover the characters often encourage *over* consumption of goods. Jai, during a fashion show in Episode 119, comments, "Too much couture." To that Carson responds, "There is no such thing as too much couture." Yet on the show, excessive consumption is only acceptable when it is in the realm of fashion; for example, the overconsumption of food is not acceptable. For example, in Episode 229, Fab made over friends Adam and Steve. The makeover took several months and the goal was to help the two men lose weight. Interestingly, Carson describes Adam and Steve as the poster-boys of overindulgence, yet one could argue that the only difference between the straight friends and Carson is not how much, but what items they choose to consume.

Consumption as a Tool to Shape Identity

Goods become an intrinsic part of creating an identity, creating an image and telling a personal narrative. Personal choices in the various categories (food choices, attire, fashion, living space and design) are conceptualized as being a reflection of one's inner being. Often the Fab Five are presented creating personal stories and narratives through the use of objects.

For example, in Episode 101, Brian is an aspiring artist and therefore it is determined that he has to communicate his lifestyle through his choices of appetizers and the way he wears his shirts. In reference to the foods served during the event, Ted advises Brian that his food choices must reflect his artistic side by choosing a menu that is both visual and expressive. Similarly Carson counsels that his clothing should reflect his "cool and rock and roll" lifestyle. In this episode, goods are used to represent Brian's creativity and the cool expected of an artist.

Throughout the series the Fab Five use goods to position individuals, construct a public persona, and refine their identity. The Five create an identity based on "stuff" and general narratives of what it means to be an artist, a jock, a groom, a man. Consumption is also used to gain independence. Thus, in Episode 123, Ted explains that the goal of the makeover is to set the guy up with all the things he needs to be independent and cool.

The idea that items can create an identity is especially interesting in Episode 302. During this episode, the Fab Five use goods to help a female to male (FtM) transsexual become a better man. The Five suggest that clothing, grooming, and a juicer are the essence of masculinity. Carson explains, "We should prepare you with clothes that every man needs." According to Carson, the transformation from FtM can be achieved with clothing that will fool the eye and give the impression that he is bigger than he really is. Moreover, furniture is also essential for the transformation, as evidenced when Thom describes his design as a "cool new Brooklyn dude apartment" because, as he later explains, "guys like gadgets" (Episode 302).

Danny, described by the Fab as a "tecno-hippie," was made over on Episode 212. The Five make it clear that his long hair is not appropriate for corporate America when Ted describes his look as being more appropriate for selling bongs than for representing a non-profit. Not only does the show create narratives for the individuals they make over, consumption as an intrinsic part of one's identity extends to venues and events.

At the end of Episode 101, as the Fab Five reflect on the success of the transformation, their words are evidence that for them consumption, as opposed to education or merit, is what facilitates social mobility. During Episode 101 Ted, Kyan and Carson cheer Brian for adopting the vive, look and lifestyle they proposed.

For the Fab Five, acquiring objects is something used as a reward to communicate wealth, as shown in Carson's argument that the best way to convey success is by purchasing expensive fabrics at designer stores; in fact he says that purchasing some nice cashmere shows that you are successful, you have arrived. Thus, acquisition is represented as a merit-based reward that communicates social status and economic success. Consumerism is depicted as a form of self-discovery. In the closing of Episode 120, Carson says, "Cheers to us for helping him find the real Rob." That quest of realization, that journey to discovering one's own identity through consumption, is finalized after the makeover.

The relationships between the object and the self are also in question. During Episode 119, Carson comments, "Listen to the store," as if consumers could engage in a dialectic relationship between the product and themselves. When I listen to stores they usually don't say much; however, my Master-Card seems to notice. That the show depicts and encourages the development of personal relationships with brands and products as part of the process of self discovery suggests a relationship with goods that goes beyond their function.

Consumption as a Desirable Skill to Learn

Consumption is represented as a desirable skill that one must learn. The Fab Five serve as normative agents of the institutional power in charge of the pedagogy of consumption, an instructional process by which the participants learn to "refine" their criteria when selecting goods. It not only involves learning the proper way of selecting, maintaining, and using goods, but it also includes lessons on brand preference and creation of needs.

In the area of fashion, Carson during Episode 119 explains to the audience and the recipient of the makeover how to be a "wise shopper." In this episode he explains how to find couture treasure at discount stores. The lessons of consumption conclude with Carson stating all the characteristics of a bargain: style, laundering, seasons. Consumption then becomes more than selecting goods to satisfy general needs (food for hunger, clothing to cover one's body). It becomes a desirable skill — the result of knowledge, practice and aptitude.

During Episode 123, one of the Fab Five, Kyan, trades skills with James, the straight guy. James gives Kyan golf lessons, and in exchange Kyan gives James grooming lessons. The lessons crafted by the "Grooming Guru" involve learning how to use new product categories and specific brands. The first lesson is learning the craft of shaving, the second mastering the use of Crest White Strips. This particular aspect of Kyan's "proper grooming" teachings is a common theme of the show. On Episode 127, Kyan teaches the twins both how to use specific brands to clean their bathroom, and how to use L'Oreal on their skin.

The show represents consumption as something one must learn how to do and a necessary skill for performing masculinity. This is most evident in Episode 302, when the Fab five give a makeover to a female to male (FtM) transsexual. Carson attempts to explain how clothing can be used to perform gender; he explains the performance of masculinity must include cashmere and pants that "give you a nice package." Here not only can you learn the skill of shopping, but also how to be a man through consumption.

The pedagogy of consumption often leads to a process of self discovery. Consumption is also represented as a way to connect with one's hidden qualities or aspects of one's personality. Often after the makeover, the students realize all the goods they need to include in their daily routine. Often they realize that there are a series of objects that they never thought to buy, but that are now essential to their daily lives.

Conclusion

The television program *Queer Eye* has had an enormous influence on television, advertising and popular culture. *Queer Eye's* low cost of production made it a particularly profitable property for Bravo. It became a cultural phenomenon because it revolutionized product placements, changed media buying techniques, had a local and international reach, and affected society's discourse on masculinity in the United States.

In the show *Queer Eye*, goods become an intrinsic part of creating an identity, creating an image and telling a personal narrative. Personal choices in the various categories (food choices, attire, fashion, living space and design) are conceptualized as being a reflection of one's inner being. Moreover, the role of the experts in *Queer Eye* is to create social needs and the narratives necessary to satisfy those needs through consumption. Thus, materialism becomes an instrumental tool to solve family disputes, conciliate relationships, celebrate events, unite cultures, transcend phobias, and mark changes.

The social impact of *Queer Eye* is particularly troublesome as the television show encourages the over-consumption of goods, and depicts five hedonistic characters that completely disregard the impact of immeasurable materialism. Moreover, this makeover show proposes a classification system to determine the value of individuals that is based on consumption and image.

Queer Eye rates men and identifies the many areas in need of repairs. However, the Fab Five's solution to a boorish masculinity — lack of personal hygiene, personal style or decoration sense is always consumption. Thus, every week the five-some proposed new ways in which "aesthetically challenged men" could purchase their way into a new lifestyle and acquire services that would facilitate their interactions with their wives and girlfriends. The Fab Five rating system of the participants helps identify them as normative agents of the institutional power in charge of altering and guiding the selection of goods. Products form an essential part of the narrative and help shape the identity of the participants by presenting specific brands that are associated with an idealized lifestyle.

BIBLIOGRAPHY

Allatson, Paul. "*Queer Eye*'s Primping and Pimping for Empire Et Al." *Feminist Media Studies* (2004): 208–11.

Allen, Ted, et al. *Queer Eye for the Straight Guy: The Fab 5's Guide into Looking Better, Cooking Better, Dressing Better, Behaving Better and Living Better.* New York: Clarkson Potter, 2004.

Atkinson, Claire. "Comeback Trail: Broadcast TV Storms into Fall. Stronger Lineups, Better Talent Fuel Ratings Growth and Ad-Rate Hikes." *Advertising Age* 2 Oct. 2006. 6 July 2007 <http://adage.com/index.php>.

_____, and T. L. Stanley. "*Queer Eye for the Rich Guy.* Marketers Waving Money Chase Fab Five." *Advertising Age* 29 Sept. 2003. 6 July 2007 <http://adage.com/index.php>.

Bateman, Robert B. "What do Gay Men Desire? Peering Behind the Queer Eye." *The New Queer Aesthetic on Television: Essays on Recent Programming.* Ed. James R. Keller and Leslie Stratyner. Jefferson, North Carolina: McFarland, 2006. 9–19.

"Compose Yourself: Warren L." *Queer Eye for the Straight Guy.* Prod. David Collins and David Metzler. Bravo Television. 2 Mar. 2004.

Friedman, Wayne, and Richard Linnett. "Jay Leno Slated for *Queer Eye* Makeover. Gay Product Placement Show Draws High Ratings." *Advertising Age* 4 Aug. 2003. 6 July 2007 <http://adage.com/index.php>.

Gallagher, Mark. "Queer Eye for the Heterosexual Couple." *Feminist Media Studies* 4.2 (2004): 223–225.

"Getting Kicked Out from the Garden of Eaten: Adam and Steve." *Queer Eye for the Straight Guy.* Prod. David Collins and David Metzler. Bravo Television. 5 Sept. 2006.

"Hair Today, Art Tomorrow: Brian S." *Queer Eye for the Straight Guy.* Prod. David Collins and David Metzler. Bravo Television. 15 July 2003.

Heller, Dana. "Taking the Nation 'from Drab to Fab': Queer Eye for the Straight Guy." *Feminist Media Studies* 4.3 (2004): 347–50.

Kavka, Misha. "Love'n the Real; Or How I Learned to Love Reality Television." *Spectacle of the Real: From Hollywood to Reality TV and Beyond.* Ed. Geoff King. Bristol, UK: Intellect, 2005. 93.

Linnett, Richard. "TV Show with Highest Priced Ads: *Friends.* NBC Tops Charts of Most Expensive Prime Time Programs." *Advertising Age* 15 Sept. 2003. 6 July 2007 <http://adage.com/index.php>.

"Meeting Mildred: Rob M." *Queer Eye for the Straight Guy.* Prod. David Collins and David Metzler. Bravo Television. 16 Mar. 2004.

Miller, Toby. "A Metrosexual Eye on Queer Guy." *GLQ: A Journal of Lesbian and Gay Studies* 11.1 (2005): 112–7.

NBC Universal Media Village. "Broadcast Marks a Television First as Foreign Version of U.S. Originated Show Hits American Airwaves." Press release. NBC Universal, Inc. Ed. Bill Brennan and Zenon Dmytryk. 2 Aug. 2007 <http://nbcumv.com/release_detail.nbc/bravo>.

_____. "'Queer Eye' Charges Into Season Three with Emphasis on Straight Guys' Unique Stories Plus a New Umbrella Title." NBC Universal, Inc. Ed. Dan Silberman. Aug. 2, 2007 <http://nbcumv.com/release_detail.nbc/bravo-20050531000000-queereye charges.html>.

Pearson, Kyra, and Nina M. Reich. "Queer Eye Fairy Tale: Changing the World One Manicure at a Time." *Feminist Media Studies* 4 (2004): 229–31.

Serpe, Gina. "Bravo Shuts Queer Eye." E! Entertainment Television, Inc. 2007. March 26, 2007 <http://www.eonline.com/news/article/index.jsp?uuid=2ad9d1fa-790c-44ef-8db8-ac042eb8f342>.

"Taking on the Twins: Brandon and David B." *Queer Eye for the Straight Guy.* Prod. David Collins and David Metzler. Bravo Television. 1 June 2004.

"Training Day: James M." *Queer Eye for the Straight Guy.* Prod. David Collins and David Metzler. Bravo Television. 23 Mar. 2004.

"Trans-form the Trans-man: Miles G." *Queer Eye for the Straight Guy.* Prod. David Collins and David Metzler. Bravo Television. 1 Aug. 2006.

"Trump-ed To Triumph: Danny K." *Queer Eye for the Straight Guy.* Prod. David Collins and David Metzler. Bravo Television. 16 Aug. 2005.

New Blouse, New House, I Need a New Spouse

The Politics of Transformation and Identity in Television Makeover and Swap Shows

SHIRA TARRANT

Television makeover and swap shows seduce us with the possibilities of a whole new life. The message is that all we need is a new wardrobe, a new spouse, or a remodeled home — and *voilà* — we can experience the power of personal transformation. We are promised that by changing our hair, our partner, or our interior décor, we can change our experience of life itself. If we can transform ourselves, these shows suggest, then all things become possible. New wardrobes and made-over lifestyles open the door to lofty goals like becoming righteous or realizing our true potential. At the same time, though, it is clear that shows like *What Not to Wear*, *Wife Swap*, and *Extreme Makeover: Home Edition*, reproduce powerful and repressive ideological messages about the politics of identity.

It is these meta-stories — our cultural mythologies about identity and transformation — that are most compelling. Underneath the surface of these trashy, flashy, and instantly stimulating television shows is serious ideological content about gender, race, class, and sexuality (Parenti 30). As Herman and Chomsky note, while pop culture media can distract our attention from political conflict around the world it is also true that television fluff embodies real political struggles of its own.

Television makeover shows are seductive and so potent because in one slick move they give to us with one hand while they are taking away with the other. Viewers can escape for an hour by uncritically indulging in bits of hope, dream, fantasy, and train wreck. We can vicariously shop (*What*

171

Not to Wear), buy (*Extreme Makeover*), or trade (*Wife Swap*) our way to personal transformation. There is the potential for shows like these to communicate anti-oppression concepts to a huge audience. The problem is that the options offered for achieving this change do not include political participation, economic parity, or even spiritual contemplation. There is no mention of structural inequality. And these issues remain invisible by presenting what are actually "privileged social arrangements as part of the natural order of things" (Parenti 2005). In other words, the highly charged politics of transformation become naturalized.

Television makeover and swap shows entice us with the possibility that we can change and reinvent ourselves. Yet with their themes of commodity trade and consumer indulgence, these shows also contain harmfully narrow tropes about gender, race, and class. There is an almost relentless heternormative impulse. Never mind that our collective anxiety increases every time we internalize the cultural message that our old selves are not good enough and never will be. These shows reward the so-called worthy and implicitly leave the rest of us to fend for ourselves.

If television makeover and swap shows like these seem to fly in the face of feminist politics and social justice efforts — or simply challenge the basic tenets of self-respect and personal esteem — then why do so many of us like to watch? Quite simply, because they're fun. Some of the pleasure comes from the over-the-top victory of good over evil, where improved fashion, behavior, and décor triumphs over sweatpants, selfishness, shag carpeting. And then there's The Reveal, the money shot of reality shows such as these, in which the makeover is made public with huge flourish and fanfare. The Reveal keeps us glued to the end, and this addictive entertainment factor is also what makes the invisible ideological messages in shows like this so powerful.

While makeover and swap shows bolster dominant ideals about what makes individuals valuable, they also reinforce restrictive limitations on the ways in which we perform our self-identities. This process targets women in specific ways. *Wife Swap* and *What Not to Wear* tell us that women are obsessed with personal relationships and with the physical adornment of the home and body. Both *What Not to Wear* and *Extreme Makeover* naturalize consumerism and fetishize commodities. Because American culture expects and encourages women to be the primary shoppers, this takes on a gendered hue. Even weirder is the fact that in *Wife Swap* women *are* the commodities — wives are items that can be bought, sold, bartered — or, in this instance, quite literally, swapped.

The makeover show is terrain where amazing transformations of the body and home take place, and where participants live out a *Prince and the Pauper*-type experiment. But this experiment lacks any critical reflection on social injustice that Mark Twain would have found relevant. Television makeover shows are today's fables that transmit our culture's dominant ideas about how to act and who to be — or how *not* to act and who *not* to be. These modern fables are filled with repressive prescriptions about who we are or might be; in short, a component of what bell hooks calls the politics of domination. These mass media fables work on us by telling "stories, images, and whopping rationalizations that shape how we make sense of the roles we assume in our families, our workplaces, our society." Like fun-house mirrors, these stories "distort and warp 'reality' by exaggerating and magnifying some features of American life and values while collapsing, ignoring, and demonizing others" (Gitlin in Douglas 16).

What Not to Wear

In *What Not to Wear* an unsuspecting subject is secretly nominated to appear on the show. She is ambushed off the street, shown footage that was filmed on the sly, and summarily confronted with her fashion faux pas. The video is proof that she dresses either too sexy or too frumpy; she presents herself as too old or not old enough. The point is never raised that taping this footage involves following someone around for weeks to spy on them at work, on the street, or lounging around their backyard. Under different circumstances this would be called stalking. At last count, *What Not to Wear* featured a woman in 78 out of 83 shows. Given statistics that women are the victims in the vast majority of all stalking cases, this point is especially alarming.

After the fashion intervention, Stacy London and Clinton Kelly, the show's hosts and stylists, whisk the subject away to New York where she is given $5,000 and instructions on how to reinvent herself through proper wardrobe, hairstyle, accessories, and makeup. Her old wardrobe is unceremoniously tossed in a big trash can. The Reveal at the end of the hour showcases her new look. It is also a manipulative moment designed to evoke awe in the television viewer. The not-so-hidden message is that women need to be changed, that women should *want* to be changed, and that transformation requires cash.

Shows like *What Not to Wear* also convey specific cultural messages about what women can and cannot be. The options are very limited. Examples gleaned from TLC's episode guide include the following. Note the gender snarkiness: Gina owns her own business, but dresses more like a hooker than a businesswoman. She likes miniskirts, tube tops, spandex, feathers, and fringe. Stacy and Clinton help Gina create a professional image. A second episode features Laura who has a wardrobe full of big, baggy clothes. She thinks they make her look thinner, but Laura's boss and family think she's hiding beneath these grubby, shapeless clothes. They'd like to see Laura look more feminine. Firefighter Kristine would rather dress like "one of the guys," but Stacy and Clinton help bring out her "feminine side." Finally, there's Niya. Stacy and Clinton convince her that high heels and halter-neck dresses are not appropriate for a 24-year-old mother of two. The sexually expressive woman must become more restrained while the wallflower learns to forefront her cleavage and curves. In the search for a perfect wardrobe, *What Not to Wear* clearly lets women know that we are never okay exactly as we are. We are damned if we do sex it up; we are damned if we don't.

The irony is that when all is said and done, the show's participants often do look quite good. At the end of the show, the primped and primed emerge for The Reveal cooing over their new look and swearing they feel suddenly ready to get that dream job, be a better mom, or ask for a promotion. Critical viewers are left, however, with the unsettling question of whether individual constraint is the price that must be paid for personal transformation. For women, these tradeoffs are high.

But if this point is left unsettled, what *is* clear is that the forces of consumerism and market capital are alive and well. Change has a price tag. Its initial cost, as we know from the show's budget, is $5,000 per person. This amount is unaffordable for most, yet American women are increasingly willing to go into debt just to achieve the consumer ideal. We know how to buy status. As Juliet Schor points out in her film *The Overspent American*, shopping is no longer about keeping up with the Joneses. Today it's all about keeping up with the Paris Hiltons, Kanye Wests, or the next new media darling getting pimped out by TMZ. If we're not sure how to keep up with these wealth-driven fashion standards, Stacy and Clinton help us along.

We are lured into thinking that $5,000 really is a reasonable price to pay for realizing our better self. We can buy true potential at the mall. And next season, we can do it again. What remains dangerously unaddressed and reinforced here are the politics of class. Its logic goes like this: If we can buy our way to personal transformation, and if we can pay to discover our True Self, then culturally it becomes very easy to believe in the idea that the poor who cannot buy a new wardrobe therefore must not have access to their higher self. The misguided conclusion is that those who cannot afford the price of a new wardrobe must not really be as good as the rest of us. And by this logic, those of us who can only afford to buy knock-off versions of brand name and designer duds might look glam, but the message is that we really only achieve the simulacrum of our full human potential.

While it's easy to find the show entertaining, *What Not to Wear* naturalizes ideas about class and poverty, worthiness and unworthiness. Its reasoning is insidious: If you buy you can become. If you cannot buy, you cannot become. Because transformation is something you *buy*, not something you *are*, the poor can never *become*. This has a powerful impact on our cultural belief systems. The question is, who is worthy of transformation, personal improvement, and self-realization — and who is not?

Wife Swap

Wife Swap (ABC) shares with makeover shows its themes of transformation, commodity trade, and the recreation of dominant ideology. The Reveal at the end of the show highlights couples' epiphanies about their relationships and lets us know that when wives trade places families can improve.

Dahlia Lithwick of Slate.com describes *Wife Swap* as a show that allows the viewer to both escape her home and family, and to make them over. Having learned that it's impossible to achieve a perfect balance of home, kids, and jobs, *Wife Swap* offers women a chance to escape from the constraints of their own "impossible choices, and an opportunity to completely remodel someone else's." Watching another woman on television who has utterly failed to "have it all" with her own family, then switching lives with another woman who has also failed at this, is fobbed off on us as entertainment. The husbands on *Wife Swap* "are almost universally caught sitting on couches, looking expectant. They rarely step up to show their new 'wives' the ropes, or suggest any sort of household partnership. It's not because these men are lazy," Lithwick explains, but simply because it is made clear to us that home is still the province of women.

Although many women on the show have paid jobs outside the home, many do not. And even if they do, it doesn't matter. The whole premise of the show relies on the assumption that a woman's place is in the home. Their paid jobs are often hushed up or avoided, which means that *Wife Swap* only shows half the lives of the wives. In other episodes, women's jobs become a focal point of the program and incentive for attacks on wage-earning mothers. British writer Natasha Forrest comments that the preoccupation with cleaning — does she do it too much or not enough? — functions to create more and more excuses to keep women indoors and certainly reinforces the notion that housekeeping is a woman's job. As Lithwick points out, in the world of *Wife Swap*, and in the lives it emulates and reinforces, whether we're a "'neat' family, a 'rules' family, a 'fun' family, or a 'takeout food' family, still depends mainly on mom's choices." What's more, mom is unremittingly heterosexual.

Virtually all of the episodes of *Wife Swap* feature heterosexual families. The exception is one show featuring a lesbian couple. The good news is that this single episode creates a small fissure in the hegemony of heteronormative prime-time television. The possibility that we might continue to see loving, caring same-sex couples on network television is expanded ever so slightly. The Gay and Lesbian Alliance Against Defamation (GLAAD) applauded *Wife Swap* for its February 9, 2005, episode that centered on lesbian mom Kristine Luffey who traded families with heterosexual mom Kris Gillespie — who is also a conservative Christian.

Here again, though, is an instance of the media giving with one hand while taking away with the other. The end of this episode culminates in a face-off between the two couples with Gillespie insinuating that her 12-year-old daughter's safety was at risk because a lesbian was living in her home. GLAAD argued that the public benefits by seeing the prejudice that many same-sex families face in everyday life. Perhaps. But where some might be horrified by Gillespie's homophobia, homosexist viewers may find reinforcement for their misguided beliefs about same-sex partnership. This episode of *Wife Swap* cannot alone tip the scales of public opinion in favor of same-sex families. It might help, but it's not enough. And one lesbian couple notwithstanding, *Wife Swap* is still premised on the idea that women are wives, that wives come with children, and that women can be traded like baseball cards — or baseball players, for that matter.

The setup for *Wife Swap* is that two women trade places for two weeks. To make the show entertaining, they're chosen from extremely different backgrounds. In one episode, for example, a gun-toting Southern matriarch is swapped for an anti–NRA animal-rights activist. For the first week in her new life, the swapped wife has to follow her new family's rules. During the second week New Wife gets to run the show and begins to impose her own rules on the household. The Reveal takes place when the wives are returned to their rightful partners and the two couples sit down to discuss the experience. The two-week encounter causes both families to confront their spoken and unspoken expectations of partnership and parenthood. This meeting is the time for exploring what they learned from the process, what they could accept, and what they insist must be changed.

If we know that *Wife Swap* is taking away with its one hand, what positive messages could a show like this possibly provide with the other? First, there is the slight chance that *Wife Swap* might subvert heteronormative dominance. Second, by the end of the show, some people really do seem willing to rethink their relationships. Husbands may come to realize they've been dumping the housework on their wives. Wives recognize the value of spending time with their children instead of offloading the job onto the nanny. One wife realizes that her compulsive shopping is selfish and hurts her family while another wife comes to understand that her children appreciate a shopping spree at the toy store now and then. Third, where generations of women have struggled with awesome challenges regarding childcare, work, and home, *Wife Swap* hints that we might learn a lot from how other women address these choices. However, when the couples reconvene after the swap to rehash their experiences, these promising features are quickly overshadowed by gendered accusations that are lobbed about like so many wet diapers.

This segment is predictably confrontational if not humiliating, and emphasizes what Kathleen Collins calls the "talk-show confessional therapy" aspect of the show in which everyone airs their grievances (23). The woman who doesn't listen enough to her husband is chastised. The woman with an unclean home is berated. The woman who doesn't get sole satisfaction from her family is told that she should. Instead of using the conversation at the end of the show as a chance to strengthen the bonds of sisterhood, the television editing process ensures that wives are shown as blaming each other and pointing out the other's flaws. Like a verbal mudfight, they attack each other's lifestyle choices and angrily defend their own, notes Forrest.

Each woman walks a fine line between being crowned Good Mommy or Bad Mommy. The moral of the story in this modern fable is that a good woman is a compassionate wife and mother. She is physically available for her children. She bakes cookies. She meets her family's emotional needs. She doesn't shop too much — that would mean she's selfish. But she does shop just enough to let her husband and kids know she cares about them. She cleans her house (because she is sanitary and hygienic), but she doesn't clean it too much (which would mean she's rigid and obsessive). By talking with her husband she tends to his emotional needs. But she's careful not to be overly chatty. That would make her husband henpecked and prove she's a nag. Apparently, the double-bind of oppression is still alive and unwell (Lithwick 2004; Frye 1983). .

Extreme Makeover: Home Edition

Extreme Makeover: Home Edition (ABC) is a home remodeling show featuring Ty Pennington and his Home Design Team. The show begins with Ty behind a blowhorn "surprising" the deserving family who is about to receive a massive home renovation. The Reveal takes place about a week later when Ty, The Team and family, friends, and neighbors gather to see the revamped home. With money and good, old-fashioned elbow grease the ugly duckling house becomes a swan.

Gender-role stereotypes remain largely intact on *Extreme Makeover*. Pink is for girls; blue is for boys. Girls quietly contemplate, serenely gaze at their reflections, and gently play dress-up. Boys rock out, love cars, and mess around with electronic gear. It's a classic example of Simone de Beauvoir's thoughts on the gendered aspects of imminence and transcendence, being and doing.

Rare is the gender-neutral or gender-transgressive home makeover on this show. A little girl who dreams of becoming a ballerina comes home to find her room transformed into a dance studio complete with ballet barre, mirror, and pink tulle. A teenage boy who loves music is outfitted with a guitar-themed bedroom. His sister finds a pastel butterfly flitting across the wall of hers.

The Design Team re-fashions every room in the house by taking into consideration the hopes, dreams, aspirations, and special needs of each family member. A young-adult paraplegic, for example, is outfitted with a wheelchair-accessible apartment adjacent to the family home that provides him with the autonomy and independence he's been wanting so badly. His mother no longer has to help him into the shower. He can comfortably join his family for dinner at the newly fitted dining table.

In each episode, the family chosen is proven to be a worthy recipient for a home makeover. For instance, one show features a patriotic vet from the Iraq War. A second involves a Los Angeles couple crowded into a small house after adopting nieces and nephews who were orphaned when their parents were killed by random gang violence. One woman struggled to keep her family intact after becoming widowed by her husband's premature death. Another family adopted special-needs kids and wanted to accommodate their range of physical abilities.

Surely, these are all worthy recipients. But the question is *who was not chosen to be on the show?* Embedded in this ode to consumerism is the implicit message that some people are *worthy* of change and assistance and others are *unworthy;* in other words, some people are simply better. This has pernicious implications.

On *Extreme Makeover: Home Edition* we do not see immigrant day-laborers struggling to meet the needs of life with cash paid under the table. We do not see family members facing serious drug or alcohol problems. Nobody is a gang member underserved by the schools and living in substandard housing. We see the mother who's been laid off after years on the job, but we do not see the unemployed who have a series of low-income jobs or who have simply given up looking. The unspoken message is that if these folks are not getting on the show then perhaps they are not worthy or deserving of our help.

The idea that we can divide potential recipients of community and social support into worthy and unworthy classifications has a long history in American society. It means that we think certain people deserve our help because they have needs through no fault of their own. The others are people whom society judges for making themselves poor by allegedly not trying hard enough, by doing illicit drugs, or by choosing to have too many children. Left out of these assumptions is any critical analysis of how institutions, race, class, gender, and prejudice convene to produce and reproduce need and poverty in our society. We look away from the complicated social, political, and individual forces at work here. Instead, the story left intact by *Extreme Makeover* is that moral people (who try really hard) deserve our help; immoral people (who are lazy) do not. *Extreme Makeover* reinforces this idea as much through its omission — whom they do *not* choose for the show — as much as by showing us the worthy recipients who *are* selected for a home remodel.

In a parallel story, by selecting construction crews implicitly portrayed as native born or English-speaking, *Extreme Makeover: Home Edition* leaves out of the picture the work of thousands of poor immigrants who actually do this type of work each day. In the current wave of immigration into the United States, most migrants are Hispanic and they are the ones providing the physical work that has remodeled so many homes across the country. But *Extreme Makeover* disregards this, essentially making the immigrant laborers invisible. Out of sight, out of mind is the point made (Lagunas 2007).

These stories about worthiness and socioeconomic status, and about visibility and invisibility, that are told through *Extreme Makeover* easily dovetail with prejudiced views about skin privilege and ethnicity. When these factors merge, they feed into the already racist imagination of what bell hooks refers to as the White Supremacist Capitalist Patriarchy (hooks). We know our society creates a disproportionate number of Black and Latino working class and poor. Therefore, reinforcing ideas about who is worthy or unworthy of aid is particularly dangerous. With Hurricane Katrina, we saw a public that was willing to help the so-called deserving in need — such as those who sat politely on their rooftops waiting for help. But too many of the American public quickly rejected the idea of helping others they thought behaved badly. Rumors of looting in the streets and mayhem in the Superdome were enough to deem entire groups of people undeserving of assistance. These folks were blamed for their own problems, or at least for lacking the self-control to prevent matters from getting worse.

Of course *Extreme Makeover* is a far cry from disaster in the Gulf Region. The provocative parallel, however, is the unspoken process of sifting and sorting entire groups of people into the worthy good and the unworthy (or even demonized) bad. The invisibility of this process on *Extreme Makeover* contributes to the ideological tools of domination that played out so harshly after Hurricane Katrina and that continue to impact the politics of everyday life.

*   *   *

In the end, television makeover and swap shows provide powerful stories about the potential for personal transformation. Who might we — the participant-voyeurs — become after pretending for an hour that we've been the ones who were made-over, made-up, or traded in? How many of us rethink our relations by pretending that other people are watching like they do on *Wife Swap*? I know that I get an urge to rearrange the sofa cushions and repaint the living room walls after watching *Extreme Makeover*. I've definitely weeded through my closet and tossed out lumpy sweaters thinking how proud Stacy and Clinton would be. When I shop for clothes I play a private little game with myself called *What Not to Wear*. And I'm pretty sure I'm not the only one who's doing it. The point is, television makeover shows seep easily into our daily lives. Along with them come these common themes of commodity and consumerism.

What we learn from makeover shows is that becoming new and whole and realizing our maximum potential is facilitated by a Sears home appliance (the sponsor of *Extreme Makeover*) and Crest White Strips (the sponsor of *What Not to Wear*), along with the many other consumer items that we oddly crave after watching these shows. In the case of *Wife Swap*, women *are* the commodities being traded, and transformation becomes possible via this transaction. The consumerist story embedded in television makeover shows is that transformation and realizing one's true human potential can be bought at the store. This creation of false wants and needs helps keep capitalism moving its goods and services at a rapid pace around the globe. We know that with the feminization of poverty and sweatshop labor, these issues matter in women's lives. With the restrictive messages about gender and the pressures to conform, these issues matter for men, as well.

It is fair to say that that pop culture television gives to us with one hand. And the possibility remains that it could give to us much more in the future. If the media has improved from what it used to be, there is still, however, a long way to go. With millions of people watching shows like *What Not to Wear*, *Wife Swap*, and *Extreme Makeover: Home Edition*, these become powerful vehicles for transmitting hegemonic ideals. While it's true that pop culture can function to distract us from serious political struggles taking place around the world, it is also the case that pop culture embodies real political struggles of its own. And where pop culture is itself an instrument of power and domination, it's important that we understand the ideological mechanisms at work.

BIBLIOGRAPHY

Beauvoir, Simone de. *The Second Sex.* Trans. H.M. Parshley. 1952. New York: Vintage Books, 1989.

Collins, Kathleen. "Compromising Positions: Gender by Design on *Merge* and *Mix It Up*." *Bitch* 23 Dec. 2003: 21–24.

Douglas, Susan. *Where the Girls Are: Growing Up Female with the Mass Media.* New York: Three Rivers Press, 1995.

Extreme Makeover: Home Edition. ABC. Exec. prod. Denise Cramsey, Tom Forman. 15 Feb. 2004–.

Forrest, Natasha. "Wife Swap." 16 Feb. 2003. 21 Dec. 2007. <http://www.thefword.org. uk/reviews/2003/02/wife_swap>.

Frye, Marilyn. *The Politics of Reality: Essays in Feminist Theory.* Freedom, CA: Crossing Press, 1983.

Herman, Edward S., and Noam Chomsky. *Manufacturing Consent: The Political Economy of the Mass Media.* New York: Pantheon Books, 2002.

hooks, bell. *Cultural Criticism & Transformation.* Dir. Sut Jhally. VHS. Northampton, MA: Media Education Foundation, 1997.

Lagunas, Oscar. Unpublished Paper. Dec. 18, 2007.

Lithwick, Dahlia. "Girls Just Wanna Be Swapped: Why Post-Feminist Women Enjoy *Trading Spouses* and *Wife Swap*." 30 Sept. 2004. 21 Dec. 2007 <http://www.slate.com/ id/2107510>.

Parenti, Michael. *The Culture Struggle.* New York: Seven Stories Press, 2005.

Schor, Juliet. *The Overspent American: Why We Want What We Don't Need.* Ed. Kelly Garner. DVD. Northampton, MA, 2004.

What Not to Wear. TLC. Ex. prod. Abigail Harvey. 18 Jan. 2008–

Wife Swap. ABC. Ex. prod. Michael Davies, Stephen Lambert. 29 Sept. 2004–.

Revealing Western Norms of Gender Identity in *What Not to Wear*

Idealizing Femininity in Visual Culture to Win the "War on Terror"

ELLEN W. GORSEVSKI

"People size up your patriotism by how you act. It is very simplistic to believe fashion is trivial."
— Katell le Bourhis of the Costume Institute at the
Metropolitan Museum of Art, New York

I will begin this chapter with an experience I had with an assignment I gave students while I was teaching an upper division college course in communication and gender. In using Julia Wood's text *Gendered Lives: Communication, Gender, and Culture*, I had asked the students to respond to a discussion prompt on respecting differences among cultures. To my surprise, instead of taking the assigned reading as a means to appreciate international and intercultural differences in expressions of femininity, several students commented, in effect, that they were "glad to be in America where women aren't repressed by having to be covered up by a *burqa* like women in many Middle Eastern countries are." It got me thinking: what prompted this rather uniform, ignorant, and xenophobic response from students who were supposed to be increasing their understanding and respect for difference between and among women in all their glorious diversity, domestically and internationally? Why did the veil, also called the *hijab*, or in its long form the *burqa*, seem to stand out for students as a symbol of their belief of how repressed women are purported to be under Islam? I also wondered how the *not* wearing of the *hijab* or *burqa* became for these students equally a symbol of freedom because they remarked that American women did not have to suffer this alleged "indignity" of having to be covered. By extension, this caused me to ponder that as avid television watchers and absorbers of popular culture, how and why do Americans maintain such stereotypical views of gendered representations of femininity and freedom? In mulling over these questions, scholars have reported how certain kinds of images or television shows reiterate and confirm dominant discourses and political ideologies that foster the circumscribed views my students expressed (Droogsma; Cloud; Fisk). Such imagery via photography and television shows is highly situated in the current geopolitical context (Cloud 286; Droogsma 294–295).

In a time of national crisis, with America's global War on Terror featuring two bloody, and by many standards losing, wars in Afghanistan and Iraq, television programming has turned forcefully to celebrating cathartic themes: one theme features savvy, high-tech crime sleuths solving mysterious, gory murders (shows in the *CSI* genre); the other theme features actual and symbolic gore occurring through the purposeful reconstruction of one's appearance via plastic surgery, home renovation, or the destruction and subsequent reconstruction of a person's (or a group's) wardrobe, hairdo, makeup, and personality.

This chapter will focus on this latter form of programming that has become an increasingly popular staple of prime-time television: the wardrobe makeover. In particular, the popular program, *What Not to Wear* will be analyzed from a rhetorical-critical perspective to reveal the power of visual rhetoric to be cathartic and galvanizing to popular conceptualizations of feminine gender identity, which in turn serves to solidify and strengthen the collective national identity during these uncertain times (Cloud 300). This chapter will explore the transformative potential for unifying national identity that occurs when viewers watch a representative individual become engendered in a more feminine and archetypal way. The viewers see the person who is represented, in a series of highly edited scenes, as someone who is working through deeply embedded psychological crises and lowered levels of self-confidence that constitute the direct result of an unfashionable wardrobe. For viewers of this process, the individual's journey becomes a metaphor for the nation's crisis of confidence and its ability to prevail. Television accomplishes this sense of triumph through mainly visual rhetorical means.

First, I will describe the basic plot of a typical episode of the program, establishing the conceit for the ranking of the marked individual. Second, I will establish how this kind of popular program operates ideologically by offering a review of key literature on mediated and televisual imagery as it relates to ideology. Third, the ideological significance of the veil, conflated in the American context to include both the *hijab* (headscarf) and the *burqa* (the garment covering a woman's entire body from the top of her head to her calves or sometimes on down over her feet). Finally, conclusions about this program and its ideological significance as it is representative of the broader genre of television makeover programs will be offered. I argue this program — and the entire genre of makeover programs that it represents — works through a process of unconscious persuasion to galvanize American political support for the War on Terror.

The Generic Formula of What Not to Wear

Like many programs in its genre, *What Not to Wear* (hereafter referred to as *WNTW*) employs a familiar formula. This formula stems from earlier American narratives such as the *Wizard of Oz*. The film scene of Dorothy being made over in Oz is steeped in the American psyche, so it is easily played out on television: An unfashionable, insecure person is whisked off to a glamorous location — in *WNTW* it is New York City — to undergo the dramatic and emotional process of becoming remade as fashionable and newly self-confident. *WNTW* is similar to other programs in its genre, such as *Queer Eye for the Straight Guy*, or *Ambush Makeover*. *WNTW* also shares themes with related contest programs such as *American Idol, Dancing with the Stars*, or *America's Next Top Model*, in which a nerdy, badly dressed unknown (*Idol*), an out of shape has-been celebrity (*Dancing*), or an awkward beauty (*Top Model*) becomes remade and refashioned with the help of a phalanx of experts such as dietitians, trainers, fashion stylists, plus hair and make-up experts.

In this genre of televised makeovers, the marked individual, usually a woman, is led in her transformation by the modern fashion equivalent of the Good Witch Glenda character from *The Wizard of Oz*: the charming, witty, handsome hosts of the program. In *WNTW* the hosts are the gay man and straight woman duo, Clinton Kelly and Stacy London. The significance of the sexuality of the hosts is that the conversational styles of a gay man and a straight woman would typically be aimed at feminine gendered speech communities (Wood 123). Also, Kelly and London are assisted, much like Dorothy's team of Tin Man, Scarecrow, and Cowardly Lion, by other supporting cast members: a hairstylist, Nick Carrojo, and a make-up artist with a single name (like Cher or Madonna), dubbed Carmindy. The program begins with the unfortunate woman's friends identifying her as unfashionable and in desperate need of a makeover. Her friends have already ranked her as a fashion zero. Once marked as such, she is tailed by a secret paparazzo who films her doing everyday things in public like eating or shopping, while wearing her unfashionable outfits and hairdo. The woman is presented in specific categories of unstylishness, such as Michele, who is "trapped in the 1980s" ("*WNTW*: Michele"). Numerous other categories of outmoded dress include ones such as the too- casual-youthful dresser who is in dire need of more professional garb for law or medical school; or the sloppy grad student who is headed for a job but whose clothes do not reflect professionalism; or the deluded woman who dresses in clothes that are too large or too small for her body size or type. The show thrives on humor, such as this comment: "Laurie wears baggy clothes that make her look old and disheveled.... [She] also has a mullet she hasn't cut in 15 years" ("*WNTW*: Favorite Makeovers"). Typical of the show's humor, the undertone here is a class-based dig at working class women with unfashionable hairdos and clothes.

Next, the marked woman is surprised by the sudden and unexpected appearance of Kelly and London, who inform her that if she agrees, she will be flown to New York and given a credit card she may use to spend five thousand dollars on a whole new wardrobe, plus she will get a new hairdo and make-up. The only catch is that the hapless woman must agree to bring *all* of the contents of her old wardrobe with her to be relinquished in exchange for the new clothes, hairdo and make-up. As in Michele's case, she may also have to have her cherished long locks chopped off short. The most humorous part of the program is the trash can scene. In this scene, *WNTW* employs the classic coercion technique from propaganda that Jacques Ellul refers to as the "struggle session," in which one's peers wheedle and cajole the marked individual into agreeing with their views, in this case, their views on fashion. In the "struggle session" presented in *WNTW*, the hosts, in a witty and sarcastic way, lampoon the woman as she tries on, models, and then is compelled to throw into a symbolic trash can all of the ugly, outdated clothes from her wardrobe. Whether the marked woman wears clothes that proclaim her to be a hippy, a punker, a preppy beach chick, a throwback to the 1980s, and so on, she will argue for the merits of her unfashionable looks, but this is an argument she will always lose.

Following this often quite comic-tragic scene, during which the viewer is invited to laugh at the poor woman as her eyes well up with tears in parting with her awful duds, which represent her soon-to-be-former timid self, the flamboyant and charismatic hosts, Kelly and London, coach her on the kinds of clothes and outfits that will better suit her body type, lifestyle, and

career. This coaching session functions like the Biblical self-sufficiency para-
ble of "give a man a fish and he can eat for one day; teach a man to fish and
he can feed himself for the rest of his life," albeit in the capitalistic context
it becomes "teach a woman to shop." So after she has been trained by the
fashion experts on what she should and should not wear, she is sent, again
tailed by a paparazzo's camera, to be filmed as she tries on and purchases her
new wardrobe, all while being spied on and drolly critiqued by Kelly and
London.

Finally, the woman gets a hair and make-up session and is then returned
to her friends and family to be revealed as a new, improved woman, free from
the shackles of her ugly, unfashionable former self. Not only are her wardrobe,
hair, and make-up positively changed, but so too has her personality been
emboldened. The viewer is led to believe that as a result of her external
makeover she has also become internally remade into a more confident, successful person. The implication is that she is now free to pursue a more full
and successful life both personally and professionally. Now that she has been
newly remade, *WNTW* concludes with the newfound *fashionista* twirling
about in her new get-up, the embodiment of American can-do gumption,
will power, and openness to change.

Nationalism, Femininity, and Freedom

How can such an apparently innocuous and vacuous plot, repeated
countless times with an endless array of badly dressed women, serve as a
strategic socio-cultural imperative to support a dominant political agenda?
Fashion has long been used as a tool of ideology and propaganda, especially
in wartime (Doonan; Kron 1–3). Nonetheless, writes Joan Kron, "The idea
of vanity during wartime makes many people uneasy. In a period of growing moral righteousness, many people question the propriety of talking about
fashion when ... missiles are flying and exploding before our eyes through
the magic of television" (1). Yet history bears out the importance of fashion
as a political tool during wartime. In France during World War II, for example, "being fashionable was also 'an act of rebellion,'" since it showed the
occupying German army that the French could not only make do, but actually thrive in conditions of great scarcity (Kron 2). Indeed, in 1941 fashion
served as a "morale builder"; British *Vogue*, for example, commanded its
readers: "Beauty is your duty" (Kron 2). Following World War II, the luxurious drape of full skirts exemplified the abundance of materials in the
United States and in much of Western Europe, thus serving as a political

contrast to the drab, uniform-like garb then popularly perceived by Westerners to be prevalent in Communist bloc nations such as Soviet Russia or China. During the Vietnam War era, the sexy go-go boots of the day symbolized the crushing of the Communist Viet Cong enemy, as sung by Nancy Sinatra in "These Boots Were Made for Walking." Today, during the War on Terror, fashion continues to be a means of showing strength and of expressing support for the troops abroad. Simon Doonan, an expert on American fashion, comments on the significance of the outfit worn by a major American journalist in Iraq:

> After watching [CNN's] Anderson Cooper's intrepid reports last week, I am totally convinced that there is room for style on the battlefield.... Gloria's [Vanderbilt's] handsome lad, while dodging bombs in Lebanon, became a style icon.... He looks so wickedly handsome and *au courant*! His preferred garments — a cobalt-blue sports shirt under a matte-black top-stitched bulletproof vest — have a definite whiff of the Belgian fashion designer Raf Simons or vintage Helmut Lang about them. As a result, Mr. Cooper gets my fashion-in-the-face-of-adversity award.

Thus fashion is firmly ensconced in the visual dialogue of the War on Terror. Whether it be dashing and courageous reporters in harm's way on the ground, or the rest of the populace trying to build morale back at the homeland by being more beautiful, fashion plays a role in the politics of how war is represented.

In its hour-long time slot, *WNTW* is able to offer a gender-specific narrative of strengthened and remade gender identity by taking a frumpy woman and transforming her into a feminine "super woman" archetype (Wood 179). Rhetorical analysis of the loser-to-winner narrative has implications for America's current climate of hyper-nationalism: *WNTW*'s final product, its fashionable woman, is the feminine version of men on television wearing the ubiquitous stars and stripes flag lapel pin. A woman's femininity is tied to her spirit of nationalism because by enacting the gender performance of fashion metamorphosis, she is ranked as being more American, more "free," and thus more desirable. The viewers of *WNTW* are drawn into a participatory process of ranking the woman who is being changed. For the viewer of programs like *WNTW*, ranking mere superficial clothing takes on an ideological meaning; a woman is seemingly being ranked on how truly American she is by what she wears and by the swagger that results from her newfound sartorial splendor.

The significance of the feminine transformation for national identity within the context of the post–9/11 years is subtle but clear: the dowdy woman casts off her ugly external baggage (sad clothes, obsolete hairstyle) to become confident and remade. The program invites viewers to now rank her as being replete with professional and personal potential, both superficially and — viewers are led to believe — substantively. National identity is gendered as the archetypal American woman; freedom is engendered as the ability to buy, wear, and do whatever she wants.

The impact of a feminine gendered visual rhetoric during a time of war is significant for ideology. Rhetorical scholar Dana Cloud has drawn on Michael Calvin McGee's work on the ideograph, which is a symbolic representation through words or imagery that advocates and reconfirms an ideology for audiences. "Either visual or verbal, an ideograph is a commonplace abstraction that represents collective commitment, it warrants power and guides behavior, and it is culture bound" (Cloud 288). Cloud has examined how the ideograph (a word represented inside brackets) of the <clash of civilizations> between a putatively modern West and a backwards Islam works rhetorically to galvanize audiences to support the current American political agenda (288). This discussion builds on Cloud's work by focusing more closely on the related ideograph of <freedom>.

For the feminine gendered side of the United States' national psyche, the freedom to transform one's self is a deeply empowering message because it exists in contradistinction to the stereotypical visual message for women of the Islamic and Arab world, particularly in places representing the ongoing War on Terror, such as Afghanistan, where women are often totally covered up by the *burqa*, the garment veiling women head to toe (Cloud 293). Thus the performative aspects of *WNTW* take on deeply cultural and political meanings. The role of the symbolic binary of veiled/unveiled for the ranking process in makeover programs needs to be understood in light of the highly pejorative connotations that being veiled tends to carry for Westerners (Cloud; Droogsma).

Veil = Oppression; Unveiled = <Freedom>

Because "clothing can be used as an experiment to study trends that reflect social and political attitudes," and since there is a "relationship between power and political influence on clothing," the importance of the literal and symbolic valence of the veil needs to be considered (Shirazi 116). Also, before addressing the significance of *WNTW* as an ideological tool that functions, albeit perhaps unintentionally, to bolster the homeland during the War on Terror, it is necessary to closely examine the social-psychological and ideological functions of the veil, *hijab*, or *burqa* as a symbol of oppression for many Westerners, and, in the case of the audience of *WNTW*, for Americans in particular. The veil, in the context of the War in Afghanistan, for example, symbolizes the oppression of women (Cloud 294). Drawn out further into a larger ideological context, the veil symbolizes "no freedom of consumer choice between one ... *burqa* and another" (Cloud 295). In the context of the War on Terror, the veil symbolizes both the personal, very individual lack of agency attributed to each woman who lives under a patriarchal Islamic state; at the same time, the veil "invites lamentation" because a veiled woman "exemplifies a pitiable absence of fashion choice in contrast to a modern conception of freedom as individual choice in the modern world of market capitalism" (Cloud 291–295). Thus in *WNTW*, the shopping sequence of the program functions as an ideological indicator to reassure viewers of America's modernity and capitalism. Being unveiled and having choice in fashion implies having <freedom>.

Conversely, wearing a veil "carries multiple meanings and interpretations" (Shirazi 115). The veil, especially in the context of the United States and the War on Terror, equates to a woman's somehow having the self-destructive attitude of choosing to be oppressed. The veiled woman functions rhetorically as one who perversely chooses what American ideology would characterize as what not to wear. For many Americans in the current political climate, the veil is a symbol of opposition to <freedom>. New research from Rachel Droogsma indicates that "since September 11, 2001, Muslim women in the United States who wear headscarves face greater scrutiny and suspicion due to a generalized fear of Muslims" (294). Indeed, reports Droogsma, for "Americans, the veil often represents a tangible marker of difference, in terms of religion and often ethnicity as well" (295). In addition to being a visible marker of religious or ethnic *Otherness*, "the *hijab* (Islamic headscarf) is an item of dress with immense political-sociological importance, as well as coded cultural significance" (Brown 105). Particularly in the Western context, for developed nations such as France, Germany, or the United States, much "opposition to the *hijab*" on the part of the populace stems from "xenophobic reaction or exclusion" (Brown 105). This sensibility of exclusion serves as one of the ranking criteria for viewers of makeover programs such as *WNTW*.

In *WNTW*, the symbolically loaded concept of the veil operates subconsciously to invite viewers to rank a woman's patriotism through her willingness to cast off her veil of ugly garb. The veil serves as a symbol and marker of all that is different or other, and therefore it is simply unpatriotic behavior to wear a veil, regardless of whether or not it is a real *hijab* or *burqa*, or if it is the Western equivalent of a veil: an ugly outfit compounded by bad hair and make-up. Thus a woman is rankable by audience members on the criteria of how veiled she is, or, in the program's closing sequence, how free she is from the figurative veil of ugliness.

The veil works both through metonymy and synecdoche. The metonymy of the veil is that a veiled woman stands in for an oppressed woman, such as the images of women that popular media have captured as representing the poverty and hardships of Muslim women in Afghanistan covered head to toe by the *burqa* (Cloud). The synecdoche of the veil is that a veiled woman is not doing her part as a vehicle for capitalism because she is not buying or wearing what she should: a new wardrobe to demonstrate she has kept up with fashion by wearing the latest trends and being a good consumer to feed the machine of capitalism. Thus the viewer of *WNTW* is invited to rank the marked woman at the start of the show as a woman veiled in ugliness and as a poor consumer, since she is not doing her patriotic duty. She starts out by figuratively scoring a zero. By the end of the program, however, the viewer is invited to see that a major transformation has occurred: The woman has cast off her symbolic veil through the literal trashing of her ugly wardrobe that stands in for the perceived political tyranny of the *burqa*. Thus she is shown to merit a higher ranking both as a fashionable, feminine woman and as a patriot.

One's patriotism is tied up in the performativity of one's gender, and in the case of *WNTW*, that gender is feminine. To be feminine, performing a feminine gendered style means going shopping and knowing what and how to make purchases. Likewise, ideologically, to perform a feminine gendered patriotism, the woman must do her modern capitalistic duty by shopping well. Indeed, "fashion is specific to capitalist economies, political practices and cultural formations" (Craik 7). Thus in *WNTW* the shopping scenes, which are both visually and emotionally engaging, invite the viewer to participate in the feminine gendered aspects of patriotism through shopping, the utmost vital activity of capitalism. One's patriotism is thus also ranked by viewers as one's ability to buy both correctly and in large quantities.

In addition, the white woman who is usually the show's chosen target is the symbolic representation of the Christian West. This archetypal woman is transformed through being updated into trendy fashion: she is the vehicle for American ideology of democracy and capitalism as it purports to modernize a behind-the-times Islamic world through military intervention and occupation. She casts off her psychic and physical *burqa*, her unfashionable covering of outmoded attire that is portrayed and perceived by society to be ugly and hurtful to her identity and sense of self confidence, and therefore, to her agency; in casting it off she thus becomes empowered. This process of the transformative enactment of <freedom> on the part of the individual undergoing this change is highly participatory and framed to be cathartic for the viewers of *WNTW*. As Dana Cloud says, "Women's oppression is a marker of an inferior society" (289), hence when the individual is shown to have the <freedom> to be remade, she is casting off the oppression of her unfashionable dress, her symbolic *burqa*, thereby enacting the highly ideological presupposition of the superiority of American culture and society through its ability to continually improve and remake itself, even as it expands itself through occupation of foreign lands and domination over their obstreperous peoples. Just as such transformation through "images possesses the capacity for visceral emotional appeal" (Cloud 290), so the televised process of a woman's transformation in *WNTW* becomes all the more engaging for viewers.

Conclusion

WNTW and other shows in its genre serve an ideological function by representing the feminine gendered side of the American archetype. The buffeted national consciousness of crisis and malaise — as body counts of American soldier casualties in Iraq and Afghanistan continue to rise — is deconstructed and reconstructed. The feminine gendered identity of America's super body politic, in the form of a now super woman, is made whole again. America, as a gendered concept symbolized through the visual rhetoric of feminine archetypes such as the Statue of Liberty, is strengthened as a republic. In the absence of the masculine, dual phallic symbols of New York's Twin Towers that were traumatically destroyed on 9/11, the stalwart, reassuring feminine symbol of the Statue of Liberty took precedence in the media's reconstruction of a healing America. Shows like *WNTW* endlessly repeat the visual destruction and reconstruction process, repeating and confirming the ideological notion that the feminine side of American society, along with associated politics, stands strong. The rhetorical narrative subtext is that, unlike her masculine symbolic counterpart, the Twin Towers, Lady Liberty survived 9/11 and continues to be a beacon of democracy for immigrants and for millions of persons under her symbolic and political aegis in lands like Iraq and Afghanistan that are occupied by American forces.

Makeover programs such as *WNTW* serve as vehicles through which a weakened national sensibility and loss of confidence is remade through the symbolic makeover of an average but representative American woman. The

undercurrent of pro–Western rhetoric that constitutes an anti–Muslim ideology is upheld and normalized. The White, Christian woman archetype is
held up as the gendered identity norm for America as a symbolically gendered being. Lady Liberty is not shrouded head-to-toe in a *burqa*, but rather,
she is remade as a sexy, empowered vixen. Her agency in her realm, the world
stage, is thus symbolically reconstructed. <Freedom> as ideograph is
reconfirmed not just by what a woman wears, but rather by what she actively
chooses not to wear, with requisite prodding and witty verbal hazing by the
show's hosts.

In *WNTW*, the symbol of the veil, "despite [its] complex meanings" in
terms of "historical and anthropological research" is reduced to a mere symbol of oppression; "Dominant conceptions of veiling assume that *hijab* functions to oppress women" (Droogsma 295). *WNTW* along with programs in
its shared makeover genre — however unwittingly — use ugly fashion as a
subtle, subtextual but nonetheless ideological metaphor for the veil and all
of the presupposed backwardness that such entailments of Islam are represented through dominant discourses to engender. Because "clothing plays a
vital role in displaying one's identity to others" (Droogsma 296), the veil
therefore plays an equally important role in confirming and reassuring one's
identity as a consumer, a citizen, and, in a capitalist market context in which
purchasing power reveals political power, a patriot (Cloud 295). For "many
Americans ... images of veiled women ... justify their belief in the inferiority and barbarism of Arabs" (Droogsma 296; see also Cloud 294–299; Steet).
Thus, the show invites the viewer to rank the initially poorly garbed, thus
veiled and oppressed woman, with a low score. The show concludes with
the newly made-over woman unveiling herself of her ungainly duds and
availing herself of trendy, fitting, fashionable vestments.

This happy ending crescendos in *WNTW* and other shows of its genre
with the "reveal," which is the television industry code word for the "unveiling" of the newly remade person. Ideologically speaking, it is no accident
that the word "reveal" is used by television industry executives, producers
and writers as a noun and not a verb. Examining the etymology of the word
as a noun, however, redirects us back to its more political meanings and origins as a verb: "circa 1375, from O.Fr. *reveler* (14c.), from Latin *revelare*
'reveal, uncover, disclose,' literary 'unveil,' from re- 'opposite of' + velare
'to cover, veil,' from velum 'a veil,' see *veil*" (Harper). The television lexi-
con of "reveal" serves an ideological function by actually being the "unveiling" of someone who had been not just physically or superficially an
unattractive person, she is also portrayed symbolically as having been an
"ugly" person. This newly refashioned woman is now remade through Amer-

ican socio-cultural power, which in turn is backed by its political might that is derived from its capital market strength and military puissance. The "reveal" is then the metaphorical "unveiling" of the stand-in for the stereotypical "evil Arab" who lurks deep within the American subconscious (Steet). This narrative proceeds through the familiar, *Wizard of Oz* formula that reiterates American can-do power. In this narrative, through the good witch's superpowers, the "Arab evil" is displaced symbolically by the feminine "good Christian" archetype. Over the course of the program, the marked woman becomes a good Western woman standing strong. She has engendered the "super woman" archetype (Wood), thus fulfilling the rhetorical need for transcendence and supremacy that is characteristic of the "anti–Arab" ideology of the War on Terror (Droogsma 296).

In this manner viewers of *WNTW* are invited to rank the woman initially as being unfashionable = un–American = unfree and then participate in the visual and "visceral" pleasure of the unfolding process through which she becomes unshrouded as she casts off the symbolically metaphorical and highly visual, palpable veil, *hijab* or *burqa* of ugly garb. The culmination of the program arrives at the final ranking of the woman, who now is fashionable in the following equation: fashionable = American = free. So ultimately she embodies <freedom>. The ideological twist is complete at the end of the program when the viewers compare her old, hideously swaddled and unfree self to her now contentedly free self. She has been freed from the fetters of her former fashion *faux pas*. Ideologically, the visual rhetoric of *WNTW* functions to render the woman being remade as an archetypal American everywoman. As such, the finally free and fashionable woman engenders American <freedom>. As ideographic symbol, she then embodies the political and ideological agenda to create "mass public support for the war" (Cloud 290).

Dana Cloud has shown how highly emotional photographic images in *Time* magazine have functioned to illustrate a "before-and-after sequence that suggests that before the U.S. attacks" as part of the War on Terror, Muslim women "wandered in chaos or lived, invisible and indistinct, at the mercy and discretion of irrational and autocratic men," and, following the U.S. interventions abroad, the women have become free (294). These before-and-after images reaffirm that as Muslim women have been "unveiled," the logical conclusion must be that American intervention provides <freedom> to women of Islam (294). Likewise, just as the before-and-after formula works visually in the *Time* photographs in Cloud's study, so, too, does the before-and-after sequence in *WNTW* function to highlight <freedom>.

The highly visual rhetorical framing of the War on Terror has created a rhetorical climate of highly charged political stakes. As Americans and as television viewers, we can no longer sit back and enjoy watching a "guilty pleasure" makeover program such as *WNTW*, thinking that it is merely a pleasant but value-free diversion. For the subtle ideological subtext of the program, while ostensibly inviting viewers to rank people as merely and trivially unfashionable or fashionable, in actuality serves a darker political and rhetorical purpose. It serves to engender patriotism by calling for American women to perform citizenship through acts of shopping that help foster political aims. In the genre of programs such as *WNTW*, the feminine version of an American patriot is embodied by the "reveal" of a newly "unveiled" woman. Ironically, by having her spackle on gobs of make-up and undergo torturous hours of hair cutting, dyeing, curling or straightening, as well as an emotional "struggle session" to "teach" (reprogram) her fashion sense, the viewer is invited to see this fake woman as somehow a representative of a bona fide American woman. She perfectly embodies the American myth of being able to buy happiness.

As a tool of ideology, makeover programs such as *WNTW* are highly persuasive. Repetition, which, according to Jacques Ellul, is a hallmark of propaganda, enables the ruse to slip by unnoticed. Each time we see a new woman remade we are being slowly inculcated and implicated more deeply into the War on Terror's ideology. Each time viewers see a new "her" recreated before their eyes, they are invited to see her as a bright new self, not as someone all covered up in a superficial way. Likewise, each time viewers see her covered in trendy clothes, make-up, and hairspray, they are invited to avert their eyes to the fact that this is simply just another form of *hijab* or *burqa*, albeit a Western one. Feminist scholars have argued that being culturally enslaved to fashion and make-up, and in more extreme cases plastic surgery, is no less oppressive to women than having to wear the veil (El Guindi; Wood). The increasing use by American women of Botox to smooth wrinkles, and the epidemic of their choosing to use plastic surgery to be fashionable is elided in makeover programs by a discourse of make-up and wardrobe as acceptable "modern" veiling leading to <freedom>. The message is that American women are urged to enact their <freedom> to reshape their bodies through at the least destructive end, uncomfortable and expensive fashion (*WNTW*) and, at the most destructive end, violent and bloody chopping, cutting, suctioning from, or, insertion of unhealthy silicone implants into their bodies (*Nip/Tuck*). All this painful activity is done so American women may conform to Western socio-cultural norms of beauty. The popularity of euphemizing such socio-cultural violence against women in terms such as "enhancements" is a testament to the strength of makeover programs and their ideological rhetorics that sway vulnerable populations to at minimum, spend a lot of money on superficial trappings, and at worst, risk life threatening surgeries to achieve a fleeting and unrealistic ideal of beauty. The recent plastic-surgery death of Donda West, the mother of rap music star Kanye West, is just another reminder of the casualties of 'beautification' whose numbers mount each year.

Orthopraxy, that is, the urging of the masses to behave in similar ways, is also a highly persuasive activity (Ellul). In the case studied in this chapter, orthopraxy includes activities such as watching the same popular television shows, ranking other people in the same culturally prescribed ways, and shopping for the same trendy fashions. In the wake of 9/11 and in the context of the ensuing politics of the War on Terror, the actual freedoms of Americans are shrinking: the freedom to maintain personal privacy, to travel by airplane without being searched, to have internet and phone communications go unexamined. Yet the dominant discourses of popular television preferences and ranking systems for beauty and social acceptability encourage us to look the other way. Our <freedom> as Americans to pursue these activities without reflection bears further inquiry. Future research beckons scholars to observe how other social practices are represented in media in ways that serve to confirm or resist ideology.

BIBLIOGRAPHY

Brown, Malcom. "Multiple Meanings of the 'Hijab' in Contemporary France." *Dressed to Impress: Looking the Part*. Ed. William Keenan. New York: Berg, 2001. 103–105.

Cloud, Dana. "To Veil the Threat of Terror: Afghan Women and the Clash of Civilizations in the Imagery of the U.S. War on Terrorism." *Quarterly Journal of Speech* 90 (Aug. 2004): 285–306.

Craik, Jennifer. *The Face of Fashion: Cultural Studies in Fashion*. New York: Routledge, 1994.

Doonan, Simon. "Anderson's Wartime *Chic* Is *De Trop* on Wall Street." *The New York Observer Online*. 30 Jul. 2006 <http://www.observer.com/node/52488>.

Droogsma, Rachel A. "Redefining Hijab: American Muslim Women's Standpoints on Veiling." *Journal of Applied Communication Research* 35 (Aug. 2007): 294–319.

Edwards, Janis L., and Carol K. Winkler. "Representative Form and the Visual Ideograph: The Iwo Jima Image in Editorial Cartoons." *Quarterly Journal of Speech* 83 (1997): 289–310.

El Guindi, Fadwa. *Veil: Modesty, Privacy, and Resistance*. New York: Berg, 1999.

Ellul, Jacques. *Propaganda: The Formation of Men's Attitudes*. New York: Vintage, 1973.

Fiske, John. "Television: Polysemy and Popularity." *Critical Studies in Mass Communication* 3 (Dec. 1986): 391–408.

Harper, Douglas. "Reveal." *Online Etymology Dictionary*. Nov. 2001 <http://www.etymonline.com/index.php?search=reveal&searchmode=none>.

"Kanye West's Mom Dies after Surgery: 58-Year-Old Had Cosmetic Procedures After One Surgeon Refused to Operate." MSNBC.com. 30 January 2008 <http://www.msnbc.msn.com/id/21742159/>.

Kron, Joan. "When Beauty Was a Duty." *The New York Times Online Archive*. Feb. 1991 <http://query.nytimes.com/gst/fullpage.html?res=9D0CE5D8153DF93BA35751C0A967958260>.

McGee, Michael C. "The Ideograph: A Link Between Rhetoric and Ideology." *Quarterly Journal of Speech* 66 (1980): 1–16.

"Our Favorite Makeovers: Laurie Pratt." *What Not to Wear*. TLC. 30 January 2008 <http://tlc.discovery.com/fansites/whatnottowear/bestof/mostshocking/mostshocking.html>.

Shirazi, Faegheh. "Islamic Religion and Women's Dress Code: The Islamic Republic of Iran." *Undressing Religion: Commitment and Conversion from a Cross-Cultural Perspective*. Ed. Linda B. Arther. New York: Berg, 2000. 113–116.

Steet, Linda. *Veils and Daggers: A Century of National Geographic's Representation of the Arab World*. Philadelphia: Temple, 2000.

"*What Not to Wear*: Michele." TLC. 3 Dec. 2007 <http://shopping.discovery.com/product-65564.html >.

Wood, Julia. *Gendered Lives: Communication, Gender, and Culture*. Belmont, CA: Thompson Wadsworth, 2007.

15

Reality Television, Body Cult and Identity Metamorphosis in Brazil and the United States

BIANCA FREIRE-MEDEIROS
AND ANDRÉ BAKKER

As reality shows escape rigid aesthetic agendas and blend elements from different genres — melodrama and documentary, talent contest and news, game shows and music videos — they provoke analytical, commercial and financial instabilities. Blooming from the convergence of new media technologies and what Alain Badiou framed as a "passion for the real" (35), reality television redefines debates on the ethical boundaries which separate pedagogical curiosity from voyeurism, educational documentation of ordinary interactions from social control. It eloquently expresses a present fascination for the "authentic" and "true" which, although not being completely original*, acquires a distinctive aura in our contemporary world. This "passion for the real" which reality shows stand for has accompanied not only TV, but also cinema since its origin, finding a privileged expression in the documentary genre.

The popularity of reality-based programming is by no means limited to U.S. or European broadcasting, and in fact, most of these shows are either imported or produced locally in different corners of the world. In Brazil, *No Limite*, adapted from CBS's *Survivor*, is considered to be the first locally produced reality show. Nevertheless, the format found its greatest popularity

In order to apprehend "life as it is," post-war European directors have imposed on themselves the task of filming on location, without professional actors, with significant results, as in La Terra Trema (1943), Roma, Città Aperta (1946) or Ladri di Biciclette (1949). With the emergence of the portable cameras and the direct sound, those theoretical premises have found even more radical possibilities of realization in the so called American "direct cinema" and the French cinema verité.

amongst Brazilians not in the adventure but in the confinement sub-genre, with Endemol's *Big Brother* concept. Premiering on January 29, 2002, as *Big Brother Brasil,* the show has run for seven highly successful seasons, turning some of the participants into national celebrities.

This article focuses on the *makeover* genre, with special emphasis on two programs: *Extreme Makeover* (CBS) in the U.S. and *Buying Beauty* (Beleza Comprada, GNT/GloboSat) in Brazil. In both countries, a so-called "body cult"—featuring the adoption of certain rituals and artificial mechanisms considered adequate for achieving the goal of a "perfect body"—has become highly fashionable and several plastic surgery-centric shows can be seen on cable and satellite television. This is not surprising if one keeps in mind that the U.S. and Brazil are the world leaders as far as aesthetic surgeries are concerned: according to the Brazilian Society for Plastic Surgery, in the year 2000, 350,000 people went through at least one aesthetic surgery procedure, which means that in every 100,000 people, 207 were operated on for aesthetic purposes (Castro 7). Brazil is followed by the United States, where the rate is 185 people undergoing cosmetic surgery in every 100,000 (Castro 22).

Comparing *Extreme Makeover* and *Buying Beauty* invites discussion of how the relationship among the fragmentation of identity, the desire for distinction, and the media field plays out in those two cultural settings. Especially interesting is the way in which the new social arrangements, based on the expert systems, allow the reprogramming of the body and a supposed identity metamorphosis to be performed on TV.

The next section, which is based on the work of Giddens and Bourdieu, analyzes the role played by the media as one of the most influential cultural systems in terms of constructing identities and legitimating the knowledge issued by the "new experts" (personal trainer, stylist, dietician and so on). The ways in which reality shows act on claiming a body that is transformed from a container for the soul to a self-constituted, reformatable and reprogrammable entity are examined. Section three focuses on the content analysis of selected episodes of the two shows. This essay concludes with some remarks on the relationship between body cult and media in both countries.

Authorizing Beauty: Experts, Media and the Spectacle of Identity and Distinction

In contemporary society, identity is a transient project. As Peter Berger (60) points out, one does not know any longer what to expect from a person as a political leader, a parent, an educated person or what it means to be "sexually normal." In order to deal with the consequential anxieties, the "experts" emerge, telling the public how to live in the center of this kaleidoscope of fleeting roles.

To depict this general unsteadiness in institutional arrangements, truth regimes, ethics and aesthetics of present-day Western societies, Zygmunt Bauman suggested the allegory of "liquidity": post-modern subjectivities would be fluent, plastic, permanently impermanent. The self, asserts Richard Sennett (322) no longer implicates individuals as actors or makers: it is self composed of intentions and possibilities. This scenery of unbounded possibilities which subjects are faced with makes the self a "reflexive project," something to be unveiled in a self-discovery trajectory in which subjects must find their identities among the strategies and options supplied by the "Abstract Systems," as Giddens puts it (126). To this *subject in process* is imposed the quest for a distinctive, authentic and socially authorized image, giving birth to a structural dissatisfaction with what one is and an unsettling uncertainty as to what one seeks to be.

It has become an ordinary feature of urban subjects' everyday diet in different parts of the world to consume the advice of specialists in emotional skills and motivational speakers, as well as the *personal* in several guises: *trainer, stylist, dietician, tutor.* With a pragmatics of immediacy and an ethics of non-guiltiness, the specialists are invested with the authority to project, by the compositional effect of their partial counseling, what one needs to have and to know in order to acquire a socially legitimate image.

As to aesthetics, the "expert-media" systems duet seems to be the key underpinning force in the field's sustenance and reproduction.* Industries of cosmetics, gym clubs, weight control drugs, plastic surgery and fashion, with all their adjacencies, have become the legitimate instances for determining what *is* and what *is not* acceptable in aesthetic terms. Such determinations remain in permanent mediatic flow, forging and propagating images of desirable bodies existing only as simulacrum. This is particularly evident in the fashion industry, but is not exclusive to it. What is at stake here is a much wider field of professionals whose legitimacy is constructed less through their recognition among peers than through their exposure in media settings. It is in this sense that Bourdieu claims that television is an extraordinary instrument of symbolic violence, able to make-see and make-believe, to determine the selection procedure through which a given repertoire of

---

The notion of "aesthetic field" is hereby employed in reference to Pierre Bourdieu's understanding of social structure as a multidimensional space, constituted by relatively independent social fields — fields which are underpinned by different social practices, logics of sociability, strategies for social action and principles of legitimacy; in one word, by distinct habitus (Bourdieu, 1989, 1998).

significations acquires an aura of objectivity and legitimacy for the single fact of being transmitted to millions of spectators.

Obviously, discourses on ways of being in the world are produced and reproduced across several fields of knowledge and social practices, but they seem to acquire a distinct *aura of realness* when displayed in modern mass media. This formative, almost pedagogic, character of the cultural industry in the constitution of distinction signs has been explored by authors who depart from diverse theoretical premises and empirical motivations (Du Gay; Egan). At large, they seem to suggest that the media imagery provides a staple menu of principles of sociability, dramatize forms of thinking, acting, relating, and outline a basic cultural curriculum.

The massive presence of the *images of distinction* displayed in the media instills fascination, admiration, identification. The "community," this center of referential structures, steadily abandons its shared territoriality and historicity to bloom in virtual settings. Communities can now be groundless spaces with no common history, circumstantially edified around circles of identification ever more mercurial and unstable. The aesthetic community, which finds in the culture industry a privileged space for the constant (re)drawing of its negotiable structures, gains prominence over the ethical communities. And while the community deterritorializes itself and sees its historicity become dispensable, the body transforms from a container for the soul into a self-constituted, reformatable and reprogrammable entity. The corporeal reality is no longer conceived as a totality, but as an assembly of components which must reflect more the fluent verdicts of the aesthetic field and less the subjects' acquiescence. This conception of the body as an accumulation of components, a surface ripe for surgery and reprogramming, forms the premise for both *Extreme Makeover* and *Buying Beauty*.

REPROGRAMMABLE BODIES AND IDENTITIES

Broadcasted from December 2002 until it was officially cancelled in May 2007, *Extreme Makeover* promised "an authentic Cinderella experience," a "fairytale of real life," as its official website puts it. "Redo" the individual, reformulate his/her image and, as a natural consequence, forge another life and a new social identity: this is what *Extreme Makeover* promised to the thousands of men and women who auditioned for the show, flaunting their deformities, complaints and aspirations in a home video. The meta-narrative logic starts already in the selection procedure: the candidate to be chosen is the one who can better "sell" the image of someone whose deserved happiness is suspended by an aesthetical prejudice.

There are, however, exceptions in the selection procedure. Ray Krone, known for years as the "Snaggletooth Killer," was arrested for murder in 1991 due to the similarity between his unaligned teeth and the bite marks found in the victim. For his peculiar teeth structure, Krone spent ten years on death row until a DNA test proved his innocence. Bringing to paroxysm the idea that a wrong look leads to misery and unhappiness, without undergoing the regular selection process, Krone was invited by the show's staff to receive an extreme makeover. "We want a candidate whose appearance has affected his/her life in a deep, negative way," explained Louis Gorfain, executive producer of the program (*Extreme Makeover* home page). After a complete restoration of his teeth, a hair transplant, a face lift, a nose job and a cheek liposuction, Krone declared he was, for the first time, prepared to face life again.

The program usually presents two participants per episode. Beyond the regular aesthetic interventions, one of the participants demands surgeries for dealing with severe deformities. In both cases, the self-contemplative look and the testimonial-talk in front of the mirror reveal anxiety and apprehension. "This is the last time I see this face," said one of the participants in a tone blending relief and tension. Another participant sighed: "I cannot believe this day finally arrived ... I will finally become a woman." The mingling of apprehension and eagerness is expressed by those who, willing to "redo" their corporeal image and, consequently, reorganize the desire others may have upon looking at them, cannot avoid the fear of not recognizing themselves anymore, of losing sight of the traces which have hitherto guided their understanding of themselves. Still lying in the surgical bed and under the effect of anesthetic medicines, 38-year-old David, member of the American National Guard, shares with surgeons and spectators his deep uneasiness with the possibility of seeing himself as "a complete stranger."

Each surgical procedure is registered in high-speed plans, although with graphic details of extreme realism: the anesthetized body waiting for the surgeon's hands, the scalpel carving the skin, the tubes sucking blood and fat, the stitches, the face covered with gauze and hematomas. The face, conceived in classic cinema as a mystical, untouchable, almost sublime surface — Greta Garbo and Marlene Dietrich are obvious examples — emerges here precisely as the most "doable" part of the body, the locus where the most drastic interventions are to take place. Before a central reference of personality and social status, the face acquires a functional plasticity to be manipulated by the surgeon, who must remake it in accordance with the dominant aesthetic standards of Hollywood.

The scenic composition of the program is divided into two well demarcated territories: the place of origin of the candidate, recovered through simple framings which stress the domestic environment and bucolic landscapes, and the destiny where the elected individual is sent: Hollywood, the symbolic scenery of glamour where the stardom and all the fetishes structuring the spectacle universe circulate. Hair dressers, dentists, personal trainers, kissing tutors, stylists, psychologists and star surgeons who together form the luxurious "Extreme Team" are now gathered for the nobodies, the nonentities who desire to be part of the spectacle of identity metamorphosis.

In general, participants have a vague idea as to what they aspire to change. During each stage of the aesthetic interventions, they deliver their bodies to the experts without great disagreements concerning what should be changed. David complains that what bothers him the most are his nose and his teeth; however, he leaves the show not only with a new nose and white teeth, but also with a reduced stomach, redrawn chin and an eye lift. The experts know better than David because they not only belong to the mainstream medical councils or academic centers, but especially because they serve the greatest Hollywood stars. The plastic surgeons, hence, are presented to the public through their diplomas and credentials to those medical councils and through their star clients. Being the "star experts," they are the most qualified agents for engineering their social recognition and stamping their passports to the "cool world."

While participants are filmed gazing nowhere or sadly contemplating their image in the mirror, a voiceover reveals stories of teen years marked by episodes of shame, humiliation, stigmatization and isolation from the world. Retold by the participant's parents, friends or by the omniscient narrator, each biography is recovered as a collection of mistakes which, far from being the responsibility of the individual, is portrayed as a consequence of the unavoidable cruelty which one's physical appearance inspires. "People would constantly slap my ears and want to fight with me all the time just because of the way I look," remembers James without apparent resentment. Christina was harassed in such a manner by her school colleagues that she had to abandon her studies, but far from willing to inflict on them an equivalent suffering, all she wants is a new look. Kimberly, presented as "the lady who never smiles" because of her teeth, speaks to an absent interlocutor: "I am unhappy since I am eight years old." Her voiceover punctuates images of an introspective Kimberley, gazing at the infinite: "This is not me. I think that if I do not resolve this situation now, I am going to get worse and worse."

All participants are constructed as sweet and lovely individuals, passive victims of their aesthetic condition, of the marks left in their lives by a disastrous genetic combination. Infantilizing the participants and repeating a recurrent pattern in castrating relations, *Extreme Makeover* smashes on a national scale the little self-esteem left in those individuals, maximizes their fragility, registers in close their deformities, to then emerge as their only hope.

In Brazil, "radical" makeover shows are nonexistent, for they bump into two obstacles: the production costs and the vigilance of the Regional Council of Medicine, which forbids the exhibition of any surgical procedures for commercial purposes on TV. Surmounting both limitations and supposedly escaping a "spectacle" over plastic surgery, *Buying Beauty* proposes to follow the daily lives of six individuals undergoing surgical aesthetic procedures in order to acquire a desired image. "More than a series about beauty," the program aims to be "a real life *novela* on the quest for self-esteem in present days," according to its official website.

Each story takes up two 30-minute episodes: the first one shows the preparations, the doubt and hesitation that pop up during the initial visits to doctors and specialists, as well as commentary by relatives, friends and colleagues on the expectations involved in the process. The second episode shows the results of the metamorphosis and the ensuing changes in the subject's life. Compared to *Extreme Makeover* and reality shows produced in the U.S., *Buying Beauty* is much less "sophisticated" as far as production values are concerned, with some audio limitations and no "special effects."

Buying Beauty follows six anonymous individuals in their visits to the doctor and aesthetic experts and in their chats with family and friends in the already conventional language of the genre, placing the individual to be made over at the heart of the narrative, recovering significant aspects of his/her biography, stressing traumas, fears and anxieties concerning the body and its future transformations. Its distinctiveness relies on the incorporation of experts foreign to the aesthetic field: consultation with plastic surgeons and participants' confessions over the drama of having tiny breasts or a large nose are mediated by "specialists in human behavior," as defined by the producers. Shot in black and white, the specialists are grouped around a TV set showing the same episode the audience is watching, inspiring complicity between "them" and "us," who also watch and judge the participants. Different from the "Extreme Team," here the group is basically composed by people identified as "intellectuals" by the Brazilian audience. The "intellectuals" are: psychoanalyst Alberto Goldin, a specialist in family therapy who writes a quite popular column in the newspaper *O Globo*; PhD in Philosophy Paulo Vaz, author of essays on body and technology; another philosopher, Charles Feitosa, who has a research project on the aesthetics of the ugly; Nizia Villaça, an anthropologist who has written extensively on media and body; and Rosa Magalhães, who doubles as historian and creative director for one of the main samba schools in Rio.

Nineteen-year-old Larissa, a prospective TV actress, was the subject of the first show. At sixteen, she'd already had liposuction, breast implants, ear correction surgery, and, most recently, she'd had her hair straightened. The invitation to be on the show came via the very plastic surgeon Larissa had visited for an estimation of the procedure's cost. The doctor thought she had precisely the requisites demanded by the show's producers: young, pretty, and still unhappy about her appearance.

When justifying her participation on the show, Larissa summarized *Buying Beauty*'s premise: "Being good-looking does not mean you can't be better-looking." Indeed, different from the characters chosen by *Extreme Makeover*, none of the six participants displayed any severe malformation or were too far from the hegemonic Brazilian beauty standard. All of them were white and could be referred to as either middle or upper-class. The only one with a health concern was Tatyana, 29 years old, who underwent not plastic surgery but a stomach reduction. She was approximately 220 pounds and blamed her unsuccessful professional career for her being overweight, a problem she'd already tried to face with diets and pills. Although defining herself as a "true shy spirit," Tatyana accepted being part of the show, believing that sharing her story would inspire "other people to take the right decision and change their lives" through a radical procedure such as that. Gastric bypasses, as discussed during the show, have become alarmingly common in Brazil since the last decade.

Sônia introduced herself as a representative of the "new Brazilian grannies," who do not allow themselves to look "old and grey" any longer; that is why she decided to go for a general face lift. The other two female participants, Darlene and Margô, in their late thirties, were contented with their professional lives, but unhappy with their small breasts and large noses. Refusing to accept her genetic code or her natural condition, Margô accused her father, with mixed feelings of resentment and tenderness, of passing on his "potato-nose" to her.

The sixth character was Pedro, a 25-year-old who had just finished college and already had a high-paying job waiting for him. But he was slightly overweight and, even worse, was considered to display some "female features": prominent breasts and a "guitar shape." With the moral support of his mother, who followed Pedro throughout the show, he underwent liposuction on the chest, abdomen and low back. He was characterized as an outgoing and intelligent young man, with many friends who also talked about their own plastic surgeries and encouraged him (unlike his father, who was completely against the procedure). Pedro was not very successful with the opposite sex: "They always want to be my friends, not my fiancées," he explained. And his mother added: "It's the fatso syndrome." In another conversation with his mother about his weight issues, Pedro said that even after liposuction he'd still have a taste for fat foods, because he has a "fat spirit." She replied, "But that's a memory issue. You can erase that one and implant another," to which Pedro retorted, "Is there surgery for that?"

As Brazilian psychoanalyst Jurandir Freire Costa argues, the real or ideological progress of science and technology has altered the profile of the corporal image idealization, not only in the core but also in the "peripheral" countries. Until very recently, what was sought was the mythical *perfection* of the sentimental past; today, it is imagined that perfection will be accomplished through the physical *perfectibility* promised by the new medical technologies. And as Pedro's words suggest, memory has become something disposable as well. It makes sense to act, hence, as if bodily and memory components could be combined in multiple formats that always allow substitutions, additions and recombinations through genetic, electronic, chemical or mechanical prostheses. Surgical interventions on the body are not only performed where medically necessary — as in the classic medicine which, as Michel Foucault observes, pursued the cure of specific harms threatening life — but also where desired — a desire which is potentially infinite.

Buying Beauty displays a variety of talk situations, but it is the monologue — the participant filmed in black and white talks straight to the camera — that is used as a truth-sign of direct access to the authentic emotions being experienced. On the evening before his surgery, Pedro "intimately" shares his anxieties with us: "I'm anxious not because of the surgery itself, but I'm very anxious to see the results. I trust the doctor and, well, this is all I can do. I am changing my life and I hope everything goes all right."

What seems to be at stake here is an *authorization process*, a recognition by the subject of the truthfulness and reliability of the experts' discourse. Pedro delegates his body and ultimately his life to the plastic surgeon who has the task of making him desirable. As Anthony Giddens has remarked (126), in modern society, it comes to be imperative to "trust" the Abstract Systems of which one is a layperson, and to perceive as legitimate what the fields' and subfields' experts conceive as so.* It is by trusting the Abstract Systems which surround these aesthetic procedures, as well as the effects to

By "Abstract Systems," Anthony Giddens refers to the process of specialization of knowledge and practice which has accompanied the constitution of modern societies: the emergence of particular scientific, professional, religious and other 'fields,' with their particular logics, institutional space, and mainly, their respective experts. For, in modern society, it becomes impossible to be an expert in all existing fields of knowledge and practice; one is necessarily forced to "trust" the abstract systems of which he/she is an amateur, and to delegate to its experts the ultimate authority on issues related to their expertise.

be generated through those very procedures, that Pedro and the other participants submit themselves to such radical transformations.

By avoiding treating surgical procedures as spectacle as well as by the absence of a judgmental narrator figure, *Buying Beauty* places itself at a somewhat more respectable distance from the subject, with some critical detachment. Although international stereotypes around Brazilians usually include fantasies of naked bodies (Freire-Medeiros), the participants' bodies are not so overtly exposed as in *Extreme Makeover* and the recovery process is focused on much more as a psychological healing than as a display of scars and stitches.

Buying Beauty supposedly has as its goal "to make an effort to understand why someone resorts to plastic surgery and to what extent this resort reveals something about each of us, articulating the "specific and the generic," as put by one of the "intellectuals" who was part of the group of specialists mentioned before. The problem at hand in regards to the participation of this so-called intellectual group is that their critique tends to be neutralized, or even obliterated, by fast-paced editing, which turns reflexive thought into unrelated quotes, by selecting only two or three minutes out of thirty-minute-long discussions.

On the last episode we follow a reunion of all participants, who gather at a restaurant to watch clips from the show, leading to confessions and a debate on their aesthetic choices as well as on the views the intellectuals had displayed towards them. And as happens in *Extreme Makeover,* it is concluded that fixing a person's appearance is the means to making him/her happier and more successful.

Conclusion

In both *Buying Beauty* and *Extreme Makeover*, the triad "look-love-life" is set out as constructs that are indissolubly connected to each other, with the "look" assuming a prominent position. In a world where visuality has become one of the most fundamental dimensions of social experience, one's looks are among the most eloquent operators of status positioning. It has become — remembering Bourdieu's symbolic capital — an "acting principle" in the construction of social space, confining the subject's possibilities of being distinctively recognized in distinct social settings. In the context of the two shows analyzed here, the "look" refers to an incompatibility between subjectivity and the exteriority of the individual, between how one perceives oneself and what one presents to others.

In order to date for the first time, Christina joined *Extreme Makeover*, undergoing a nose and ear job, tummy tuck, liposuction in the legs, treating her skin with acids, correcting her vision with laser surgery, injecting *Botox* in her lips, whitening her teeth, and undergoing drastic weight loss under the supervision of Michael Thurmon, "master in body sculpturing and in fast weight loss," as identified by the show's omniscient narrator. Presented as "the girl who has never been kissed," the 25-year-old saleswoman even had the chance to be trained by Marilyn Anderson, presented on the show as "Hollywood kissing coach" and author of the book *Never Kiss a Frog*. With the assistance of a masculine model, Anderson taught Christina — and the spectators — how to flirt, kiss and seduce in a Hollywood fashion.

Here we see a basic and widely shared premise: it is unfeasible to be recognized either affectively or professionally if one is dissonant with the standards agreed upon by the experts of the aesthetic field. The subject, whatever his or her original bodily experience might have been, must be ready to transforms his/her body through surgery. Social and sexual recompenses — without any necessary relations with sentimental, moral or spiritual ascetics — will definitely come (Costa). Indeed, both *Extreme Makeover* and *Buying Beauty*, as well as the majority of makeover reality shows, do not invest in a self-caring which leads to an improvement of life quality in the broader sense of transformations and which respects the original traces of the body of each individual. Rather, they seem to suggest that, in order to be happy, one *must* indeed conform oneself to the socially authorized standards of beauty accorded by the aesthetic experts; that precisely those experts, owners of the knowledge of what the "true beauty" is, are the arbiters of that happiness.

Extreme Makeover signals to subjects — participants and spectators — the possibility of not only transforming one's body and, by consequence, one's identity standards, but of doing so with reference to celebrities. This is quite obvious in *Extreme Makeover*, but this doesn't mean that it is structurally different in the case of *Buying Beauty*. The show relies on Brazilians' obsession with plastic surgery, which is related, as doctors and psychologists seem to agree, to the ideals of beauty conveyed by the media as well. In an interview for *Rio Mídia*, plastic surgeon Ricardo Cavalcanti Ribeiro suggests that even more worrying is that these standards of beauty do not fit with Brazilian types: "Demand for breast and hip enhancements — which are incompatible with the bodies of young Brazilian women — is one example of the influence of North American culture" (September 2007).

Both shows arouse the feeling that the tension between massification *versus* singularization, characteristic of mass societies, can be mitigated;

through current medical technologies of bodily intervention, potentially everyone can acquire the distinctive bodily features of the celebrities, if they can, of course, afford those interventions. And here we find the "democratic" projection of *Extreme Makeover, Buying Beauty* and other makeover reality shows: *anyone* is able to reverse his or her aesthetic inferiority and become happier through the aesthetic procedures offered or documented by the show. It is considered natural to make use of artificial mechanisms, which are all the better if their results look natural.

Natural *versus* artificial, reality *versus* construction. In the end, it seems impossible to speak of reality shows without at least touching on those antonymic pairs. We would like to conclude by situating ourselves in opposition to the critics of the culture industry identified with an apocalyptic view (Eco). These critics, such as those from the Frankfurt School, tend to underestimate the critical consciousness and the ethical standards of the individuals who consume what media offers them as entertainment. It is crucial to consider — without fraud or favor — that the spectators, long socialized in the simulacrum world, do not take the "reality" offered by reality shows as an untouched truth (Andrejevic). On the contrary, they do not only perceive it as a constructed product, but claim their participation in that construction, either as direct participants or by electing their preferences through interactive mechanisms.

It is not possible to ignore the power of media as a source of experiences which are simultaneously exemplary and unavailable to the private individual in whatever other sphere and that, hence, it is less a matter of falsifying the real than one of *producing* the real. Departing from contexts and situations very "unreal," programs like *Extreme Makeover* and *Buying Beauty* provoke emotional reactions which are perceived as legitimate because they are elicited by actual individuals and not by fictional characters. Expectations and anxieties are taken as credible because they are shared by participant and spectator. The critical energy, thus, should not be directed to this or that program only, but to the social contexts from which they come into being, to the arrangements of daily life which makes them attractive to their public and profitable to their producers.

BIBLIOGRAPHY

Andrejevic, Mark. *Reality TV: The Work of Being Watched.* Lanham, MD: Rowman & Littlefield, 2004.
Badiou, Alain. *Pequeno Manual de Inestética.* São Paulo: Estação Liberdade, 2002.
Bauman, Zygmunt. *Amor Líquido.* Rio de Janeiro: Jorge Zahar Editor, 2003.

_____. *Comunidade*. Rio de Janeiro: Jorge Zahar Editor, 2003.

Beleza Comprada. Rede Globo de Televisão. Prod. Jorge Espírito Santo. 2004.

Berger, Peter. *Perspectivas Sociológicas: Uma Visão Humanística*. Petrópolis: Vozes, 1996.

Big Brother Brasil. Rede Globo de Televisão. Prod. J. B. De Oliveira. 29 Jan. 2002–2 April 2002.

Bourdieu, Pierre. *A Economia das Trocas Simbólicas*. São Paulo: Editora Perspectiva, 1998.

_____. *O Poder Simbólico*. Lisboa: Difusão Editorial Ltda, 1989.

_____. *Sobre a Televisão*. Rio de Janeiro: Editora Zahar, 1997.

Chambat, Pierre e Ehrenberg, Alain. "Les *Reality Shows*, Nouvel Âge Télévisuel?" *Esprit— Revue Internationale* 188 (January 1993): 22.

Costa, Jurandir Freire. *O Vestígio e a Aura: Corpo e Consumismo na Moral do Espetáculo*. Rio de Janeiro: Garamond Universitária, 2005.

Du Gay, Paul. *Consumption and Identity at Work*. London: Sage, 1996.

Extreme Makeover. ABC. Dir. Shanda Sawyer. 2002–2007.

Extreme Makeover. Home page. Accessed 22 March 2004 <http://abc.go.com/primetime/extrememakeover/index/html>.

Foucault, Michel. *História da Sexualidade I: A Vontade de Saber*. Rio de Janeiro: Graal, 1980.

_____. *A Microfísica do Poder*. Rio de Janeiro: Graal, 1981.

Freire-Medeiros, Bianca. *O Rio de Janeiro que Hollywood inventou*. Rio de Janeiro: Zahar Editor, 2005.

Giddens, Anthony. *As Conseqüências da Modernidade*. São Paulo: Editora UNESP, 1991.

Hobsbawn, Eric. "The Cult of Identity Politics." *New Left Review* 217 (1996): 36.

Kilborn, Richard. "'How Real Can You Get?': Recent Developments in 'Reality' Television." *European Journal of Communication* 9 (1994): 421–39.

McCarthy, Anna. "Stanley Milgram, Allen Funt and Me: Postwar Social Science and the 'First Wave' of Reality TV." *Reality TV: Remaking Television Culture*. Eds. S. Murray, and L. Ouellette. New York: New York University Press, 2005. 19–39.

No Limite. Rede Globo de Televisão. Prod. J.B. Oliveira. 23 July 2000–23 Dec. 2001.

Ribeiro, Ricardo Cavalcanti. Interview. *Rio Mídia*. Sept. 2007.

Sennett, Richard. *O Declínio Do Homem Público: As Tiranias Da Intimidade*. São Paulo: Editora Companhia das Letras, 1993.

Weber, Brenda. "Beauty, Desire, and Anxiety: The Economy of Sameness in ABC's *Extreme Makeover*." *Genders Journal* 41 (2005): 4.

About the Contributors

André Bakker is a Ph.D. candidate in the Department of Social and Cultural Anthropology at the Vrije Universiteit, Amsterdam. His research explores the nexus between cultural heritage, media and conversion to Pentecostalism among the *Pataxó* indians in Brazil. He is affiliated with the NWO research project *Heritage Dynamics: Politics of Authentication and Aesthetics of Persuasion in Brazil, Ghana, South Africa and the Netherlands*. His main publications and areas of interest are in anthropology and the sociology of media, religion, the body and the senses.

Joan L. Conners is an associate professor of communication at Randolph-Macon College, Ashland, Virginia. She teaches communication courses in law and ethics, gender issues, political campaigns, media diversity, writing and public speaking. Currently she is researching aspects of the 2008 elections, including debate coverage, political cartoon representations, and online campaign communication. Conners is the coauthor of *Perspectives of Political Communication: A Case Approach* with Lauren Bell and Ted Sheckels. She has also recently authored "Pain or Perfection? Themes in Plastic Surgery Reality Television" (in *Women, Wellness and the Media*) and "'Faking' Intelligence? Representing Intelligence in TLC's *Faking It*" (in *Common Sense: Intelligence as Presented on Popular Television*).

Margaret O. Finucane is an associate professor of communication and theatre arts at John Carroll University in Cleveland, Ohio, where she has taught interpersonal communication, media effects, communication theory, and public speaking courses since 1998. She also directs the university's Center for Service and Social Action. Her research focuses on mediated interpersonal communication. She has examined such contexts as parent-child television co-viewing, married couples' use of television, and friends' co-viewing.

Bianca Freire-Medeiros is an assistant professor of sociology at the Center for Research and Documentation on Brazilian Contemporary History (CPDOC) at the Getulio Vargas Foundation (FGV) and a content researcher for TV Globo, Latin America's main television station. She has published extensively on visual culture (film, photography and television), urban sociology and travel culture and is currently developing a documentary based on her research project on tourism in poverty-stricken areas. It is titled *A Favela with a View*.

Ellen W. Gorsevski is an assistant professor at Bowling Green State University, where she teaches courses on peace and conflict analysis and the rhetoric of globalization. Her research interests are in contemporary rhetoric, especially the communication practices and artifacts of leaders in peace and social justice movements, international/intercultural rhetoric, political and social movement rhetoric, media criticism and propaganda, and nonviolent conflict communication. She is author of *Peaceful Persuasion: The Geopolitics of Nonviolent Rhetoric*. She has also published book chapters on the interactive, gendered rhetoric of *Second Life* and on the rhetoric of Jon Stewart's *Daily Show*. She is currently working on a book on the rhetoric of the women Nobel Peace Prize laureates.

David Gudelunas is an assistant professor of communication at Fairfield University in Connecticut where he also directs the Internship Program in Communication. He researches and teaches in the areas of critical and cultural studies, gender, sexuality and communication, media history and communication industries. He is the author of *Confidential to America: Newspaper Advice Columns and Sexual Education* and is widely published in the areas of popular communication as well as the intersections of sexuality and communication. He is currently working on a book about the history of shopping from home.

Shana Heinricy is an instructor in communication studies at Xavier University in New Orleans. She is currently completing her dissertation in communication and culture from Indiana University. Her publications include "The Cutting Room: Gendered American Dreams on Plastic Surgery TV" in David S. Escoffery's *How Real Is Reality TV? Essays on Representation and Truth* and "I, Cyborg" in Josef Steiff and Tristan Tamplin's *Battlestar Gallactica and Philosophy*. Her research focuses on television and the body. Her current project explores the ways that the particular bodily style presented on makeover television is constituted as the style of a good consumer-citizen.

Cary W. Horvath is an associate professor and chairperson of the Department of Communication at Youngstown State University in Youngstown, Ohio. She teaches interpersonal, organizational, group, and presentational communication. Her research helped to spawn the communibiology paradigm. She is the author of book chapters on communication and biology, use of media during 9/11, reality television, and business communication. Her research has been published in *Communication Quarterly, The Journal of Broadcasting & Electronic Media, and Communication Research Reports*. She serves on the editorial board for *Communication Teacher* and the *Journal of the Ohio Communication Association,* and has reviewed for *Communication Reports, Communication Research, Communication*

Research Reports, Journal of Broadcasting & Electronic Media, and *Mass Communication and Society.* Her current research interests involve the nexus of media use and interpersonal communication.

Matthew Johnson is a Ph.D. candidate at Temple University in Philadelphia. He is the Allen F. Davis Public History Fellow at the Atwater Kent Museum in Philadelphia. His research focuses on the intersection between constructions of gender and sexuality, and mass consumption. His dissertation is titled "Managing Diversity: The Rise of Multiculturalism in the United States."

Judith Lancioni is an associate professor in the Department of Radio, Television, and Film at Rowan University in Glassboro, New Jersey, where she teaches courses in media research and criticism, television scriptwriting, and images of women in film. She has published articles on Ken Burns' *The Civil War, Billy Elliot* as fairytale, the ethical implications of *Survivor,* and history in *Star Trek.* Currently she is researching the construction of the historical process in a PBS documentary titled *Sins of Our Mothers.*

Narissra Maria Punyanunt-Carter is an associate professor of communication studies at Texas Tech University, Lubbock, Texas, where she teaches the basic interpersonal communication course. Her research areas include mass media effects, father-daughter communication, mentoring, advisor-advisee relationships, family studies, religious communication, humor, and interpersonal communication. She has published over 30 articles in peer-reviewed journals, including *Communication Research Reports, Southern Journal of Communication,* and *Journal of Intercultural Communication Research.* She has also published numerous instructional ancillaries and materials.

Elizabeth Ribarsky is an assistant professor of communication at the University of Illinois at Springfield, where she teaches both undergraduate and graduate courses in interpersonal communication. Her research interests include dating communication and the intersection between mediated and interpersonal communication. Her research has been published in a wide variety of academic journals and books including the *National Forensic Journal* and *Teaching Ideas for the Basic Communication Course.* She also has made numerous presentations at regional and national communication conferences and has won several top paper awards.

Christopher D. Rodkey is a lecturer in religion at Lebanon Valley College in Annville, Pennsylvania, and pastor of Zion "Goshert's" United Church of Christ in Lebanon, Pennsylvania. His recently-completed Ph.D. dissertation, "In the Horizon of the Infinite: Paul Tillich and the Dialectic of the Sacred," investigates Tillich's influence on theologian Thomas Altizer and feminist philosopher Mary Daly. Rodkey's scholarly interests include pastoral and philosophical theology, bioethics, religious education, and the philosophy of religion. He has previously published in the journals *Doxology, Sacramental Life, Youth Worker Journal, Journal of Youth and Theology, Journal for the Study of Radicalism, Philosophical Practice, Journal of Cultural and Religious Theory*, and *Newsletter of the North American Paul Tillich Society*.

Julie-Ann Scott teaches communication, women's studies, and higher education at the University of Maine, where she is the Chase Distinguished Research Assistant. She does research in the areas of communication studies, performance studies, and feminist studies. Her article "Performing Unfeminine Femininity: A Performance Analysis of Bulimic Women's Personal Narratives" was published in *Text and Performance Quarterly*. She is also co-author of "ReAf[Firm]ing the Ideal: A Focus Group Analysis of the Dove Campaign for Real Beauty," which appeared in *Advertising and Society Review*. The subject of her current research is physically disabled professionals' personal narratives as performances of identity.

Shira Tarrant teaches pop culture, masculinity, and feminist theory in the Department of Women's, Gender, and Sexuality Studies at California State University, Long Beach. Her books include *When Sex Became Gender, Men Speak Out: Views on Gender, Sex and Power*, and *Men and Feminism*. She has published in *Bitch* magazine, *off our backs* and *Women's Studies Quarterly*, and she is the column editor for "The Man Files" at the popular blog *Girl with Pen*. Her next book is *Fashion Talks: Undressing the Power of Style*.

Yarma Velázquez Vargas is an assistant professor at California State University, Northridge, where she teaches public speaking and media courses. Her research interests include gender, queer studies, Latina studies, and political economy. Her current research explores issues of media representation and sexuality. Her work examines the manner in which the representations of queer culture in television reinforce the binaries of sex, gender, and sexuality. She is the author of "Marco Said I Look Like Charcoal; A Puerto Rican's Exploration of Her Ethnic Identity," published in *Qualitative Inquiry*.

Frank H. Wallis currently works at Nielsen in corporate support. His publications include "eBay and the Limits of Commodification," *Civilisations* and *Économie et Culture*. His book on British imperial conquests in Afghanistan and India, 1838–1845, is forthcoming. Currently he is translating Élie Berger, *Histoire de Blanche de Castille, Reine de France* (Paris, 1895).

Index

215